Dan Vinai

The

Refugee

Camp

DATE DUE

Ban Vinai

The

Refugee

Camp

Lynellyn D. Long

Columbia University Press

New York

Columbia University Press
New York   Oxford

Library of Congress Cataloging-in-Publication Data

Long, Lynellyn.
    Ban Vinai, the refugee camp / Lynellyn D. Long.
        p.   cm.
    Includes bibliographical references (p.   ) and index.
    ISBN 0-231-07862-5 (hbk.). — ISBN 0-231-07863-3 (phk)
    1. Refugee camps—Thailand—Ban Vinai.   2. Refugees—
Thailand—Ban Vinai.   I. Title.
    HV640.4.T5L66   1992
    362.87′09593—dc20   92-22251
                                                          CIP

Casebound Editions of
Columbia University Press books
are Smyth-sewn and printed
on permanent and durable
acid-free paper.

Book design by Teresa Bonner
Printed in the United States of America

10   9   8   7   6   5   4   3   2   1

To

the

People

of

Ban Vinai

Contents

Illustrations

Figures

Tables

x

Acknowledgments

A book is very much a social construction as I have learned in writing this one. There are many people who helped write this book and who through their faith in me and in this project made it possible. Theirs are the contributions, the errors are my own.

Five people, in particular, stood by me and kept this work going from the beginning to the end. They are Dennis Long, Shirley Brice Heath, Gilbert Herdt, Ellen Basu, and Father John Blanchard. They were always willing to share their theoretical insights, experiences, and good judgment. Dennis, most of all, believed in me and believed that this project was important. He helped in countless ways. Shirley and Gil taught me to be an ethnographer and to think critically about the larger meanings of refugee situations. Father John Blanchard taught me the importance of many different ways of knowing and always reminded me to remain open to other points of view. Ellen provided a critical eye and was always willing to read yet another draft.

Many others shared their experiences and knowledge of the Lao, Thai, and Hmong peoples and of Southeast Asia. Among those I would like to thank are: Father Yves Bertrais, Marie Helene Bourhis-Nedellac, Arthur Dommen, Ruth Hammond, Thom Huebner, Bouttry Janetvilay, Giang Ly, Father Michel, Araya Niemloy, Seeng Noiwan, Ann Norman, Wadtanee Phitakpao, Jittiya Prompitag, Souksomboun Sayasithsena, Robert Textor, Nipa Thorudomsak, Chalermsri Udomphant, Suchitra Vai-asa, and Long Yang. Arthur Dommen, in particular, thoughtfully shared his knowledge of Laos and the war. Long Yang spent long hours of his own time helping me to translate and interpret several Hmong tapes. Souksomboun Sayasithsena and Seeng Noiwan of the Foreign Service Institute helped me with the Lao and Thai transliteration, respectively, while Ruth Hammond carefully corrected my Hmong spelling. Araya Niemloy and Nipa Thorudomsak and their families took me in and made Thailand a second home.

Several people provided important insights about international relief and helped me to see this project in a broader context. They include: Wendy Bateson, Lois Cecsarini, Chris Elias, Charles Ferguson, Erica Hagen, Joan Horne, William Horne, Rita Katarowski, John Lewis, Moira Lucey, Milbrey McLaughlin, Lotte Marcus, Don Ranard, Willie Rifkin, Court Robinson, Paul Stekler, and Jim Tollefson. Lotte Marcus, in particular, from her own experiences as a refugee made me aware of the political and personal suffering and reminded me that I had made a long-term commitment. Jim Tollefson provided good advice on writing about these issues, and Charles Ferguson shared his wisdom when it was needed.

In addition to Shirley, Ellen, and Gil, many anthropologists helped me to question the interpretative method and to think critically about my own interpretations. They include Victor Caldarola, Jane Collier, Art Hansen, Carl Kendall, Robert Mather, Karen Plisken, Dale Rezabek, Sophie Ricard, Patricia Vondal, and Joseph Westermeyer.

Several organizations through their support made this work possible. They include the Catholic Organization for Relief and Refugees (COERR), Wenner-Gren Foundation for Anthropological Research, MacArthur Foundation (through an International Peace and Security Fellowship at Stanford's Center for International Security and Arms Control), and the American Association for the Advancement of Science (through an AAAS Diplomacy Fellowship). Many people at the Agency for International Development (A.I.D.), State Department Refugee Bureau, and UNHCR have also supported my interest in refugees along the way and should be thanked.

Gioia Stevens, my editor at Columbia, has provided the needed encouragement and careful editing. She, Tim Cooper, and Dee Horne have taught me a lot about writing and the creative process. Erica

Hagen, Yang Ger, and Nhia Za Vang provided their perspective on camp life through their photographs, and Ava Dahlstrom made a map out of my scrawls of the camp. Bryerly Long should also not be forgotten. She accompanied me back to Ban Vinai and was a very patient traveler.

Finally, I wish to thank the people of Ban Vinai—both refugees and relief workers. My greatest debt is to you, wherever you may now be.

Phonetic Symbols for Lao and Thai

Vowels

ɔ as in caught

ɛ as in cat

ə like o with a smile

y like u with a smile

Consonants

ŋ -ng

Tones

ˆ low falling

ˉ mid-tone

ˋ high falling

ˇ low rising

ˊ high

[no tone] low

Description of vowel sounds are taken from J. Marvin Brown, A.U.A. Language Center, Thai Course, American University Alumni Association Language Center, Bangkok, 1967.

Ban Vinai

The

Refugee

Camp

The people and events reported here are as I recorded and remembered them. However, I have combined the narratives of certain refugee households of the same ethnic group. I have also protected the identities of public figures, such as the priest or the UNHCR field officer, by creating composite portraits of several people in that position. My purpose is to protect those who remain in Ban Vinai and particular decisions reflect my own understanding of the sensitivities of organizations and governments who have power over these people. Unless otherwise indicated, all conversations with refugees in Ban Vinai were in Lao, and with relief workers in English or Thai.

The Road to Ban Vinai

In the cool, dry season of late winter, the land is parched. The thick reddish earth dusts the tall teak trees that line the banks of the Mekong River. At daybreak a fog rolls in over the river that flows between the mountains of Laos and Thailand. On the Thai side, a silent procession of saffron-robed monks passes from house to house of villagers who offer alms of rice. Shrouded in the early morning mist, they appear ethereal.

Waiting for the van to Ban Vinai, I wonder if the monks will come to my side of the street, but as in times past, they ignore the foreigners. Watching them pass silently by, I suddenly know that I am back in Thailand, back in Chiang Khan. On first glance, little has changed since my departure four years earlier. There are a few more houses than there were in 1982, but the appearance of a small, quiet farming town remains.

In another century, Chiang Khan was part of a vast river trade network linking northern Laos to the ports of Siam. The upper Mekong River valley formed a boundary line for competing French and Siamese claims to the region of Lan Chang, the kingdom of a million elephants, which became present-day Laos. By the mid-nineteenth century, the Siamese had extended

1

their influence over the river region as far north as Luang Prabang. The French, looking for a potential overland trade route to China, in all likelihood recognized the importance of the Mekong as a link in this route. By playing off regional rivalries and displaying their naval strength off the coast of Bangkok, the French eventually gained control of Laos. The Franco-Siamese Treaty of 1893 ceded them the left bank of the Mekong and established Laos as a protectorate. Although the trade route to China never developed as the French hoped, they encouraged the beginnings of an opium trade from northern Laos to Thailand and beyond.

In the late nineteenth century, towns such as Chiang Khan continued to develop as river traffic brought Laotian products to Thai regional and national markets. However, the building of the railway from Bangkok to Nong Khai, a large town in Northeast Thailand, in the early twentieth century created an alternative overland route. In the ensuing development, Chiang Khan and other towns in the region were bypassed. The paved road extended only as far as Loei, the provincial capital, south of Chiang Khan. Laos on the opposite shore was a backwater in the French Indochinese empire. The French also encouraged the Laotians to establish ties with Vietnam rather than Thailand. When the French withdrew in 1954, Laos was extremely poor and undeveloped, which provided little incentive for the Thai to develop trade in the northeast.

Great changes to Chiang Khan came again toward the end of the Vietnam War in the early 1970s. Gunboats roared up and down the Mekong and American planes from the newly constructed air bases in Ubon and Loei flew overhead on bombing missions to Laos. The Thai established a military base in the town that served as a center for their naval operations on the Mekong. The river cargo flow between Chiang Khan and Sanakham, the Laotian village on the other side, was over 1,100 passengers daily.[1] The traffic included military personnel and villagers who travelled back and forth to market, to visit relatives on the other side, and/or to work. The United Nations, with Western assistance, funded the beginnings of the Mekong Valley River Development Project.

When the war ended in 1975, the Lao People's Democratic Republic, the new Communist regime, again looked eastward to their Vietnamese allies for trade and foreign assistance.[2] The main flow across the Mekong became refugees—lowland Lao who had been associated with the Royal Lao government, ethnic minorities, such as the Hmong, who had fought for the Americans during the war, and other Laotians fleeing economic and political hardships. Relationships between Thailand and Laos deteriorated and in the early 1980s, the border was officially closed. The customs building in Chiang Khan lay empty and in disrepair. The town, which had always been on the periphery of Thailand's economic activity, became even more of a backwater. Unlike other parts of Thailand, Chiang Khan and much of the northeast were relatively unaffected by the massive postwar boom sweeping throughout the country. With the border closed, Chiang Khan became an outpost, the last stop for an overnight coach tour from Bangkok.

In 1986, when I come to Chiang Khan for the second time, the overnight air-conditioned coach, which arrives at five each morning, and a daily bus are the town's main transportation links to the larger world. Chiang Khan is also the residence of some fifty or sixty international relief workers who sleep there at night and work in Ban Vinai, a Laotian refugee camp sixty kilometers away.

Watching the monks disappear down the street toward the temple, I enjoy the moment of peace one feels living in Chiang Khan. It is a deceptive peace, because the political situation can change at any moment. In comparison to Ban Vinai, Chiang Khan seems timeless and the conflicts far away. The sun has not yet appeared to warm the chilly air and the street is quiet again.

The villagers disappear inside their houses. The houses, two-story unpainted wood structures with television antennas, lean out over the river bank. Their brown hues shrouded in the early morning gray fog add to the sense of remoteness I always feel on first reaching Chiang Khan. Relief workers sometimes compare the town to Siberia. But, the contrast with Sanakham, the Laotian village on the opposite shore, is striking. On the Laotian side, there are few houses and many more trees, which the Thais, who are beginning to suffer the effects of massive deforestation in the northeast, occasionally slip across the river to cut. On Sunday mornings, the Laotians on their side can be seen panning for gold on the river banks. To their neighboring kin in Chiang Khan, the time and willingness to search for the occasional, microscopic fleck of gold symbolizes the poverty of the socialist regime.

Breaking the morning stillness, a woman swings open the large front doors of her house. As they clatter apart, she begins setting up her small shop of batteries, soap, and other items bought in Loei. A man appears and builds a fire to warm them in the chilly morning air. The smoke curls up through the fog adding to the opaqueness. The van for Ban Vinai suddenly appears around a corner. Coming fast, it momentarily dominates the narrow street. The driver stops briefly and I board.

Three men sit in front: the Thai driver, Pere, an elderly French priest, and Paul, an Englishman. Behind sit three Thai women, two

French Catholic nuns, and a Dutch woman. They work for COERR, a Catholic voluntary agency (commonly known as a "Volag") on various relief projects in the camp (see table 1.1). As I join the other women, Pere introduces me. He is a very tall man with large feet and hands that express his magnanimity. I greet the women in Thai and French. The Thai women look surprised. "She speaks Thai better than you," says Boonchan, a young Thai woman, to Anika, who is Dutch. Looking annoyed, Anika turns away and opening a Bible, begins reading.

"Do you have a husband," asks Boonchan, using the Thai word [fɛɛ́n] for boyfriend as well. "Yes, in San Francisco," I reply. "When is he coming?" I explain that I have come alone to do field research and that my husband, Dennis, will visit later in the year. The women look surprised. Boonchan asks my age and whether we have children. Responding that I am thirty-three and childless, I add, "But, I want children." The women nod sympathetically. The nuns stop listening and begin reading psalms. Pere is already asleep in the front seat.

The driver has left late and he speeds quickly along the winding paved road bordering the river. He weaves the van deftly past market vans, diesel trucks, animals, and blue-uniformed school children. The van passes through several small hamlets punctuating wet rice fields that lie between the mountains surrounding the river valley. Tall palm trees shade the road. The sun, a bright fiery red, appears through the morning haze from side to side as the road bends and turns with the

TABLE 1.1.

Organizations of Ban Vinai

ADRA	Adventist Development and Relief Agency (originally Projects Asia)
CAMA	Christian and Missionary Alliance (U.S.A.)
COERR	Catholic Office for Emergency Relief and Refugees (Thailand)
ESF	Ecoles Sans Frontières (France)
FHI	Food for the Hungry International (U.S.A.)
ICA	International Christian Aid
IRC	International Rescue Committee (U.S.A.)
JSRC	Japan Sotoshu Relief Committee
MOI	Ministry of the Interior (Thailand)
OHI	Operation Handicap International (France)
PPAT	Planned Parenthood of Thailand
TCRS	Thai Chinese Refugee Service (Taiwan)
UNHCR	United Nations High Commissioner for Refugees
ZOA	Zuid-Oost-Azie Refugee Care (Netherlands)

SOURCE: Field Office, United Nations High Commissioner for Refugees. *Brief on Ban Vinai Refugee Camp,* 1986 and 1988.

river. Fishermen in long thin boats glide up and down the Mekong's receding banks and skirt along an invisible line separating Laos from Thailand. At Pak Chom junction (a village east of Chiang Khan), the driver turns southward onto a dirt road leading into the hills and Ban Vinai.

Fieldwork

Prior to fieldwork in Ban Vinai, I had spent fourteen months living and working in refugee camps in Southeast Asia. From December 1980 to February 1982, I worked as an United Nations Volunteer relief worker with Laotian, Vietnamese, Hmong, and Cambodian refugees in the Philippines Refugee Processing Center and later, as a consultant, for a voluntary agency (Volag) in Ban Vinai, Thailand. During that period, I visited several other camps in the Philippines, Hong Kong, and Thailand and at one point, assisted some 40 Vietnamese, primarily children who arrived by boat, in obtaining asylum.

Upon returning to the United States, I worked with Southeast Asian refugees and other immigrants in Boston and San Francisco from 1982 to 1986. Working with resettled refugees, I witnessed the effects of the refugee camp's institutionalization as I saw former refugees struggling to adjust to a new society in their daily interactions with welfare systems, schools, hospitals, and with other Americans. Relief workers, too, I discovered had to deinstitutionalize as well as cope with the usual cross-cultural adjustments of returning. Conducting ethnographic research in the lowland Lao community in San Francisco, I also saw increasing gender and generational differences within households— trends that I suspected had begun in the camps.

At the same time, I wondered about the much greater effects of camp life for those who remained behind, who were more likely to be rural, poor, less educated, and without powerful outside connections. I wondered what happened to refugees who remained in camps for many years. In 1986, I decided to return to Ban Vinai to conduct, as part of my research, an ethnography of refugee camp life.

During fieldwork in Ban Vinai, I documented the daily lives of five households and typical interactions of camp life: interviews, market transactions, voluntary agency meetings, ceremonies, etc. I interviewed refugees, relief workers, and officials in Lao, Thai, French, and English.[3] The majority of my interviews with the five households were conducted in Lao.

5

In trying to capture the complexity of life in the camp, I found myself doing an ethnography of the relief community as well as of the Laotian refugees. As a member of the dominant group, I consciously examined my own role as a relief worker and ethnographer in various dialogues and interactions.[4] During fieldwork, I also conducted interviews and observations in four other refugee camps along the Thai-Laotian and Thai-Kampuchean borders—Chiang Kham, Site Two, Khao I Dang, and Panat Nikom. The data gathered in these camps allowed me to compare and contrast refugee experiences and to some extent, generalize certain observations and findings.

Obtaining permission to conduct research in a refugee camp is usually difficult.[5] Fortunately, the Catholic Organization for Emergency Relief and Refugees (COERR), a Thai voluntary agency, sponsored my research and obtained the necessary permissions. In return, I provided statistical training for COERR's workers, periodic reports on my findings, and a copy of my final dissertation. I also analyzed a campwide survey and interviewed refugee leaders and Volag staff. The majority of my time, however, was spent in conducting the ethnographic study.

From February through December 1986, I interviewed the five households almost daily. Of the Hmong households, two came from major clans and one from a minor clan. The three Hmong households consisted of extended families, and one was polygynous. The lowland Lao household was a childless couple (who later adopted a son), while the lowland Lao/Khmu household was a nuclear family.

The five households also varied by socioeconomic status. One was well off by camp standards, three reported average incomes, and two were poor. In one household, the people were unregistered, "illegal" refugees. The majority of the children in all five households were born in Ban Vinai; a few were born at the end of the war or during their flight to Thailand. Members of the households had lived an average of seven years in the camp, as had most Ban Vinai residents. The demographic and social characteristics of the five households were fairly representative of the larger camp population, as determined by a 1986 camp survey.[6]

From prior experience as a relief worker, I was aware of the need to have a well-defined role that addressed the daily needs of camp life. Unfortunately, research is often suspect in refugee situations. At best, it is seen as peripheral to the more compelling humanitarian needs of a refugee situation and at worst, as threatening to a political status quo. Having specific responsibilities as a relief worker and being part of COERR undoubtedly determined my vantage point, even as that role also made me an insider in this situation. COERR's Thai relief workers

6

helped me understand and appreciate the Thai perspective on refugee issues, while the priests and nuns, who came from several countries, shared their many years of experience of Hmong and lowland Lao culture, history, and language with me. Because I was a COERR worker, it is likely that some households were initially more willing to welcome me, while others kept me at a distance. Over time, I observed that refugees and relief workers alike cared less about my relief work and more about the findings from my research.

During 1986, I spent the majority of my days in the camp and the majority of the evenings in Chiang Khan, living with other COERR workers. After the first month, I stayed a night or two each week with a Hmong household in the camp. Later, in 1989 and 1990, I returned to Ban Vinai in two brief visits to conduct follow up interviews.

Refugee Consciousness

By staying and working in refugee camps over time, I became aware of how camp life creates what in this book I will call "refugee consciousness." Consciousness, a quality or state of awareness, is defined in social and political life through our relationships to others. Consciousness becomes alienated when more dominant and external others impose their own forms of awareness on the self.[7] In Sartre's terms, consciousness is transformed from *être-pour-soi* (being-for-self) to *être-pour-autrui* (being-for-others).[8] The usefulness of this concept in the refugee context is that it allows us to see the mechanisms by which relations of dependency affect both individual and collective identities. When the survivors of war adopt a refugee consciousness, they become refugees not only for themselves, but also for others. Relief workers likewise may choose to treat these survivors as refugees or empathize by recognizing that the circumstances of war can happen to anyone.

Many studies of refugee camp life to date have focused on the traumatic effects of the experience from a psychoanalytic perspective.[9] Psychoanalytic theory helps to explain the long-term effects of the experience on individual consciousness and inter-generational relationships, particularly in the case of young children who have suffered or witnessed traumatic events in refugee situations.[10] At the same time, remaining at the individual and psychoanalytic level can lead to placing responsibility for good mental health on the refugees and relief workers themselves, rather than on the governments and those in power who both create refugee situations and the need for camps.[11] Traditional psychoanalytic theory also does not suggest which strategies allow peo-

7

ple to survive this experience and/or to adapt to long-term camp situations.

The sociocultural research demonstrates the need to look at the particular contexts of refugee situations to identify "normal" beliefs and practices.[12] By analyzing daily routines and relationships between different actors within a sociocultural system, it is possible to see how people adapt over time to the camp experience. Recognizing that camps may be extreme environments (but increasingly common), explains why certain forms of aggression, for example, may be a normal reaction for particular individuals and groups over time. Much of the research (both sociocultural and psychoanalytic) also suggests that there may be positive outcomes of the refugee experience: increased receptivity to new ways and ideas, strengthened sense of self and collective identity, greater sense of altruism, and a greater inner rootedness and/or security.[13]

From a sociocultural perspective, refugee camps, such as Ban Vinai, may also be seen as total institutions, which pattern relationships between refugees and relief workers.[14] Although refugee camps have existed since earliest recorded time, the modern camp more closely resembles other total institutions—the asylum, prison, hospital—than it resembles its predecessors. Such institutions structure relationships of dependency between refugees and relief workers as a means of controlling the inmates. In Foucault's terms, the modern camp is a technology of power, specifically a mechanism for containing and managing conflict.[15] At the same time, camps are asylums for those whose lives are threatened.

Much of the research on refugees as well as numerous reports document the political and economic circumstances of refugee situations. However, few specifically analyze the role of camps within the larger international political economy. Because the refugee, as a category, is often assumed, there is little discussion of what this category means both individually and collectively to those who become refugees. Many studies also document the political, economic, and historical events leading to the formation of refugee camps, but there is little discussion of the internal processes that perpetuate them.[16] In proposing alternatives to camps, however, it is important to ask whose and what interests are served by these situations? In the literature, refugee situations often appear static and immovable. However, as in all social life, these situations are constantly evolving and changing. Because refugee camp situations are increasingly long term, it is important to know how the refugee experience shapes individual and collective identities.

In this book, I analyze the refugee camp experience along three dimensions: political economic, sociocultural, and psychoanalytic. In the broadest sense, the "refugee" is a modern political economic and legal construction in an international system of nation states. From this perspective, refugees share common characteristics: their poverty, disenfranchisement, alienation, and dependency on international organizations, etc., across all refugee situations. From a sociocultural perspective, refugee camps are unique human environments. Refugee camps share characteristics of other total institutions: prisons, asylum, and hospitals. These camps enforce a dominant Western bureaucratic and rationalized system on their inhabitants. Like inmates of other total institutions, refugees resist the institution's enforced socialization. Each refugee group also brings unique cultural traditions, beliefs, and practices, which allow them to resist the more Western forms of modernization. Refugees' cultural understandings and traditions also frame personal interpretations of the camp experience and interactions. The refugees' potential for freedom, and thus, the profound effects of camp life, are evidenced most clearly in the personal expressions and interactions. From a psychoanalytic perspective, certain key events and relationships, particularly those that form one's earliest memories and impressions, frame individual interpretations of this experience.

In the following chapters, I address each of the three dimensions— the political, sociocultural, and psychoanalytic—by describing and analyzing both the larger context of international relief and daily life inside Ban Vinai. In chapters 2 and 3, I describe the formation of the international relief system and its role in the regional politics of Southeast Asia. These chapters provide the political, economic, and historical context of Ban Vinai and situate the camp in the larger politics and structure of international relief. In chapters 4 through 10, I depict life inside Ban Vinai and portray interactions between refugees and relief workers. In chapter 4, I describe the camp setting and contrast the ideologies and world views of refugees and relief workers. In chapters 5 through 7, I depict the daily lives of different generations and describe their varying relationships to relief workers and to the institution. These chapters are based on the life histories of three women: a young Hmong student, a 33-year-old Khmu mother, and an elderly Hmong shaman. In chapters 8 through 10, I then show how various generational and institutional relationships play out in three characteristic events of camp life: 1) a resistance meeting, 2) a processing interview, and 3) an annual festival. The first depicts both the symbolic as well as organizational forms of resistance. The processing interview is the institution's own rite of passage, while the annual event, New Year's, is a festival of reckoning and remembrance. Finally, in chapter 11, I explore the policy and theoretical implications of this research. I review alternatives to refugee camp life for the Laotian refugees and discuss how the Ban Vinai experience informs our broader understanding of refugees and international relief.

By necessity the camp inhabitants were well aware of how larger political and economic relationships affected their lives and they reflected this knowledge in their interrogations of me. Including their questions throughout the narrative brings home the de facto counter-ethnography of those about whom I write.[17] Their questions made me aware of the larger forces that limited our capacity to change the situation. My responses, in turn, at times, reflect my own limitations as a relief worker to comprehend their lives. While there are many conventions for reporting on ethnographic research, I chose the narrative genre to capture the complexity and reflexivity of the refugee camp experience.[18]

I also organize the narrative around three seasons—the hot, the rainy, and the cool—to show how the camp alters inhabitants' temporal and spatial relationships. Their ties to the land and a planting cycle traditionally defined these relationships for most highlander Hmong and lowland Lao peasants. The disjunction between seasonality and productive life in the camp contributed to the inhabitants' dependency on an institutional structuring of time and to a need for reestablishing ceremonies, such as New Year's, in new ways to provide meaning to their daily lives.

The Ban Vinai refugees, as other indigenous and migrant peoples who live in border zones, are caught in a transitional state.[19] Because the refugee experience of conflict, flight, and uprooting is attenuated in the camp, this experience prolongs the refugees' liminality.[20] As other rites of passage, the time spent in the camp marks the refugees' changing awareness and status.

Erikson, a refugee, observed that a great tragedy of the refugee experience is the disruption it creates between different generations.[21] The experience of uprooting and conflict disrupts the transmission of knowledge from one generation to the next and traditional forms of knowledge may be lost. In prolonged refugee situations, differences develop that reflect each generation's particular historical experiences. As I will show, the elders in Ban Vinai, remembering life before the war, seek to reestablish the traditional patterns of life they once knew. They dream of returning to their homeland. For the middle generation, the experiences of war and conflict predominate. Caught between the desires of the elders and their own hopes for their children, the "war generation" seeks security. The youngest generation, the "camp generation," knows only life in the camp. Recognizing their limited educational and economic opportunities, they hope for a better life beyond the camp and want to immigrate. Thus, in prolonged camp situations, there are often marked differences in how each generation patterns its daily life and in how each envisions life beyond the camp.

Relationships between the sexes may also be affected by camp life. While sexual division of labor is common in many agricultural settings, women's work in Ban Vinai becomes increasingly domesticated. Women spend much of their day in maintaining the household and in insuring its survival. A few find employment with voluntary agencies (Volags). Women are also expected to transmit and maintain the traditional practices through their daughters and granddaughters. Men's workload, on the other hand, is reduced and many men are unemployed. Men find work with Volags, trade with local people, and/or become involved in black marketeering. With the loss of productive employment, they become increasingly involved in resistance organizations and activities.

The refugee camp transforms not only relationships at the local level, but also the inhabitants' relationships to the larger world. Although this transformation begins during the war and flight, the camp continues to alter the inhabitant's relationship to time and space, framing them in a Western institutional context. Camps, such as Ban Vinai, become meeting points for families and households split apart during the war, but the process of relocation and resettlement again extends kinship ties across national boundaries. The camp itself is both a local and transnational community.

As refugees, the people of Ban Vinai are part of a larger political and economic world order. Their refugee status, while placing them outside the nation state, affords them certain rights and protections. The refugee status also sanctions contemporary national boundaries and identities.[22] At the same time, the growing number of refugees living in Ban Vinai and other camps over long periods of time calls into question the legitimacy of the nation state and its boundaries.

TWO

Creation of an International Relief System

Asylum

The generation portrayed in these verses neither returned to Egypt nor found the promised land. As a minority people, they fled a powerful, tyrannical state to preserve their way of life. Like so many refugees of modern times, they lived between what they had lost and what they had not yet found, in a state of fear and waiting. Their hope lay in the next generation, their memory and frame of reference in the past.

Until the nineteenth century, the mass migrations and flights recorded throughout history were rarely defined as refugee movements. The flights of the Israelites from Egypt, Huguenots from France, or Hmong from China, to cite only a few, were motivated by social and political economic forces similar to those underlying many contemporary refugee movements.[1] Such movements, however, were unimpeded by national boundaries, although these early refugees often came into conflict with indigenous peoples in places where they sought sanctuary. From the early seventeenth century to the twentieth, the European monarchies extended their national boundaries over territories in Asia, Africa, and the Americas.

Would God that we had died in the land of Egypt! Or would God that we had died in this wilderness! And wherefore hath the Lord brought us unto this land, to fall by the sword, that our wives and our children should be a prey? were it not better for us to return into Egypt?   Numbers 14:2—3

13

The legacy of this colonialism was artificial, often untenable borders that continue to provoke human population shifts today.

The modern concept of asylum, which evolved in the nineteenth century, corresponded to the beginnings of modern warfare and the rise of nationalism in Europe. Although asylum had its roots in biblical times, the concept changed from saving individuals from family and tribal feuds to protecting victims of national and international conflicts.[2] As national boundaries became more fixed, national governments increasingly assumed the asylum responsibility.[3] Asylum, however, was not a new concept and the idea of aiding the victims of war originated earlier in the legal and philosophical treatises of Erasmus, Grotius, and Helvetius, but found little public acceptance.[4] The liberal social reform movements of the latter part of the nineteenth century provided more favorable grounds.

In 1859 Jean Henri Dunant, a Genevan entrepreneur, conceived of the idea of aiding victims of war. While seeking an audience with Napoleon III for his projects in Algeria, he became involved in the Battle of Solferino in the Crimea.[5] The battle, which claimed more than 40,000 Austrians and Frenchmen, overrode his own financial concerns and led to his founding of the Red Cross. Dunant aided the victims and dressed in a white suit, became known as the "Man in White."[6] As relief efforts are often entangled in conflict, his suit became splattered in blood and the red and white became the symbol for the Red Cross. From his experiences, Dunant, in *Un Souvenir de Solferino,* argued: "Could not the means be found in time of peace to organize relief societies whose aim would be to provide care for the wounded in time of war by volunteers of zeal and devotion and properly qualified for such work?"[7] While applauding his work, Florence Nightingale pointed out that civilian medical services could relieve nations of their responsibility for going to war.[8] Her concern continues to haunt relief efforts today.

The eventual outcome of Dunant's vision, the International Committee of the Red Cross (ICRC), a private Swiss organization, played a major role in organizing early relief efforts (see table 2.1). During the First World War, ICRC assisted in refugee repatriation and prisoners of war correspondence. In 1919, ICRC founded the League of Red Cross Societies to coordinate international relief work and became guardian of the Geneva conventions protecting war prisoners.[9] Immediately following the First World War, the need for international assistance became apparent when for the first time thousands fled economic and social upheaval.[10]

Modern technology would change the nature of warfare. Even be-

TABLE 2.1.
A Chronology of Selected Relief Events

1859	Battle of Solferino in Crimea
1863	Founding of Red Cross Societies at Geneva Conference
1920	Nansen appointed League of Nations' High Commissioner for Refugees
1938	Conference at Evian
1943	United Nations Relief and Rehabilitation Administration (UNRRA)
1947	International Refugee Organization (IRO)
	Partition of India and Pakistan
1948	United Nations Relief and Works Association (UNRWA)—creation of the Palestinian refugee camps
1950	United Nations High Commissioner for Refugees (UNHCR)
1951	United Nations Convention Relating to Status of Refugees
1956	United Nations Refugee Fund (UNREF)
1957	Hungarians flee to Western bloc
	Algerians flee to Tunisia and Morocco
1959	Tibetans flee to India and Nepal
1960	World Refugee Year
	African refugee movements (throughout the 1960s and early 1970s): Togo, Zaire, Burundi, Tanzania, Senegal, Uganda, Central African Republic, Zambia, Bostwana, Sudan, and Ethiopia
1967	Biafran War in Nigeria
1969	Organization of African Unity (OAU) Convention Governing the Specific Aspects of Refugee Problems in Africa
1971	Bangladesh Crisis
1972	UNHCR operations open in Thailand
1975	First Wave of Southeast Asian refugees
1978	Vietnamese Invasion of Kampuchea
	Second Wave
1979	Geneva Conference on Indochinese Refugees
	Soviet-backed coup in Afghanistan
1982	Third Wave
1984	Famine in the Horn of Africa
	Karen (Burmese) flee to Thailand
1989	Second Geneva Conference on Indochinese Refugees

fore the First World War Dunant, in witnessing the Crimean carnage, foretold the changes: "If the new and frightful weapons of destruction which are now at the disposal of the nations seem destined to abridge the duration of future wars, it appears likely, on the other hand, that future battles will only become more and more murderous."[11]

The concept of total war developed during the First World War when, with the use of aerial warfare, the distinction between military and civilian populations was no longer respected.[12] As nuclear and

15

guerrilla warfare technologies developed, this distinction would become increasingly meaningless. Of the victims of the First World War, an estimated 5 percent were civilians; of the Second, 50 percent; of Vietnam, 80 to 90 percent; and of the civil war in Lebanon, 97 percent or more.[13] Reflecting the changing technologies of war, the concept of asylum changed from protecting the single dissenter fleeing state persecution to protecting thousands fleeing to survive. In response to large-scale movements, the international community increasingly specified refugee rights and treatments through international relief efforts.

In the 1920s Fridtjof Nansen became the League of Nations first High Commissioner for Refugees and was immediately faced with the problem of assisting a million and a half refugees from the Russian Revolution.[14] Many fled to Europe, others lived in camps in Turkey and Asia Minor, while still others escaped to China (only to flee again during the Second World War). Following this crisis in 1922, the Greco-Turkish conflict displaced 320,000 Armenians and in the Middle East, 30,000 Assyrians, Assyro-Chaldeans, Kurds, and other groups under Turkish rule. Nansen convened an international conference in Geneva. At the conference, he persuaded sixteen nations to accept the Nansen Passports, which provided refugees with travel and identity documents. Eventually, fifty-two nations recognized these documents.[15]

The history between the wars witnessed a series of setbacks. Larger political and economic forces held sway and, characteristically, relief efforts played a minor role until after the Second World War. Between the wars, an international convention to protect civilian victims was drafted but never promulgated. Such protection was relevant to the new aerial warfare that left civilian victims in London, Dresden, Hiroshima, and elsewhere, but most likely could never have been enforced. In 1933, a second refugee high commissioner, James G. McDonald, was appointed to assist refugees fleeing Nazi Germany. Two years later he resigned, disgusted with the failure of governments to protest the Nazi regime or to grant haven for its refugees.[16]

International Institutions

In 1938, as the Second World War approached, President Franklin D. Roosevelt convened thirty-two governments at Evian to discuss ways of assisting escapees from Nazi-dominated territories. At the conference, the international community failed to offer asylum beyond already limited quotas, and Evian is remembered primarily for its failure to save the Jews. In response, the international community created the Intergovernmental Committee for Refugees (IGCR). IGCR initiated discussions with the Nazi government on ways of securing the exodus of refugees. These discussions continued for eight months, but terminated abruptly when the Nazis invaded Poland.[17] During the Second World War, IGCR continued working with other international organizations to assist underground movements and at liberation, issued the London Travel Documents similar to the earlier Nansen Passports.

In late 1943, foreshadowing the end of the war, Washington with forty-four governments established the United Nations Relief and Rehabilitation Administration (UNRRA). Predating the formation of the United Nations Organization, UNRRA's task was to "plan, coordinate, administer or arrange for the administration of measures for the relief of victims of war in any area under the control of any of the United Nations through the provision of food, fuel, clothing, shelter, and other basic necessities, medical and other essential services."[18] The Allies intended UNRRA to be a temporary *ad hoc* organization to repatriate displaced persons, but the refugee problems proved to be far greater. UNRRA's accomplishments, however, were impressive. In its first year alone, it repatriated over six million people and eventually, ten million.[19] Employing almost 50,000 people, UNRRA spent $4.23 billion on supplies, programs, reconstruction, and aid, in what was one of the most effective massive relief efforts ever undertaken.[20]

Incipient cold war politics, to some extent, compromised the neutrality of the emerging international relief system. Moscow refused to support any organization not solely concerned with repatriation.[22] Ceding to strong Soviet pressure, UNRRA refused to aid those who had participated in resistance activities hostile to their government or who did not want to return to their country of origin.[23] When the Western allies repatriated thousands of Soviet citizens, many were incarcerated and murdered by Stalin.[24]

In 1947, as UNRRA's mandate expired, the UN General Assembly created the International Refugee Organization (IRO). IRO was given a broader mandate to assist enemy nationals who had become refugees. Optimistically, the General Assembly also expected IRO to bring about, "the prompt liquidation of the post-World War II refugee situation" and accordingly, limited its mandate to three years.[25] IRO negotiated resettlement agreements, provided overseas transport, and prepared refugees for their new countries with vocational training, health services, and a welfare program. IRO also administered a network of camps. By 1951, IRO had resettled more than a million people (1,038,750) into permanent homes.[26]

Probably the first large-scale resettlement program, IRO was plagued with many of the same problems faced in later resettlement efforts. The costs for postwar resettlement were astronomical. IRO spent $428,505,335 over four and a half years.[26] Many refugees also spent long years in camps awaiting resettlement. Upon accepting the 1947 Nansen Award for her work with refugees in postwar Europe, Eleanor Roosevelt commented that she was depressed to know that 70,000 refugees remained in camps.[27] In 1955, ten years after the war, the majority of these same refugees were still waiting in the camps.

In 1948, the General Assembly created the United Nations Relief and Works Association (UNRWA) to assist Palestinians evicted from Israel. Between 1950 and 1969, UNRWA spent almost $700 million to assist approximately 1.4 million people.[28] With UNRWA funds, several relief agencies, ICRC, the League of the Red Cross, and American Friends Service Committee (AFSC), also assisted 750,000 Palestinians, who fled to Jordan, Syria, Lebanon, and the Gaza strip. Unwilling to address the Palestinian people's claims to a homeland, the General Assembly continued to renew UNRWA's mandate. From its inception, the Palestinian refugee situation was highly politicized. In contrast to other relief organizations, UNRWA reported to a Special Political Committee of the General Assembly. Several generations and almost half a century later, Palestinians continue to live in the UNRWA-built camps.[29] For the international relief community, " 'Palestinization' stands as the world's prime object lesson in what a refugee emergency can lead to if not handled responsibly by the international community and the governments most directly involved."[30]"Palestinization" is also a poignant reminder of the enduring human costs when there is an absence of political will.

In 1950, the General Assembly established the United Nations High Commissioner for Refugees (UNHCR) to take over the legal and political protection of refugees remaining when IRO ceased to function. UNHCR became the major organization in the international relief system. UN member states realized that the postwar refugee problem they thought would be short-term had not yet been solved. In establishing UNHCR, their representatives hoped they would be able to solve the refugee problem and find a permanent solution within a few years.[31] In the optimism of the postwar, however, little did they realize that national liberation movements in Asia, Africa, and Central America would again challenge the validity of nation state solutions.

In 1951, UNHCR produced the Convention Relating to the Status of Refugees, which defined the refugee as,

Any person who, as a result of events occurring before 1 January 1951 and owing to a well-founded fear of being persecuted for reasons of race, religion, nationality or political opinion, is outside the country of his nationality and is unable or, owing to such fear or for reasons other than personal convenience, is unwilling to avail himself of the protection of that country; or, who not having a nationality and being outside the country of his former habitual residence, is unable or, owing to such fear or for reasons other than personal convenience, is unwilling to return to it.[32]

The convention established refugees' rights to religious freedom, gainful employment, property and work in "liberal professions" (i.e., to continue practicing as doctors, lawyers, teachers, etc.). It also accorded refugees the same standard of treatment as other foreign nationals. Most importantly, the convention established the right of non-refoulement; that a refugee cannot be forcibly repatriated. The 1951 Convention was later appended to include persons without a nationality, and a 1967 Protocol amended the time limits to cover all refugees after the Second World War.

As a coordinating body, UNHCR had little power to enforce the 1951 Convention, particularly the principle of non-refoulement, without government cooperation. Occasionally, high commissioners used their "good offices" to act quickly in an emergency. They would also use this authority to assist displaced persons and returnees.[33] From its inception to the present time, UNHCR has had to enlist government cooperation.

Although twenty-four countries unanimously adopted the convention, UNHCR had trouble getting governments to accede to the convention their representatives had signed.[34] The convention was eventually recognized in 1954. By the late 1970s, however, only seventy-eight countries had ratified the convention and only seventy-two the 1967 Protocol.[35] Even today, many Asian and Eastern European countries still have not ratified the convention.[36]

UNHCR receives no regular budget allocations and initially could not obtain government or private support without prior permission from the General Assembly.[37] A distinctive feature of UNHCR's budgetary process is its dependence on voluntary government and private, as opposed to assessed, contributions.[38] Potentially, large donor countries, such as the United States, can influence the organization's priorities. An analysis of UNHCR aid to African states during 1963 to 1981, however, showed that humanitarian rather than political factors determined UNHCR's allocations during that period, and UNHCR's assistance was based primarily on the number of refugees.[39]

The drafters of the 1951 Convention defined refugee protections primarily in terms of the European refugees of those times. Although

UNHCR's mandate was broader than its predecessors', the convention only applied to refugees after they had been granted asylum. The convention never guaranteed asylum, and the international community has no effective mechanism for intervening in the internal affairs of a government to protect against human rights' violations.[40] According to one senior UNHCR administrator, "UNHCR cannot involve itself directly with the underlying causes of refugee movements and can do nothing overtly to prevent them."[41] The 1951 Convention also conceived of refugees, as individuals to be treated on a case by case basis. Most refugee movements in the postwar period, however, have been large-scale movements.

The early postwar relief movement was solidly aligned with the Western bloc, and this alignment was reflected in interpretations of the 1951 Convention. As one UNHCR observer notes: "In the post World War II era there was evidently a common consensus that those who flee communism are assumed to be *bona fide* asylum claimants, and even if they could not establish a well-founded fear of persecution, they were not turned back."[42] Determining refugee status in the early postwar era was easier; those fleeing Communism were refugees. This suited the politics of the cold war, but proved to be outmoded in the changing realities of North-South relationships.

Soon after its founding, UNHCR's first task was to protect refugees remaining from the war.[43] UNHCR had little funding and appealed to outside sources. In 1954, the Ford Foundation provided a grant for projects "intended to finding permanent, radical, and final solutions to the problem of refugees" (p. 52). The projects were implemented by fifteen voluntary agencies, including the World Council of Churches, National Catholic Welfare Conference, American Friends Service Committee, and Young Men's Christian Association (YMCA). The General Assembly also established the United Nations Refugee Fund (UNREF) to achieve "permanent solutions for refugees" (p. 57). Although the UN set a target of $16 million in voluntary contributions for 1955–1958, they characteristically fell short (p. 57).

UNHCR sought to integrate the postwar European refugees in first asylum countries. Integrating refugee camp inhabitants, like obtaining government support, proved to be a difficult and lengthy process. The so-called residual refugee population included a high proportion of elderly, physically or mentally disabled, and chronically ill people, who had been denied resettlement. An estimated one-quarter of refugee households had a disabled member, which made it difficult for families to leave without leaving that member behind. Lengthy stays in camps also created problems of depression and apathy. UNHCR rhetorically claimed, however, that its goal was to "help the refugees help themselves" (p. 48).

By 1956, 75 percent of the refugee camp population had been settled, but resettlement funds had been expended. Lindt, then UN High Commissioner, made permanent solutions for the refugees a major objective and worked to close down the camps. Some voluntary agency staff opposed their closing, because they feared many refugees outside the camps were worse off than those inside.[44] UNHCR, however, argued that the isolation of camp life was particularly bad for children.

Camp clearance gave contributors a measurable goal and UNHCR set 1960 as the target date. From 1956 to 1959, the organization raised $14.5 million, three-quarters of which was spent for permanent resettlement. Approximately 15,000 European refugees in China made their way to Shanghai and were evacuated through Hong Kong. These funds also assisted a new wave of refugees, the Nationalist Chinese in Hong Kong. In 1959, UNHCR raised another $3 million for camp clearance.[45] Official history does not record the last refugee's resettlement, because by 1960, UNHCR was already engulfed in new, more massive refugee crises throughout the world.

In the postwar period, there were only two more major European refugee movements. In 1957, several thousand Hungarians fled after the Soviets put down the anticommunist uprising. Again in 1968, thousands of Czechoslovakians fled when the Soviets invaded and took over the government. During the Hungarian crisis, UNHCR recorded, "On a single night at the height of the emergency, 8000 people crossed the frontier" (p. 67). A year and a half later, the high commissioner was able to report 170,000 Hungarian refugees had been resettled in thirty countries. The Western powers responded equally quickly and sympathetically to the Czech refugees. In both cases, accepting these peoples served Western interests in the cold war.

Following the Second World War, the Western powers expanded the role of relief institutions in international affairs. The increasingly complex system was designed primarily to deal with a trans-European refugee flow, to help displaced persons return to their homelands, and to solve short-term problems. Western relief organizations often portrayed the refugee as a helpless victim, whose plight was nevertheless temporary. Relief itself was primarily conceptualized in Western terms to aid the postwar refugees and those fleeing communism.

The architects of the international relief system assumed government good will and support. They also assumed uncontested national

21

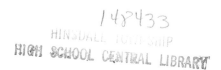

boundaries. Little did they realize that nationalism in the new states of Asia and Africa would provoke massive refugee movements. In ensuing years, the international relief system they established would be severely strained by new, large scale population movements throughout the world.

Refugees from New Nations

From the early 1960s to the present, refugee crises have increasingly been located in the non-Western world. Distinguishing the new refugee movements from earlier ones in Europe, UNHCR observed: "The post-war refugees in Europe were, in general, town or village folk—artisans and craftsmen, small shopkeepers and merchants, intellectuals and professional men. The majority of African refugees are rural people, peasants and herdsmen, hunters and cultivators" (p. 111). While many rural peasants and nomads had historically migrated in times of famine or conflict, the proliferation of the nation state system meant that these traditional migrations came to be defined as refugee movements.

In the late 1950s and throughout the 1960s, the formation of new nation states in Africa provoked new migrations throughout the continent. Although the Algerian refugee crisis began in 1957, the same year as the Hungarian one, it evolved very differently and in ways that would characterize many subsequent non-Western refugee movements. During Algeria's struggle for independence, many agrarian peasants fled to Tunisia and Morocco. Characterizing that movement, UNHCR noted: "The Algerian refugees were mostly women and children and older men, many were farmers or village people, others were semi-nomadic. They had brought their flocks of sheep and camels with them, but they did not want to settle, only to survive until they could return home in safety. What they needed most were medical services, food and clothing" (pp. 77–78).

Over the next two years as the crisis worsened, UNHCR assisted local Tunisians impacted by the crisis. The evolution of the Tunisian crisis would characterize many later refugee movements in the new nations of Asia and Africa. UNHCR coordinated the effort, while voluntary agencies established food distribution centers. By 1959, the flight of some 250,000 refugees surpassed the Hungarian one (p. 79). A large proportion of the refugee population, 90,000 (36 percent) were children. Despite their own poverty, however, the Tunisians, by traditional custom, offered asylum and expended their own resources to help the refugees.

In 1962, UNHCR and the voluntary agencies arranged for the Algerians to be repatriated. They organized milk distribution centers, clothing, tents, shelters, and schools in the process. As most refugees returned home, UNHCR hailed the "miracles achieved by organized international assistance" and observed that countries of all ideological persuasions, the United Arab Republic, France, United States, and USSR, provided assistance (p. 81). Significantly, in providing assistance to Tunisia and Morocco and in keeping with its neutrality, the General Assembly made no reference to the recipients as refugees.

The Algerian crisis exemplified the different priorities UNHCR would follow in Africa in attempting to achieve durable solutions. Unlike the European refugees who settled in the asylum country or resettled in third countries, most Algerians eventually returned to their home country. UNHCR argued that these refugees were fleeing a temporary conflict and wanted to repatriate (p. 81). As in most African refugee situations, third-country resettlement was not an option. In ensuing years, UNHCR would continue to work toward repatriation or local integration of many African refugees. As one UNHCR field officer later explained their priorities: "UNHCR believes that the best solution is first, repatriation; second, local integration; and third and *last,* third-country resettlement."[46] By third-country resettlement, the officer meant that refugees who had sought asylum in one country (the second country) would then be resettled in yet another (the third).

During the early 1960s, UNHCR and voluntary agencies assisted many refugees in Africa as new states gained independence. In 1961, 6,000 refugees fled from Ghana to Togo, some 150,000 from Angola to the Bas Congo, and several thousand Watutsi from Rwanda to northern Congo. During the same year, UNHCR was also involved in refugee situations in Uganda and Tanzania. Most African refugees eventually returned or found asylum in a neighboring country. By 1965, UNHCR reported being involved in fifteen different African refugee situations. Between 1965 and 1969 this trend continued. Total assistance increased $200,000 each year and by 1969, the number of African refugees totaled 240,000.[47]

Voluntary agencies likewise played a growing role in the various relief efforts. Although a few agencies, such as the American Jewish Committee, American Friends Service Committee, and the YMCA, were founded around the First World War, many more evolved after the Second World War.[48] In March 1962, the International Confederation of Citizen's Voluntary Associations was organized in Geneva to coordinate and provide a forum for relief efforts. UNHCR served primarily as a coordinating body, while day-to-day operations were carried out by the voluntary and other non-governmental agencies in the field.

In contrast to the UN organizations, the voluntary agencies by being in the field could often respond more quickly to a crisis.[49] However, many local religious missions were not initially equipped to deal with large relief operations. During the 1960s, the voluntary agencies' role in relief efforts grew and several—Catholic Relief Services, World Council of Churches, Lutheran World Federation, and the YMCA—became involved in relief work in Africa. Other agencies—the Danish Refugee Council and Oxfam—helped raise funds for various crises. UNHCR took on the role of coordinating their diverse interests to ensure an efficient allocation of services.

In the early years of its operation, UNHCR's mandate was limited and among the UN organizations it was considered the "Cinderella" agency with low prestige and leverage in the UN system (p. 882). Refugee situations in Africa, however, increased UNHCR's role and visibility and required more interagency cooperation. In 1961, the high commissioner reported that: "The increasing varied nature of this Office and the extension of its activities to many parts of the world has further enhanced the need for close cooperation with some of the main specialized agencies and offices of the U.N." (p. 882). Over the years, UNHCR would coordinate its relief efforts with the International Labour Organization (ILO), UNESCO, UNICEF, the World Food Programme (WFP), the Food and Agriculture Organization (FAO) and other UN bodies.

In the late 1960s, UNHCR played a significant role in getting African states to work together on refugee issues. Dr. Schnyder, the high commissioner reported proudly: "Perhaps the outstanding advance, viewing the problem of refugees in Africa on the broadest front, is this: there has, in this continent, been no repetition of the misery and degradation of the refugee camps that were so tragic a feature of the European scene in the early years of the work of the Office."[50]

Prince Sadruddin Aga Khan, the subsequent high commissioner, developed a good working relationship with several African heads of state. The prince was instrumental in persuading the Organization of African Unity (OAU) in 1969 to draft the "Convention Governing the Specific Aspects of Refugee Problems in Africa." The OAU Convention broadened the definition of refugee to protect those fighting for independence or fleeing civil wars—circumstances underlying many African population movements. The convention also covered ethnic minorities without nationality, who were forced to flee their homelands. Recognizing the mass character of refugee movements, the convention expanded the UN definition to include generalized conditions of violence.[51] Specifically, the OAU Convention (1969) defined the refugee as "every person who, owing to external aggression, occupation, foreign domination, or events seriously disturbing public order in either part or the whole of his country of origin or nationality, is compelled to leave his place of habitual residence in order to seek refuge in another place outside his country of origin or nationality."

The OAU Convention further provided for refugee asylum and defined mechanisms for voluntary repatriation. Forty-two African nations signed the convention, and that, along with the 1951 UN Convention remain the primary international legal instruments protecting refugees.

In the late 1960s, the Biafran refugee crisis in Nigeria attracted major international attention. Although the war began in 1967, it did not attract public attention until spring 1968. During the conflict, relief organizations supported different sides. UN organizations, except UNICEF, were reluctant to side against the Nigerian government. UNHCR was not mandated to assist internal refugees and could assist only those who fled to neighboring countries. However, UNHCR eventually repatriated some 5,000 children who were flown out of the war zone.[52] The Catholic Church and several other religious organizations supported the Ibo majority, many of whom were Christian. Religious and other nongovernmental organizations also played a major role in mobilizing public support for the relief effort. The International Committee of the Red Cross asserting its neutrality attempted to assist both sides. Relief officials appealed dramatically to save millions who would die without food, but no one knew exactly how many people were involved and much of the food aid fed rebel forces. The relief assistance allowed the Biafran rebel forces to avoid a negotiated settlement and thus may have prolonged the civil war.[53]

In 1971, another refugee crisis in Bangladesh drew world attention. From an historical perspective, the conflict was the outcome of an earlier unresolved refugee situation, the British partition of India and Pakistan in 1947, which uprooted eleven to twelve million people overnight.[54] Some thirty years later, Bengali nationalists with India's support fought to establish the independent state of Bangladesh. Military buildups by both India and Pakistan led to a full-scale war.

The aftermath left some ten million East Bengali refugees, many of whom were Hindu, who sought refuge in India. India asked for international assistance and involved UNHCR in "one of the largest and most difficult humanitarian emergency actions" in its history.[55] Although, In- 25 dia had already granted asylum to some 40,000 Tibetan refugees in the north, India's Prime Minister Indira Gandhi insisted from the beginning that the Bengali refugees would not be allowed to remain permanently in India.

The Indian government initially housed 6.8 million refugees in 896 camps and provided rations for another three million registered refugees (p. 754). The government also provided 600 million rupees (US$80 million) in refugee aid and another 300 million for the affected states. From the beginning, however, the program was organized with the goal of refugees' eventual repatriation. Prince Sadruddin Aga Khan, the high commissioner, warned: "We cannot afford to just set up huge feeding programmes and temporary housing that tends to be permanent. . . . We have to find out quickly what the ultimate solutions will be, and no one has to be a prophet to see that the best solution would be to help the people return to their homes, if and when the situation allows [this] to take place" (p. 759).

Bangladesh was one of the most successful large-scale repatriation programs ever undertaken in a relief effort. The Bangladesh experience demonstrates just how quickly a large-scale effort can be mounted if there is a negotiated settlement. Even before the cease fire in 1972, some refugees began returning to Bangladesh. The ultimate success of the program, however, depended on the political settlement and the cooperation of the governments directly involved. The Indian government with the Bangladesh authorities in Dacca organized the refugees' return and provided transport. Refugees received two weeks basic rations for the journey and some provisions for their first few weeks home. The relief operation also established staging camps in transit and some 271 camps in Bangladesh (p. 779). Of the ten million refugees, more than seven million repatriated by March 1972 (p. 760).

The Indian government eventually accepted the remaining refugees who shared common linguistic and cultural roots with their kin in the Indian state of West Bengal. Yet, that asylum was costly. When the Southeast Asian refugee situation was defined as a crisis eight years later, there were still far more homeless refugees in West Bengal, living on the Calcutta train tracks and in other impoverished circumstances, than all those in Thailand combined. Periodic unrest between local Indian communities and these refugees continues to the present time.

Refugee movements, such as Biafra and Bangladesh, may not have attracted much public attention were it not for the media. During the 1960s and 1970s, UNHCR and other relief organizations began enlisting performing artists to raise money for refugees. One of the first media events was "World Refugee Year" organized by *Crossbow*, a British journal in 1960. Jean Cocteau designed a refugee stamp that brought in $1.5 million for relief and Yul Brenner encouraged other performers to participate in a recorded "All-Star Festival" to benefit UNHCR. This event was followed by an International Piano Festival in 1965 and a third record in 1969 that sold over a million copies.[56]

Artists from Joan Baez on the Khmer border in 1979 to Ken Kragen, who organized the USA for Africa event in 1984, have continued to play an important role in raising money for refugee crises. While their support benefited many refugees, artistic involvement could also trivialize a complex political situation. Artists who lacked political awareness were used by various causes. In this vein, Ken Kragen, reflecting the optimism of one who raised $5 million for refugees, recounted: "Once we got into it and began to realize the scope of the problem and what we were doing to raise money and awareness, the whole thing became a much bigger task. Then we began to think maybe we could improve the world."[57]

The media also played a major role in defining refugee crises and bringing them to public attention. Voluntary agencies, such as CARE, Save the Children, Oxfam, and many religious groups used television advertising to raise contributions for their relief efforts. Although many agencies were involved in development projects, they often found it easier to raise money for relief efforts. By defining a situation as a crisis, the voluntary agencies attracted more public support. Relief also suggested a short-term commitment, while development projects often required several years of sustained effort.

Timing, however, was critical for enlisting public support for a crisis. As Shawcross, a British journalist, later observed, television executives and viewers are fickle; starving children do not necessarily become a story.[58] He noted that the Western audience was more susceptible to appeals in the fall than in summer, when many were on vacation. The international relief system's dependency on the media to raise money had definite disadvantages. The crisis mentality emphasized short-term solutions and public attention could shift before the conflict was resolved or the crops planted.

The focus on relief assistance, at times, obscured the larger political implications of refugee movements. In the 1960s and 1970s, the forces of nationalism created mass migrations throughout Asia and Africa. Many conflicts were the outcome of artificial and untenable boundaries created prior to independence. Often, the victims were minority groups, nomads, and poor peasants. That these peoples came to be defined as refugees reflected the international community's perceived need to define boundaries in the creation of new national identities. The definition of refugee also reflected a new understanding of forced migration and an expansion of the role of international relief in response to such migrations.

The nature of modern warfare had also profoundly changed. The major powers were engaged in an armament race designed to assure mutual deterrence.[59] The technology of nuclear warfare was not sufficiently developed to provide the illusion of a clean strike, nor could the survival of a defeated government be assured. Military interventions supported the nation-state system and its boundaries, even those that had only recently been established. Conflict was contained and the major powers used it to extend their sphere of influence. At the local level, for many peoples, national identities conflicted with traditional boundaries and notions of community. Conflict—specifically through guerrilla warfare—was an expression of those tensions and when supported by a major power, resulted in revolutions and counterrevolutions.

During this same period, the international relief community became increasingly complex. The various components of the international relief system included: 1) the international organizations (UNHCR and

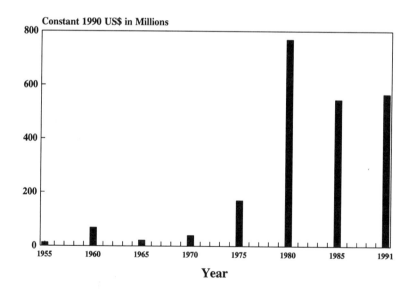

28 FIGURE 2.1. UNHCR Expenditures, 1955–1991

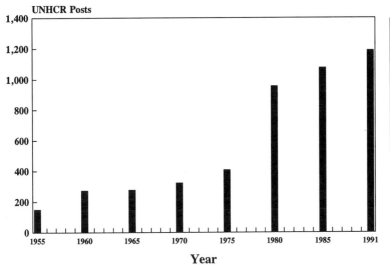

FIGURE 2.2. UNHCR Number of Posts, 1955–1991

other UN bodies), 2) national governments, 3) voluntary, nongovernmental agencies, 4) the media, and 5) the public. From 1955 to 1975, as
shown in figures 2.1 and 2.2, UNHCR expenditures and posts moder-
ately increased. From 1975 to 1980, however, with the onset of the
Southeast Asian refugee crisis, UNHCR expenditures and posts grew
exponentially. Various refugee crises also brought different voluntary
agencies to the forefront of public attention and relief efforts became an
important part of many voluntary agencies' work.

Thus, the decades of the 1960s and 1970s marked a turning point in
international relief. Increasingly, the international community realized
that the refugee problem could not be solved permanently. "As fast as
one problem is solved, another rises," one high commissioner's report
stated.[60] UNHCR's and the voluntary agencies' refugee work in Europe
shifted to the new nations in Africa and Asia. Refugee populations in
these poorer countries, often struggling to survive, were a tremendous
burden on local populations and international relief lessened that burden. Yet, sometimes international involvement and attention also
heightened or prolonged an internal conflict. Ultimately, the resolution
of these refugee crises required political solutions. As UNHCR and the
voluntary agencies' expanded their involvement, new refugee movements severely tested their resources and capacity to respond.

THREE

Camps

in

Thailand

In the 1970s, events in Southeast Asia brought a new set of refugees to the forefront of international attention. The mass movements from Laos, Cambodia, and Vietnam into Thailand were by no means the first in that region. Migrations in that area of the world have been a traditional pattern of life since prehistoric times.[1] Such migrations have created the immense cultural diversity of the region and often allowed minorities to maintain their identities in more favorable locales as different elites rose and fell in power. This time, however, the large scale movement of three nationalities, which included many different ethnic groups, reflected not only the forces of colonialism and emerging nationalism, but superpower entanglement.

In 1887, the French Indochinese Union came into being when the French annexed three parts of the former Vietnamese empire, and the protectorate of Cambodia, for administrative purposes.[2] Colonization created new boundaries and further migrations. In 1893, the French forced Siam (present day Thailand) to cede all areas on the left bank of the Mekong to Indochina. For the next fifty years, the French extended their control over the region.

In the 1930s and 1940s, several Vietnamese

31

nationalist parties, including the International Communist Party, arose in opposition to French rule. During the Second World War both the French and Japanese conscripted local populations. These conscriptions later provided additional organization and support for the Communist and nationalist Resistance.

Following the Second World War, the French returned to rule the region, but encountered growing national Resistance.[3] After 1945, the Indochinese Communist Party gained the upper hand and led the opposition. The French adopted a policy in both Laos and Cambodia of minimizing their political difficulties by supporting an elite minority who, in turn, benefited from the continuing colonial presence. In 1953, pro-French governments in Laos and Cambodia (after 1970 known as the Khmer Republic and from 1975 to 1978 as Kampuchea) became independent.[4] Meanwhile, in Vietnam, the Vietminh Communist forces controlled the north and in 1954, at Dien Ben Phu, gained a part of Laos. At the Geneva Convention later that same year, a military truce divided Vietnam into two zones at the seventeenth parallel.

As the French began withdrawing in 1954, the United States became increasingly involved. President's Eisenhower's famous "Domino Speech" in 1954 established an ideological justification for American intervention. Subsequently, Secretary of State John Foster Dulles committed strategic forces to Thailand. For thirty years (from 1945 to 1975), the region was engulfed in conflict between the Communist Resistance—Vietminh, Pathet Lao, and Free Khmer—and the Western-backed forces of the governments of South Vietnam, Laos, and Cambodia.[5] What might have remained a national liberation and small-scale regional conflict escalated into a full-scale war when the United States and Soviet governments committed troops, financing, and equipment to the war.

The refugee problems in the region (see figure 3.1) began even before the end of what came to be called the Vietnam War.[6] After the 1954 Geneva Agreements, one million refugees fled from North to South Vietnam. Continued conflict during the 1960s displaced several hundreds of thousands in all three countries. Because the majority did not cross an international boundary, they were not considered to be refugees under the 1951 Convention. As the war escalated, aid organizations and voluntary agencies established resettlement centers and provided food aid to the three countries.

In Laos, in the early 1960s and 1970s, U.S. heavy bombing of the North Vietnamese and Pathet Lao Communist troops forced highlander populations into more inaccessible mountainous areas or refugee camps

THAILAND

Chiang Kham •

Ban Nam Yao •

• Ban Vinai

Ban Napho •

Ubon •

• Sikhiu

• Kab Cherng

Site 2 •

• Site B (Greenhill)

Bangkok
Suan Plu ★

Khao I Dang •

Site 8 •

• Phanat
Nikhom

• Khao Larn

• Klong Yai

MYANMAR   LAOS

THAILAND

CAMBODIA

Andaman
Sea

Gulf
of
Thailand

VIETNAM

South
China
Sea

Songkhla

FIGURE 3.1. Map of Refugee Camps in Thailand (Source: CCSDPT 1986)

33

Number of New Arrivals (Thousands)

Camps
in
Thailand

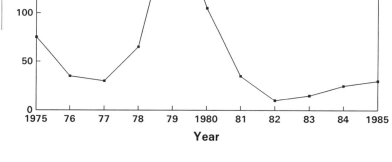

FIGURE 3.2. Total Refugees (UNHCR-Administered) Arrivals in Thailand, 1975–1985 (Source CCSDPT 1986)

in the lowlands.[7] The Hmong highlanders were caught in the crossfire and were recruited by both sides in the war. Those who were recruited by the CIA fled to the mountain town of Long Cheng, which became a secret base during the war. The heavy bombing prevented agricultural production in many areas and required Laos, which had been self-sufficient, to import food.[8] The U.S. government airlifted food supplies to the remote areas and supplied the refugee camps. Many Hmong did not flee across the border until after the war, perhaps, because the provision of aid and paid employment (soldier's pay) provided economic incentives to remain.[9] When the war finally ended in 1975, an exodus across the Mekong into Thailand began.

From 1975 to the present time, refugees from Laos, Cambodia, and Vietnam have sought refuge in Thailand. For analytic purposes, the large-scale movements of the three groups may be divided into three periods; 1) the First Wave, 1975–1977, 2) the Second Wave, 1978–1981, and 3) the Third Wave, 1982–1986 (see figure 3.2). These three waves reflect changes in the international political climate toward the refugees and in the socioeconomic and demographic characteristics of those who came in each period. The First Wave correlates with the American withdrawal and rescue operations, the Second with widespread famine and the invasion of Cambodia by Vietnam ("the Cambodian Crisis"), and the Third with continuing and cyclical conflict.

34

The First Wave (1975–1977): Former Allies

The last days of the war came rapidly and left the Americans quite unprepared for the evacuation. The first refugees were not necessarily the most likely to be persecuted by the new regime, but were those who fled immediately or who had the fortune to be plucked up by the hastily planned rescue operations.[10] In early April 1975, the U.S. government organized Operation Eagle Pull to evacuate their Embassy staff and 800 Cambodians to Thailand. Several thousand Cambodians followed by foot across the Thai border. Most were then resettled in France or the United States In a last ditch effort to bolster support for the Thieu regime in Vietnam, the Ford administration organized "Operation Babylift," an emergency program to evacuate 2000 orphans. President Ford personally held the first baby carried off the plane. The program, however, failed to gain support for an increasingly unpopular war. In mid-April 1975, the administration began plans to evacuate 150,000 Vietnamese. In the final days of April, the war ended as tragically as it began. U.S. helicopters in "Operation Frequent Wind" flew people from the rooftop of the American Embassy in Saigon to waiting U.S. naval vessels in the South China Sea, while marines beat back several thousand Vietnamese trying to escape.

The First Wave of 130,000 Vietnamese refugees were primarily urban, educated elite, many with ties to Americans.[11] The Americans evacuated 65,000 Vietnamese by air and boat and another 65,000 left by their own transport (air, boat, or overland by foot) for Thailand. The Americans then flew the refugees to four processing centers in Guam, Arkansas, Pennsylvania, and Florida where they received cultural orientation and English training. The training, however, imposed an assimilation model that proved to be unnecessary.[12] Although they arrived during a period of economic recession, the majority of the first group of Vietnamese were professional, well-educated, and highly skilled.[13] Their values also accorded well with the American work ethic.[14] Within two years of arrival, 94.5 percent of those employable had jobs as compared with 93.1 percent for the United States as a whole.[15]

Soon after their withdrawal, the U.S. government tried to internationalize the resettlement effort and encouraged refugees in the processing centers to accept other offers of resettlement. With the exception of France, European countries declined to get involved. UNHCR, who wanted a role in the postwar reconstruction of Vietnam, likewise avoided becoming implicated with U.S. efforts. Both UNHCR and the European countries held the United States responsible for the aftermath. UNHCR officials also hoped to develop a repatriation program which received little support from the United States. When 2,000 Vietnamese asked to be repatriated, the Americans were astonished. UNHCR tried unsuccessfully to negotiate their repatriation with the Vietnamese authorities. Acting without UNHCR cooperation, the United States then sent 1,500 Vietnamese back by ship who were immediately sent to reeducation centers. This action only confirmed the prevailing American sentiment that their former allies would be persecuted by the new regime.[16]

The American press, administration, and public initially supported the new Vietnamese arrivals. Their flight fit the prevailing rhetoric that people inevitably oppose Communism by voting with their feet and helped to exonerate American involvement in the war (p. 112). American support, particularly among State Department and Agency for International Development officials, also reflected a genuine mixture of guilt and concern for allies left behind. These "Old Asia Hands" and the voluntary organizations eventually became an effective lobby in enlisting massive public support for Southeast Asian resettlement.

In May 1975, the United States passed the Indochina Migration and Refugee Assistance Act authorizing a major federal role in the reception and resettlement of the Indochinese for two years. Because the refugees were resettled under the Parole Authority, they were not subject to the numerical restrictions of the Immigration and Nationality Act.[17] Conceiving of the program as a rescue rather than a relief operation, the United States expected it to be temporary. However, the 1975 Act was extended several times. In August 1975, the U.S. government again invoked the Parole Authority for Vietnamese and Cambodians who had not yet been resettled and for Laotians also closely associated with the U.S. government.

The First Wave of Laotian refugees to Thailand fled across the Mekong in 1975. From the north came several hundreds of highlanders and other ethnic minorities who had fought against the Vietminh and/or been uprooted earlier by fighting, and from the south came lowland Lao civil servants, Chinese businessmen, and Vietnamese employees.[18] Until August 1975, under the terms of the 1954 Franco–Lao Convention, Laotian citizens were not required to have a visa to enter France and some went directly to France. In spring 1975, American pilots airlifted between 12,000 and 15,000 Hmong, including Vang Pao and his chief officers, from Long Cheng to Thailand. In August that same year, the Attorney General authorized the admission of the first group of Laotians, totaling 3,466 people, under the "Lao Parole Program."[19] Vang Pao and his officers were then resettled in the United

Camps in Thailand

36

States, where the U.S. government helped them with housing and employment.[20]

The majority of the 45,000 highlander refugees who fled to Thailand were Hmong. They came primarily from Xieng Khouang province and followed their leader Vang Pao out of Laos.[21] Several thousand Hmong and other refugees settled in Ban Vinai and Nong Khai refugee camps (see figure 3.1). Until 1979, Ban Vinai maintained an average population of around 11,500 in five centers.[22]

From the United States, Vang Pao continued to direct a Resistance movement and sent marching orders to camp leaders through tape cassette and periodic visits. He promised that within a decade he would return to lead his followers back to Laos. Many Hmong believed him and although they could have qualified for resettlement, remained in the camp.

The Thai government treated the Hmong and other Southeast Asian refugees as "illegal immigrants," who had entered without a visa. Once the refugees gained admission to a camp, the government accorded them the status of "displaced persons."[23] Initially, Thailand, like many other Asian countries, was not a signatory to the 1951 Convention nor the 1967 Protocol. Thai law had no "refugee" classification and the Thai called the refugees *phūu óp-phā-njōp,* "orderly departure migrants" under their Immigration Act.

In contrast, the Thai government had historically allowed outsiders (including Japanese during WWII, 11,000 Chinese in 1945, 40,000 Vietnamese in the late 1940s and early 1950s, several thousand Laotians in the 1950s, 30,000 Burmese in 1959, and 160,000 Southeast Asians after 1975) to settle in their country.[24] The government's refusal to offer permanent asylum to the majority of the new refugees reflected their political and economic interests. The Vietnam War had generated an economic boom in Thailand, and the government was increasing its export markets. The refugees' situation discouraged potential investors. Surrounded by poor, underdeveloped countries, the Thai government also feared that their relative prosperity would provoke new refugee movements. While strongly supporting the U.S. war effort, they held the West responsible for the refugees. The international community's increasing involvement further reinforced this perception.

UNHCR's operations opened in Thailand in 1972 and by 1975, they began coordinating food, shelter, and other services for refugees in the Thai camps.[25] Initially, many voluntary agencies working in the camps were religious organizations; World Vision, Christian and Missionary Alliance Churches (CAMA), Christian Outreach, Catholic Relief Services, Food for the Hungry, Zuid-Oost-Azie (ZOA, a mission of the Dutch Reformed Church), and the Young Women's Christian Association (YWCA). A few secular voluntary agencies—Tom Dooley Heritage, Redd Barna, International Rescue Committee—were also involved from the beginning.

The first group of relief workers were primarily missionaries, development workers, and former military, who had previously worked in Laos, Cambodia, or Vietnam. After being expelled by the new Communist regimes, they rejoined the refugees in camps across the border where they renewed former relationships and ties.

The voluntary agencies were a major though not necessarily homogeneous interest group in shaping refugee life and resettlement. While many religious groups had the experience and skills to establish effective programs, a few took advantage of the situation to proselytize. The relief agencies offered employment opportunities, scarce goods, and some degree of protection and assistance in obtaining resettlement. The Thai government expelled organizations that tried to convert refugees in the camps, but this protection was not strictly enforced and the offenders sometimes returned under other auspices.

In May 1976, the U.S. government provided an "Extended Parole Program," which allowed for the resettlement of another 11,000 land refugees (primarily Laotians but also Khmer and Vietnamese).[26] U.S. criteria for admission was family ties, previous employment by the U.S. government, and close association with the U.S. government. These criteria clearly reflected the obligation Americans felt toward their wartime allies, primarily former government and military officials and their families (p. 7).

The U.S. State Department believed that they were solving the "residual" refugee problem and presented each new parole request as "final".[27] However, UNHCR argued that the Laotians were primarily fleeing economic hardship and could eventually be repatriated. When the American ambassador told Cesare Berta, the UNHCR representative, about the 11,000 parolees, Berta reportedly replied, "This is a catastrophe. This is disastrous, Mr. Ambassador" (p. 127).

The migrations across the border to Thailand continued. Between 1975 and 1977, a total of 34,000 Khmer from the east, 104,000 lowland Lao and highlander groups from the northeast and north, and 12,000 to 15,000 Vietnamese primarily by boats from the south, fled to Thailand.[28] Another several thousand people, primarily Laotians, with relatives or connections unobtrusively integrated into neighboring Thai villages.

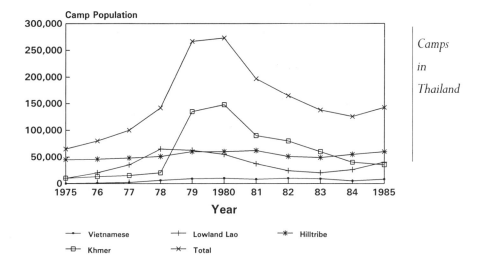

Camps in Thailand

FIGURE 3.3. Refugee (UNHCR-Administered) Arrivals in Thailand by Ethnic Background, 1975–1985 (Source CCSDPT 1986)

In 1977, the Carter administration spurred on by the Volags, paroled an additional 7,000 Vietnamese and 8,000 Laotians. This time the administration argued "compelling humanitarian reasons." The American perception of the rescue operation had gradually shifted to that of a long-term relief operation.[29] Refugee movements into Thailand likewise slowly but steadily increased (see figure 3.2). While resettlement in third countries did not keep pace with the inflow, the growing numbers did not yet threaten Thai national security.

The Second Wave (1978–1982): The Crisis

The Second Wave of Southeast Asian refugees began in 1978, with a surge of Laotian refugees, and peaked in 1979, as the Cambodians fled the oncoming Vietnamese invasion (see figures 3.2 and 3.3). Age-old rivalries between Vietnam and China had intensified as both sought to extend their influence over the region. By 1978, these conflicts erupted in what became the "war after the war."[30] The U.S. government elected not to become directly involved, but continued to exert its influence indirectly through a mounting relief effort and continued assistance to Thailand. As Nayan Chanda, a correspondent with the *Far Eastern Economic Review,* observed in his book: "In the United States a post-Vietnam indifference to Asia and strong congressional feeling ran counter to the

39

Vietnamese hope of bringing back the United States as a new guarantor of regional power balance" (p. 408). Deteriorating economic conditions in Laos, Cambodia, and Vietnam further fueled the conflicts and forced the new governments in these countries to appeal for outside support to stave off famine. Despite Vietnamese overtures for American assistance, two issues—American servicemen missing in action (MIA) and the refugees fleeing communism—dominated American foreign policy in the region.

In 1978, the migration of Laotian refugees (predominately lowland Lao) into Thailand peaked at 57,000.[31] The upsurge following the parole of 1977 provided some support for UNHCR's argument that increased resettlement opportunities, "pull factors," attracted new refugees. Deteriorating economic conditions brought on by a drought in 1977 followed by flooding in 1978 suggested even stronger "push factors."[32] In both years, Laos, which had become one of the poorest countries in the world, had to appeal for international assistance to prevent widespread famine.[33]

This Second Wave also included former Laotian officials who fled reeducation camps and many who were discontented with the new government's policies. When asked why they had left Laos, refugees cited the Vietnamese presence, the LPDR's attempts to collectivize agriculture, taxes on agricultural products, petty governmental controls and increasing bureaucratization.[34]

During the same period, Vietnam also suffered a bad harvest, a deteriorating economy, and mounting conflict with Cambodia. Attempting to take control of their economy, the Vietnamese relocated people from urban to rural areas in "new economic zones" and restructured their urban manufacturing sector. The economic reforms severely impacted the Chinese Vietnamese and middle-class Vietnamese.[35] In 1978, conflict between China, who backed the Khmer Rouge, and Vietnam intensified. With some encouragement from China, 250,000 Chinese left Vietnam for China. Beginning in April 1978, a mass exodus of people also began leaving Vietnam by boat. The "boat people" included two distinct groups: 1) urban Chinese capitalists and 2) Vietnamese, who had ties to the pre-1975 political, economic, and military order in the south.[36] The majority were under thirty-five years of age and included many young men, who left to avoid conscription. From a monthly total of 2,829 boat people in August, their numbers swelled to 21,505 in November. Initially, the Vietnamese government tried to stop them. From 1978 on, however, the refugees' stories suggested that the Vietnamese government unofficially organized and exploited the outflow.[37]

In December 1978, Vietnam invaded Cambodia, which was followed by China's invasion of Vietnam.[38] The Khmer Rouge, who had broken off relations with the Vietnamese, launched several military offensives against them. Since the Khmer Rouge had massacred several million of their own people, the Vietnamese justified their invasion of Cambodia on the grounds that they were liberating the country. The Vietnamese were therefore astonished when they were subsequently universally condemned.[39] The Vietnamese invasion precipitated the Second Wave of Khmer refugees. Escaping fighting between the Khmer Rouge and the advancing Vietnamese, approximately 100,000 Khmer fled into Thailand.[40]

Early in 1979, Poul Hartling, UN high commissioner, offered General Kriangsak, the Thai prime minister, UNHCR's help in dealing with the new arrivals. The Thai government ignored the offer, confined the new arrivals to separate camps, and began periodic push backs across the border during April and May 1979.[41] Meanwhile, the Thai press denounced the West for accepting so few refugees.

In June 1979, the border situation erupted as Thai military rounded up Khmer refugees and transported them in buses to a border further north.[42] Relief officials and diplomats rushed to the border, but the Thai military ordered them out of town. The Thai told the refugees they would be taken to transit camps for resettlement. Thai soldiers then took the refugees at dark to Preah Vihear, where they forced between 43,000 and 45,000 people down cliffs to mine fields. One young man, who survived and eventually resettled in the United States, witnessed his whole family die: "The Thai and Vietnamese shelled from both sides. They killed my brothers, sisters, and mother. I was shot. They thought I was dead. Later, when they left, I escaped."[43] Crossing mine fields for three days, the Khmer had little food or water. Several thousand died. Others remained stranded in the border zone for months.

The world press, which had been publicizing the plight of the Vietnamese boat people, quickly reacted to this incident. Thailand was widely condemned, but according to Shawcross, "From Geneva there was silence. From Bangkok, inaction." The U.S. Embassy might have been able to persuade the Thai government to halt the repatriations, but the American ambassador may have feared that by pressuring Prime Minister Kriangsak, they would bring down the government.[44] Those, who strongly protested, such as an ICRC official, provoked such anger from the Thai government that they were expelled.

The incident demonstrated the limits to international protection in Thailand. The Thai government, surprised by the reaction, criticized the West for not holding the Vietnamese responsible for the refugee situation. While asserting control of the camps, the Thai government was also responding to the growing numbers of refugees and the presence of Vietnamese troops on their border. Over the next few years, Thai policies toward refugee groups would often appear contradictory and at cross-purposes to the outside world, as they alternately opened and closed their borders. Underlying much of their policy and attitudes was fear of a Vietnamese invasion and Communist influence.

The government's ambivalence toward granting first asylum also reflected Thailand's own internal politics. Earlier, in 1976, a student dissent had led to a widespread protest. The army fired on the protesters and several student leaders subsequently joined Communist insurgency groups in the northeast, north, and south of Thailand. Among the Communist insurgents may have been Thai Hmong and other highlanders, whose lands were threatened by the Forestry Department and an encroaching lowland Thai population. More importantly, the Thai Hmong had their own disagreements with the government, which was trying hard to assimilate them into the lowlands.

The Thai leadership feared to resettle the Laotian minorities, who might have kinship ties to rebel groups in Thailand (even though these refugees were avowedly anti-Communist). They also worried that Communists could use the camps on both borders to infiltrate Thailand. Traditional animosities of Khmer versus Thai, Thai versus Vietnamese, and lowlander versus highlander underlay these ideological claims. These traditional animosities also explained variant Thai reactions to the different refugee groups. The lowland Lao refugees with whom the Thai shared kinship ties, Buddhism, mutually comprehensible dialects, and similar cultural practices would often fare better than the Vietnamese, Khmer, or Hmong.

The international relief community responded to the growing crisis by intensifying its involvement on all fronts; from inside Cambodia and Laos, on the border, inside Thailand, and through third country resettlement. In July 1979, sixty-five countries met at a Geneva Conference on Indochinese Refugees. The conference was convened primarily to discuss the problems of the Vietnamese boat people. Vice-President Walter Mondale recalled Evian and this time the international community, at least initially, responded with great enthusiasm.[45] Unfortunately, the Laotian and Khmer refugees' plight provoked little discussion, but was largely subsumed under the Vietnamese boat people's. At the end of the meeting, however, sixty-five countries pledged $160 million and twenty countries agreed to resettle 260,000 refugees.[46]

In October 1979, the Cambodian border erupted again. A renewed

Vietnamese offensive pushed several hundred thousand Cambodians, including members of the Khmer Rouge and other Resistance forces and their families, back across the border.[47] Many were severely malnourished after the years of fighting and devastation. Exhausted by the conflict, they sought sanctuary from forced conscriptions from both Vietnamese and Resistance forces. This time the Western press was ready to provide massive coverage. UNICEF and ICRC with the World Food Programme organized a border feeding operation. The Thai prime minister announced the government's willingness to provide asylum and proceeded with UNHCR-assistance to construct holding centers in Sakheo, Kamput, Khao I Dang, and elsewhere (see figure 3.1). In total, 200,000 Cambodians were allowed to enter holding centers.

To take the pressure off the border, the United States also helped establish three processing centers, in Phanat Nikhom (Thailand), Galang (Indonesia), and Bataan (Philippines). The processing centers served as interim camps for refugees accepted for resettlement in the West. At the June 1979 Tokyo economic summit, President Carter persuaded the Japanese to fund half the construction costs.[48] In return, the United States agreed to increase its refugee quota. Refugees accepted by the United States, Germany, France, Australia, and Canada were then sent from the holding centers to processing centers for medical screening and language and cultural orientation. The processing centers allowed the Western countries to buy time in resettling several thousand refugees.[49]

Images of Vietnamese boat people and starving Khmer converged together in the fall of 1979, to make the world acutely aware of what was now seen as the aftermath of Vietnam. The contemporary internal politics of the region were rarely discussed by the Western press. The Vietnamese boat people's plight was chronicled daily. Most Americans were aware of stories of piracy, forcible push backs by the ASEAN countries, and the horrors of Pulau Bidong (Malaysia) refugee camp, where 40,000 Vietnamese lived in crowded conditions. An investigation by the Australian Press provided substantive documentation of the boat peoples' harrowing experiences.[50]

In reporting the horrors of the Pol Pot regime, many journalists compared the Khmer Rouge massacres to the Nazi holocaust. Such rhetoric ignored the historical evolution of the conflict. The U.S. secret bombings of Cambodia had devastated the country's infrastructure and left a power vacuum that paved the way for a Khmer Rouge takeover.[51] In contrast to prevailing opinion, Chomsky and Herman claimed the Western press was waging a propaganda war on the Khmer Rouge.[52]

They doubted that refugee reports could be trusted. Yet, as events would demonstrate, the outside world did not really know what was happening in Cambodia, and the relief movement's holocaust rhetoric obscured rather than clarified the situation. The refugees themselves said that they fled both Khmer Rouge and Vietnamese forces and few wanted to return until they knew the conflict had ended.

Throughout these debates, there was relatively little publicity or discussion about the Laotian refugees. When large numbers of Hmong arrived in the United States, they provoked some curiosity in their attempts to maintain their customs and former ways of life. Many Hmong had little or no formal education or previous contact with Westerners. Stories in the media initially focused on the Hmong's life in the mountains of Laos. Such stories, however, ignored the radical transformations that this way of life had undergone during the war and in the camps. There was also little analysis of what was happening in Laos and/or of the Hmong's relationship to the new government.

In 1979, arrivals of Hmong in Thailand again rose dramatically. Like the lowland Lao in the previous year, many fled famine. According to one report, the upland rice farmers did not experience the effects of the widespread famine until after the January 1979 opium harvest.[53] LPDR and Vietnamese attacks on the Hmong Resistance in the Phou Bia and Phou Ta Mao (the Bia and Ta Mao mountains) during 1976–1978 may also have contributed to the 1979 exodus.[54]

During the Second Wave, refugee movements to Thailand reached their peak for all three nationalities (see figure 3.2). From 1979 to 1981, some 200,000 non-Communist Khmer, 65,000 Vietnamese boat people, and 111,000 Laotians (including Hmong) arrived in Thailand.[55] The majority were then resettled in Western countries. Resettlement rates for all three groups peaked between 1979 and 1981.

Beginning in 1979, the Western governments, UNHCR, and Vietnam also established an orderly departure program to allow Vietnamese to emigrate directly to third countries. UNHCR represented the United States in the negotiations. The program was fraught with bureaucratic delays and without much support from either the American or Vietnamese governments, was largely unsuccessful in reducing the refugee flows.

In March 1980, the U.S. Congress passed a new Refugee Act which redefined refugees in accordance with the 1951 Convention. The Act abolished former criteria which defined refugees as only coming from the Eastern Bloc or Middle East. The new act also abolished the parole mechanism and established a quota system, which was more responsive to the mass character of refugee movements. The President, in consultation with Congress, was empowered to establish an annual quota and regional allocations. The act further provided for a U.S. Coordinator for Refugees. For the first two years, Congress set a baseline quota of 50,000 refugees. Passage of the 1980 Refugee Act reflected in large part the concerns of a growing Southeast Asian refugee lobby in the United States

Although the Thai government and UNHCR saw eventual repatriation as the optimal solution, the international community, and particularly the U.S. government supported resettlement. Beginning in 1980, ICRC and UNHCR negotiated a modest repatriation program with the Laotian government (LPDR). UNHCR, who was working with displaced persons in Laos, also invested more than $2.5 million in development projects there.[56] However, fewer than 2,000 Laotian refugees over the next few years repatriated and the program never received the same financial assistance or personnel as the resettlement operation. Likewise, when the Cambodian border stabilized in mid 1980, the Thai government also enlisted UNHCR's support for a voluntary repatriation program. Approximately, 9,000 Khmer were repatriated from Sakheo, a predominately Khmer Rouge camp. The repatriation effort, however, provoked a Vietnamese attack following which 50,000 more Cambodians came across the border into Thailand.[57]

The publicity about the "Cambodian Crisis" concentrated resources in terms of funding and personnel along the border.[58] Many new voluntary agencies (Volags) opened programs during the Second Wave. Formed in 1975, the Committee for Coordination of Services to Displaced Persons in Thailand (CCSDPT) recorded a maximum of fifty-two Volags working on relief operations in the Thai camps by mid 1981. Among the new Volags were: Catholic Office for Emergency Relief and Refugees (COERR, Thai), Ecole Sans Frontieres (ESF, French), Japan Sotoshu Relief Committee (JSRC), Medecins Sans Frontieres (MSF, French), Operation Handicap Internationale (OHI, French), Thai-Chinese Refugee Service (TCRS, Taiwanese), and Youth With a Mission (YWAM, American).

During the Second Wave the number of camps reached their maximum number of twenty-one, which included processing, holding, and transit centers. Additional border encampments were not included in the official refugee counts. UNHCR, anxious to maintain good relations with the Thai government, provided assistance and protection only to Cambodians who had been admitted into Thailand.[59] In the UNHCR Cambodian camps alone, Volags had 400 to 600 workers, ICRC had 200 to 250, and the Thai Red Cross had about 100. In these same camps, some thirty-five voluntary agencies contributed $42.2 million.[60] By May 1981, Khao I Dang, the largest Cambodian camp, housed 130,000 refugees making it the largest Khmer city in the world.

The majority of the Cambodian refugees (over 200,000 people) lived in the border camps. Khmer Resistance groups organized these camps and used them as bases for their operations. Until the end of 1981, UNICEF and ICRC with the assistance of the World Food Programme (WFP) led the border relief operations. UNICEF attempted to feed only the women and children, but distinguishing the various groups proved to be difficult. The international community operated the Nong Chan Land Bridge from 1979 to 1981 to bring essential supplies, medicine, rice, and seed, to refugees until they could return home. The Volags claimed the land bridge saved hundreds of thousands of lives.[61] Since economic recovery in Cambodia remained slow, however, the border population did not diminish. A few Volags moved their operations to Phnom Penh, but the majority continued working on the border.

To prevent widespread famine inside Cambodia, UNICEF, ICRC, and Oxfam obtained access to deliver food and essential supplies.[62] Oxfam accepted the new Cambodian government's condition that the international organizations should not concurrently assist those on the border. In contrast, ICRC managed to work on both fronts and conducted secret negotiations with the Cambodian and Laotian governments, which allowed ICRC to continue its work inside both countries.

The international organizations were even less involved in Laos than in Cambodia. The Lao People's Democratic Republic (LPDR), proclaimed by the Lao People's Revolutionary Party in December 1975, was highly suspicious of Western organizations.[63] At the same time, Laos, one of the economically poorest nations in the world, was critically dependent on foreign aid. During the war, Laotians in the Western controlled zone had been among the highest per capita aid recipients in the world.[64] The massive withdrawal of foreign assistance following the end of the war in 1975 severely impacted the Laotian economy and there were few new sources of aid. From 1977 to 1979, financial assistance increased somewhat and amounted to over US$100 million.[65] From 1979 to 1982, there were again significant increases.

Earlier in 1976, Laos and Vietnam issued a joint communique declaring a "special relationship" between their two countries against the forces of imperialism.[66] In July 1977, this special relationship was given legal status in the twenty-five-year Treaty of Friendship and Cooperation.[67] By 1979, the Vietnamese military presence had visibly increased in Laos and foreign observers worried that food aid was being diverted to feed the Vietnamese troops. Relief agencies also feared that foreign aid was being absorbed by the numerous foreign technical advisers in Vientiane.[68] During the war, the revolutionary elites had developed close ties based on shared experiences. Several of the Laotian leaders had been trained in Vietnam and looked to the Vietnamese for military support, economic planning, and technical assistance.[69] Whereas the Khmer Rouge chose to align themselves with the Chinese, the Laotian leadership affirmed their relationship with the Vietnamese. Citing their domination by the Thai in the past, the Laotian leaders also claimed that their alliance reflected historical and geographical considerations, as well as the relationships formed during the war.[70]

The Second Wave refugee movements reflected the effects of Vietnamese expansionism into Laos and Cambodia and the ensuing new regional alignments. The U.S. withdrawal left a vacuum that was not replaced by Soviet aid. While supporting the new socialist countries, Soviet aid was insufficient to prevent widespread famine or to offset the flight of skilled personnel. The Soviets expanded their military presence with bases in Vietnam and advisers in Vietnam and Laos. This support gave the Vietnamese the necessary backing to extend their control over their neighbors, Laos and Cambodia. Meanwhile, Thailand and China, threatened by a Vietnamese Indochina, provided aid to anti-Vietnamese Resistance forces on both the Laotian and Cambodian borders. China trained Hmong Resistance forces in bases inside China and provided arms and asylum for the Khmer Rouge.

In the postwar period, the U.S. government maintained only an indirect influence in the region through economic and political assistance to the Thai government and other ASEAN members. Opposing the Soviet-backed Vietnamese put the Americans in the embarrassing position of supporting the Khmer Rouge in the United Nations. The U.S. government also opposed giving aid to Vietnam and the missing servicemen (MIA) issue dominated the government's relationship and policies toward both countries. By choosing to support the Resistance groups and border relief operation, the U.S. government had little leverage to influence the changing political and economic relations of the region.

By 1981, nearly 93 percent of those seeking asylum in Thailand had been accepted by the Western countries. Despite such a high acceptance rate, that summer the Thai government announced its new policy of "humane deterrence."[71] In the double-speak of relief discourse this meant detention in camps with minimal services, food rations, and no hope of resettlement. To carry out these policies, the Thai government opened a detention center, Napho, for lowland Laotians, and placed all new arrivals there. The government also began periodically closing and consolidating camps beginning with the closings of Songkhla and Laem Sing, two Vietnamese camps.

The Thai government, however, foresaw that international attention was already shifting elsewhere. Well aware of diminishing resettlement offers, the Thai sought to discourage future refugee movements. In the United States, the large influx of refugees was also beginning to provoke a domestic backlash. The American public was much less receptive to the boat people close to their own shores from Cuba and Haiti. According to Loescher and Scanlan:

> U.S. legislators and policy makers were taken by surprise when the newly framed asylum machinery of the Refugee Act broke down with the large influx of Cubans to the United States in the spring of 1980. Within the space of a few months, the United States received nearly 140,000 Cubans and Haitians, and the smooth functioning of the asylum provisions of the Refugee Act which had been envisioned by its framers was effectively sabotaged. The boat exodus from Cuba coincided with the inflow of over 200,000 Indochinese and an indeterminate number of Ethiopians, Nicaraguans, Iranians and Salvadorans seeking political asylum. In 1980 alone, 800,000 immigrants - more than those entering all the other countries in the world combined - entered the United States.[72]

The U.S. government reservedly approved Thailand's new policy of humane deterrence. In August 1981, the Green Commission, a special advisory panel for the U.S. State Department, warned that increasing numbers of refugees were fleeing for economic motives rather than from fear of persecution. The Senate Judiciary Subcommittee on Immigration and Refugee Policy likewise feared that the United States was in "danger of institutionalizing an on-going refugee/migrant flow" and advised that: "We join with others in the international community in undertaking new initiatives and new approaches to deal with both the continuing movement of people from Indochina, as well as the root causes of this continuing flow.[73]

The Third Wave (1982–1986): Continuing Conflict

48

During the Third Wave (from 1982 to the time of this study), refugee camps increasingly became semipermanent ways of life for many Cambodian, Laotian, and Vietnamese refugees. Although the majority of refugees had already resettled in third countries, some 350,000 remained in camps along the Thai-Cambodian and Thai-Laotian borders. The continuing flow of refugees across the borders fluctuated according to political policies on both sides of the border, current resettlement practices, Thai policies toward refugees, and political and economic conditions in Laos, Cambodia, and Vietnam.

During 1982, the Thai government continued to close and consolidate camps by ethnic groups. They closed several Laotian highlander camps in the north and moved the refugees to Ban Nam Yao Camp. The Ban Nam Yao refugees were later moved to Ban Vinai. In some cases, Thai guards forced refugees into the forest without any provisions and told them to leave Thailand immediately.[74] The government also closed two Laotian camps and moved the lowland Lao populations to Napho. In 1983, the Thai authorities officially closed Ban Vinai to all new arrivals (although Hmong continued to enter the camp illegally). The government meanwhile reopened Chiang Kham, a camp in the north, to create a detention center for new Hmong arrivals. These periodic shifts from camp to camp effectively terrorized the refugees, because they could never be certain when they would be uprooted again or, worse yet, sent across the border.

In 1982, on the Cambodian border, a new UN agency, the United Nations Border Relief Operations (UNBRO), formed out of the World Food Program, took over relief operations. UNHCR's abdication of the border effort paralleled the Palestinian situation. Like the Palestinians, the status of the Cambodians on the border was undetermined and they were trapped in a war zone. Various border camps served as bases for three Cambodian Resistance factions—the Khmer Rouge, the Khmer People's National Liberation Front (KPNLF) led by Son Sann, and Sihanouk's forces. In an uneasy alliance, they formed the Coalition government of Democratic Cambodia. Until the mid-1980s, the United States provided covert assistance worth $15 million a year through ASEAN to the non-Communist partners of the coalition.[75] Under the Reagan administration, the United States once again funded anti-Communist Resistance forces worldwide.

In early 1983, the political situation on the Cambodian border deteriorated. The Vietnamese attacked several Khmer border camps. Hundreds were killed, many more wounded, and thousands moved along the border.[76] In late 1984 and early 1985, the Vietnamese mounted a second dry season offensive, which drove some 243,000 refugees to Site 2, a Cambodian camp, and other border camps inside of Thailand. The

49

various Cambodian Resistance groups took over different camps: the KPNLF, Site 2; the Khmer Rouge, Site 8; and Sihanouk's followers, Site B. Although the refugees were inside Thailand, the Thai government refused to grant them permanent asylum. The government would not allow the refugees to be interviewed for resettlement and expected them to return home when the situation improved.

Although the following dry season was relatively quiet, Vietnamese forces were positioned along the border. Site 2 maintained plans to evacuate the entire population of some 135,000 inhabitants to Site 3, a site further inside Thailand, within one hour if necessary. The refugees received food supplies, but were left quite unprotected from shelling. Over the next few years, the Cambodian border stabilized with over 240,000 people living in eight camps. These Cambodian refugees were ineligible for resettlement and were periodically caught in the cross fire between various Resistance groups and the Vietnamese-backed Cambodian government. Resistance forces controlled the camps, and there was no security for their inhabitants. Rapes, robberies, and other acts of violence were common.[77]

There were fewer tensions on the Laotian border, but the Laotian refugees who remained were making a life in camps. From 1981 to 1983, new Laotian arrivals decreased and camp populations gradually declined. The Thai government credited the decline to their policy of humane deterrence, but the economy, harvest, and political situation in Laos also improved. The Laotian government also liberalized its relations and trade with Thailand. Many Laotians associated with the former regime had fled earlier and by 1985, some 10% of the population had left the country.[78]

In Ban Vinai, Laotian Hmong began to refuse Western embassies' offers of resettlement. Receiving word from Hmong relatives in America of the difficulties of resettlement, some literally refused to board the buses for Phanat Nikhom and other processing centers. Vang Pao also instructed refugees to remain there. Even though its support from Thailand and China was declining, the Resistance reiterated its promise of leading the Hmong back to Laos. The Resistance also claimed to receive funding from the World Anti-Communist League, a private, right-wing group led by retired U.S. General Singlaub.[79]

In mid-1983, the Thai government lifted humane deterrence. To ease the crowding in Napho, the government reopened the camp for resettlement interviews. Following this shift in policy, Laotian arrivals to Thailand again increased (see figure 3.2). According to Brown and Zasloff, rumors spread that 1984 would be the cutoff year for resettle-

50

ment.[80] Such rumors may have spurred on those who had kin in the United States and/or those who worried about their long-term future in Laos.

Arrival patterns during the Third Wave for Laotian refugees, as a whole, suggested that they were responding to trends in resettlement policies. UNHCR argued that lowland Lao were attracted by the expanded processing of refugees for resettlement by Western countries. The increases and decreases in movements across the border also reflected current economic conditions in Laos. Economic shortages, new taxes by the Laotian government, and a new military conscription begun in Laos were cited as push factors.[81] Cooper, analyzing Hmong arrivals in Ban Vinai, observed seasonal variations over the years 1981–1983. He reported: "Departure rate figures suggest that Hmong respond to economic factors when deciding a particular time to leave the country, in many cases completing an agricultural cycle before departure."[82] UNHCR also argued that the camps' provision of food and medical care attracted refugees across the border. The monthly food allotment was said to be worth three months' salary for a mid-level Laotian government civil servant.[83]

Beginning in 1984, the Thai were again confronted with a growing refugee population, this time on their western border. The Burmese launched heavier offensives against their own insurrectionary groups, and drove some 9,000 to 10,000 Karen into Thailand's western Tak Province.[84] Although the Karen National Liberation Front numbered about 12,000, the Burmese in several incursions during 1984 gained more control of the Karen-held territories. Karen fled to camps in Thailand where they regrouped. By 1985, the camp population numbered between 16,000 and 17,000.[85] The Thai government viewed the situation as temporary, but permitted relief agencies to operate in the Karen camps. The presence of yet another refugee group only further threatened Thai security. Refugees were arriving on three of Thailand's four borders and on the fourth border, Thailand faced opposition from its own Muslim minority.

The Thai government's policy of shifting the refugee burden to the United States and other resettlement countries was losing ground. From 1975 to 1985, 520,000 (80 percent) of the Southeast Asian refugees (i.e., accorded refugee status) had been resettled in third countries and nearly 70 percent in the United States.[86] Although the majority in UNHCR camps had been resettled, the population in the camps was growing. The Laotian camps housed 75,000 refugees, many who had spent several years in camps. In Ban Vinai, which had been open for

51

more than a decade, 45 percent of the population were under fifteen years and in Site 2, an estimated 30 percent were children.[87] The birth rate in Ban Vinai was high, averaging 4.55 percent over the three preceding years, in contrast to the Thai national average of 1.6 percent.[88]

In 1985, Thailand, with funding from UNHCR, the United States, and Canada, instituted a border screening program for Laotian refugees. The purpose of the program was to distinguish "illegal immigrants" (those fleeing for primarily economic reasons) from "refugees" (persons who participated in political and social movements against Communism and/or connected with the pre-LPDR regime). The screening program reflected U.S. resettlement criteria and screened in those with relatives in third countries (who were likely to be resettled).[89] The screening program had a high (66 percent) approval rate, but at the same time, the Thai border patrols pushed many back across the border before they were screened.[90]

UNHCR continued to press for repatriation, although money and resources were increasingly scarce. Frustrated with the lack of progress, Chetty, the UNHCR legal adviser, observed: "We have to move out from treating the refugee situation by handing out bamboo, depoprovera, and then, hope to God, the refugee situation will go away. Do we sit around and let things happen or move to active pursuance of durable solutions?"[91]

Few refugees wanted to return to Laos. From relatives and friends left in Laos, they received better information about the current situation than did UNHCR. As an UNHCR official admitted, the lack of infrastructure in Laos hampered surveillance of returnees.[92] Those who were associated with the Resistance in any way (such as by living in Ban Vinai, a known Resistance camp) could not repatriate safely. The Hmong reported that those who returned were killed.

The Western embassies also argued for the need to find durable solutions. Lacy Wright, the U.S. counselor for Refugee and Migration Affairs warned: "Because of social, financial, and demographic pressures in receiving countries, Indochinese resettlement abroad has become more difficult. Moreover, there is a growing feeling that many of those currently escaping Indochina are fleeing conditions of poverty and hopelessness, or trying to rejoin families abroad, rather than fleeing persecution."[93] The Canadian Embassy echoed his observations. The Western governments, offering no alternative, merely reiterated their support for the Thai government and the refugees.

52   By early 1986, the refugee situation had reached a stalemate. By refusing to seek a political solution, the United States and other Western

governments had little alternative, but to support camps such as Ban Vinai. The lack of development assistance to those inside Laos and Cambodia encouraged people to cross the border to seek relief. Those with family ties and connections were also drawn by the threat of diminishing opportunities for resettlement. At the same time, fearing pull factors, the United States and other Western countries diminished their assistance to the camps. Faced with the prospect of a growing permanent refugee population, the Thai government discouraged new arrivals. They made life in the camps more difficult and threatened to repatriate those remaining. The camps, however, provided a buffer zone for Thailand. Supported by conservative Thai and American factions, various Resistance groups continued to consolidate their control over the camps. Those inside the camps remained because they had nowhere else to go or because, as in the case of many Hmong, they hoped to return to their homeland.

Children walking on a main road into Ban Vinai toward the market. Taken by Yang Ger and Nhia Za Vang.

Each camp building houses approximately 100–105 people.   Taken by Erica Hagen.

A neighborhood in the camp.   Taken by Erica Hagen.

Cheng Teng Her, the leader of the COERR parasocial workers. Only the most affluent camp leaders can afford a motorcycle.   Taken by Yang Ger and Nhia Za Vang.

The International Rescue Committee (Volag) Building for Public Health and Sanitation Operations.   Taken by Yang Ger and Nhia Za Vang.

A Volag meeting. Many of the Volag refugee workers are young males. Taken by Yang Ger and Nhia Za Vang.

Hmong girls studying their lessons at home after school. The books are provided by the Volags and/or made by the camp printing press. Taken by Erica Hagen.

Hmong girls selling food and supplies in the camp market. Taken by Erica Hagen.

The ice cream man, a Thai vendor, comes through the camp. Behind are the water tanks and women sewing paj ntaub.   Taken by Yang Ger and Nhia Za Vang.

Hmong girls studying Hmong literature in an afternoon school class. In the morning they study Thai and Lao.   Taken by Yang Ger and Nhia Za Vang.

Young Hmong girl.
Taken by
Erica Hagen.

Htin and Lao children in center 9.
Taken by Lynellyn Long.

Mien
boys
playing.
Taken by
Lynellyn
Long

Lao man
making a khɛɛn.
Taken by
Lynellyn Long.

Khmu mother and children
on Volag truck.
Taken by Lynellyn Long

The cleaning crew, refugee volunteers, sweeps through the camp.
Taken by Yang Ger and Nhia Za Vang.

Road home from the market to center 3. The thatched structures are market stalls.
Taken by Yang Ger and Nhia Za Vang.

*Girls getting water
from the storage tanks
at 5 p.m. Taken by
Yang Ger and Nhia
Za Vang.*

Children bathing at one of the camp's few well-heads   Taken by Yang Ger and Nhia Za Vang.

A Volag doctor checks the child's chart in a camp hospital ward. Taken by Erica Hagen.

A young Hmong woman cares for her child at
home while preparing camp rations.   Taken
by Erica Hagen.

An elderly Hmong shaman prepares for a ceremony with joss, chicken sacrifice, and
incense. The children come and go as the ceremony begins.   Taken by Yang Ger and
Nhia Za Vang.

A Hmong woman
sewing paj
ntaub. Taken by
Erica Hagen.

A Hmong Resistance fighter preparing to return to Laos. Ban Vinai is in
the background. Taken by Erica Hagen.

New Year's ceremonial dress. The Hmong girls are lining up to play pov pob, the traditional New Year's courting game.   Taken by Erica Hagen.

Farewells: the bus to Panat Nikhom Processing Center. Also called the "bus to America."   Taken by Erica Hagen.

FOUR

A Disciplined Village

Ban Vinai is an abrupt awakening from the pastoral countryside. The road which passes through small hamlets and rice paddies suddenly climbs a hill and then rounding a bend, comes upon a vast bustling city. The contrast between the two, the tranquil countryside and the noisy, teeming camp is always a shock.

As the van rounds the bend, Pere, an elderly French Jesuit priest, stirs in his seat. Bouncing over the dirt road, the vehicle is enveloped in clouds of thick reddish dust. The sun disappears again in the haze.

I catch Pere's attention and ask, "How many people are there in the camp?" He replies: "The Volags say 45,000 but UNHCR says 43,000. There are 2,000 illegals. About 2,000 emigrate each year, but 2,000 more are born. A young population; 25 percent are under five." Pere knows these figures. Such questions are commonly asked by visitors to the camp. The difference in UNHCR and Volag estimates reflects the fluidity of the situation.

As we approach the camp gates, Pere muses about the refugees' future. Responding to the unasked question that underlies every conversation about camp life, he observes: "The governor of Loei [province in Northeast Thailand] announced that they might consider letting the

Hmong stay as third-class citizens in Thailand. This announcement must have come from someone higher up."

I nod. Unnamed higher ups are often invoked in these conversations. The unnamed "they" is part of a discourse of powerlessness that reflects that decisions made by governments in Bangkok, Washington, Ottawa, Paris, Vientiane, Ho Chi Minh and elsewhere, can over night change the refugees' lives in Ban Vinai.

At the gate, the camp administration has built a new slightly grander guardhouse, but a simple wooden barricade still bars the entrance to the camp. The driver stops behind a line of other Volag vans—IRC, CAMA, ZOA, and ESF—waiting to be admitted (see table 1.1). Two young Thai guards with M-16's desultorily ask for our blue passes. Compared to other camps in Thailand, which are surrounded by barbed wire, Ban Vinai is very accessible.

"I wonder what they are looking for," Pere grumbles. Pierre, a young man from ESF, a French Volag, borrows one of the guard's guns and pretends to hold up the vans. The French nuns look disapprovingly.

The guards wave us on. Entering the main street of the camp, the driver hedges forward through throngs of people on their way to morning market. Honking furiously, he inches ahead. Slowly, but surely he nudges aside an elderly Hmong man dressed in traditional black, who hobbles on a stick. The man turns and stares angrily at the van. Soon even he, too, is lost in the crowd that surges forward toward the market. Without appearing to notice us, the crowd mechanically gives way as we pass. Now and again, I look for a familiar face, but the faces are without expression, the civil inattention of strangers in crowded cities.[1] Through the van's smoke-paned glass, I suddenly remember the feeling of being entrapped by an institutionalized world, of living in refugee camps, and wonder why I have returned.

The van continues on past neighborhoods of long rectangular, tin-roofed, wooden barracks. Each houses ten households. The barracks are stacked along the sides of the hills and in the valleys. Around the barracks, people have built thatched lean-tos to augment their living space. There is hardly a patch of green left in the camp.

As a man leads a flock of ducks across the road, the driver momentarily slows the van. Halting at a crossroads, we pass an open photography shop, where a family in traditional Hmong dress poses in front of a painted scene of the Laotian mountains (see figure 4.1). The family stands straight and tall and, attesting to the importance of the moment, they look at the camera without smiling. Next, the van passes a few stalls and shops followed by playing fields, classrooms, and the Ministry

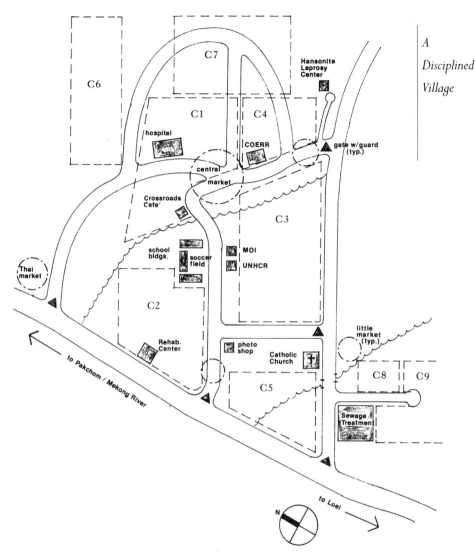

A
Disciplined
Village

C7
Hansonite Leprosy Center
C6
C1
C4
hospital
COERR
gate w/guard (typ.)
central market
Crossroads Cafe'
C3
school bldgs.
MOI
soccer field
UNHCR
Thai market
C2
Rehab. Center
photo shop
Catholic Church
little market (typ.)
to Pakchom / Mekong River
C5
C8
C9
Sewage Treatment
to Loei
N

FIGURE 4.1. Map of Ban Vinai Refugee Camp, 1986

of Interior (MOI) and UNHCR administration buildings. A small band of Thai soldiers march up and down in front of the MOI building.

As we near the center of the camp, people are already queued up outside UNHCR. The hour approaches eight o'clock and school children line up in formation outside the classrooms. A stout, middle-aged Thai woman, brandishing a stick, orders them in place.[2] Older ones

prod the younger in line and despite their dress—vestiges of sec-
ondhand clothes—the lines of children have a military precision. A
whistle blows. In perfect time, the driver stops. The soldiers stand at
attention. The Thai national anthem blares out over a loudspeaker and
the entire camp watches as a small school child raises the flag. When the
flag reaches the top of the pole, a whistle blows. The crowd surges forward again.

The driver maneuvers the van slowly across a small plank bridge that
spans a drying gully. He heads past a barbershop, restaurant, and more
Volag buildings into the main camp market. There, he stops and the
Thai women descend to the noodle stalls. Elsewhere, in the market
Hmong are selling vegetables, a Lao vendor is selling sticky rice and
papaya salad, and Hmong women are stringing up their reverse applique quilts [Hmong: *paj ntaub*] and other handicrafts. The driver hurries
on to his final destination.

Watching the world pass by, I recall images of the place I left in 1982
and am surprised how little I recognize. I left in February, in the same
month, but there were more trees then and the land was not so barren.
The camp had a village atmosphere that I no longer see. What happened
to the place that in the evening could be still and quiet? Where are the
Hmong in traditional dress who suddenly silently appeared out of nowhere for an afternoon class and disappeared the next morning to join
the Resistance across the border? These same people described war as
boring because it was a part of their lives for so long.[3] Had war continued in their lives?

The camp is more settled, dirtier, and more crowded than I remember. With 43,000 to 45,000 people living on approximately 400 acres
(slightly less than one square mile), it is one of the most densely popu-
lated places in the world. Unlike Hong Kong or Singapore, cities of
comparable density, there are no multistory buildings to create parks or
stretches of open space. The camp buildings built to be temporary are
showing signs of age and falling into disrepair. The few open spaces in
the camp, the small streams and gullies, have become open sewers. Everywhere, the thick, reddish dust blankets the land.

When I told an UNHCR relief official that I was going to work in
Ban Vinai, she called it the "country club" of refugee camps. In comparison to other camps in Thailand on the Cambodian border, she may
consider it a country club, but the Thai have more appropriately named
it Ban Vinai—"Village of Discipline"—after Commander Vinai, the
58   first Ministry of Interior (MOI) officer in the camp. The "ban" or village
part of the name fits with the outsider's first impression of a vast moun-

tain village, but the "vinai" or discipline conveys the underlying purpose and structure of the place.

When the Hmong General Vang Pao, the Thai military, and American CIA established the camp at the end of the war, they thought it would be a temporary place to house the Hmong who fought for the Americans and were fleeing the Communist government. The camp opened with some 5,000 Hmong. The 5,000 quickly grew to 12,000 as the Hmong followed their leaders out of Laos.

UNHCR and the Americans initially hoped the Thai government would allow the Hmong to resettle in Thailand.[4] Since many Laotian Hmong refugees have kinship ties to Hmong in northern Thailand, the international relief community hoped that the Thai would allow the refugees to join their kin. In supporting the camp, the Americans thought it could become a model development project for the northeast.[5]

By 1982, Ban Vinai, in comparison to the artillery fire and regimented prison life of the Cambodian border, seemed peaceful and settled. The camp resembled other Hmong villages in northern Thailand. The camp's housing and settlement pattern was organized by the Hmong themselves. At the time, the Hmong continued to observe traditional ritual and ceremonial practices. Hmong leaders also refused to accept the vaccinations and hospital services directed by World Vision, a Western evangelical relief agency. To the chagrin of relief agencies and officials, they continued to rely on traditional healers and market medicine.

In the early 1980s, Ban Vinai captured some attention in the Western press with the first reports of yellow rain. The Hmong leaders alleged that the Laotian government, with Soviet support, was using chemical biological warfare against them. Elderly former Resistance fighters described to relief workers how "poison" had been dumped on their people.[6] An international United Nations team, however, found no evidence to support such allegations, which were eventually discredited by scientists.[7] While the Hmong were being popularly portrayed in the Western press as a primitive mountain people, their leaders shrewdly manipulated the media to play on the anti-Communist sentiments of the Reagan administration to their own advantage.

In 1982, Ban Vinai was a very transient place. Each month, some 2,000 to 3,000 people arrived and departed.[8] In the interpreter training course I organized for camp medical teams and public health workers, the Hmong workers were generally young and looked ahead optimistically to life in the United States. Looking back over that experience, I wonder whether most had left, as they expected, and who had stayed behind.

Had they followed their traditional agricultural cycle, however, most Hmong would have left this fallow land by now. They, among all refugees in Thailand, had ample resettlement opportunities. Some 60,000 Hmong had resettled in the United States and a third of those had already migrated again to California's Central Valley to rejoin kin and to pursue their dreams of farming.[9] As swidden (slash and burn) farmers in Laos, many Hmong moved a short distance every three or four years and longer distances every decade or more.[10] The war intensified these movements. Fleeing the shelling, many Hmong were forced to relocate every few months. Their migrations into Ban Vinai to some extent, followed traditional seasonal migrations, peaking in early January at the end of the harvest and before the beginning of the next.[11] Why had so many elected not to continue that migration overseas?

Relief Workers

When the driver reaches the COERR offices, I descend with the remaining passengers from the van. The COERR offices consist of three concrete slab and tin-roofed buildings and a latrine block around a courtyard encircled by a bamboo fence. The courtyard is devoid of grass. Inside, Hmong and lowland Lao parasocial workers mill about waiting for the van to arrive. In one of the buildings, an older Hmong man is teaching an English class. I notice though that the parasocial workers, like many refugees who work for relief organizations, are predominantly young and male.[12] The young more quickly learn the languages of the relief organizations, but employing them only further undermines the authority of the elders. Young men are also more likely to volunteer than young women, because families fear for their daughters' physical security.

Pere introduces me to several workers. While we stand talking for a moment, a young man approaches. "Are you Lynel?" he asks. "Yes," I answer surprised, not expecting to know anyone. "Dang Chao—I was in your class in 1982—remember at the hospital," he reminds. He looks several years older and has lost the enthusiastic grin I remembered that made him stand out in a large class of many of his elders. "I thought you were going to Rhode Island, or was it Minnesota?" I ask. He nods. "Rhode Island. I want to go, but my parents don't want to," he explains.

"But, I think in the future we will go." I wonder what he means by the "future." What will be different in the future?

After a few brief introductions, Pere disappears with the French nuns to say morning mass in the Catholic chapel that is located near the far gate of the camp (see figure 4.1). Anika, a very self-assured Dutch relief worker, takes over the job of introducing me. She suggests that I work with Tou Vang, a leader of the parasocial workers, to establish research protocols and to identify households.

"She wants to go out in the neighborhoods," Anika explains, distinguishing work done inside the courtyard from that done in the public world outside. I quickly learn that there are many layers to camp life reflecting different understandings of public and private, depending on one's particular vantage point. For Anika, "going out" means venturing into a public world, whereas in the COERR courtyard she can replicate some of her familiar work habits and routines. She organizes her desk and time meticulously and watching her, I can forget that she is in a refugee camp rather than an office in Amsterdam. Gathering up her survey materials, Anika enters the next room and leaves us to work out our own schedule and plans.

Tou Vang is portly, in his mid-thirties, and accustomed to assuming command. Like many Hmong men of his generation, he fought in the war for the Americans. He attained the rank of captain and saw many of his friends killed. Although he married during the war, he and his wife delayed having children and the two youngest of his four children were born in Ban Vinai. He wants to return to Laos, but is losing hope.

He informs me, "I want my children to get a good education. When JVA [Joint Voluntary Agency, the American interviewing team] comes again, I'll interview with them."

Tou expects to resettle in Minnesota, where he has several cousins. A thoughtful person, Tou is well-respected by relief workers and Hmong of all ages. In retrospect, I realize the wisdom of Anika's choice. Unlike many parasocial workers, Tou does not derive his status from working with a relief agency and consequently is not enacting the political agenda underlying many relief worker/refugee relationships.[13] As a former military officer, Tou knows that he can be resettled in the United States and does not expect the Volag to further his case.

In Lao, I explain the purposes of my research. Tou speaks excellent English, but he appreciates my willingness to speak Lao (his second and national language) and he never speaks to me again in English. He advises me to work initially with households, where at least one person is literate in Lao.

"Then if you don't understand something, they can write it down and you can find the word in the dictionary," he explains. He suggests that in approaching the households, I offer to teach English in exchange for asking them to participate in my research study. "I understand about your research, but many people won't," he explains. "It is better to offer them something." His statement reflects the importance for many Hmong of reciprocity and in specifying the terms of a relationship in advance.

Using the initial results from a camp-wide survey that Tou is tabulating, we identify the characteristics of a representative sample of the camp population. Ban Vinai has nine centers, which have been established at different points in time over the past eleven years. Across all centers, the average length of stay (in 1986) in the camp is approximately seven years.[14] The majority of the camp population are Hmong (43,000), but other Laotian ethnic groups—Htin (900), Mien (900), lowland Lao (100), Leu (50), Laotheung (30), Khmu (20), Thai Dam (20), Musor (10), and Haw (4)—also live in Ban Vinai.

Ban Vinai's population has grown steadily. In the early 1980s, it grew as the Thai transferred highlander peoples in from other camps (see figure 4.2). Since 1984, when the Thai government closed the camp to new arrivals, the growth in population has primarily reflected high birth rates. The Hmong have one of the highest birth rates in the world (averaging 4.55 percent per annum in the camp), which greatly alarms the Thai government. In contrast, Thailand has a low birth rate (1.6 percent) and the Thai have dramatically reduced their own birth rates.

A majority of Ban Vinai's population is young (under fifteen years) and, demographically, the camp resembles other prolonged refugee

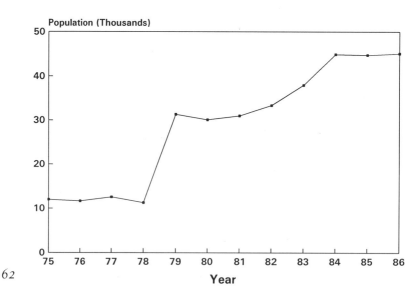

FIGURE 4.2. Ban Vinai Population, 1975–1986

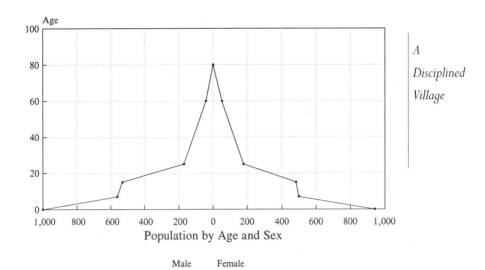

Population by Age and Sex

Male   Female

FIGURE 4.3. Population Pyramid of Ban Vinai

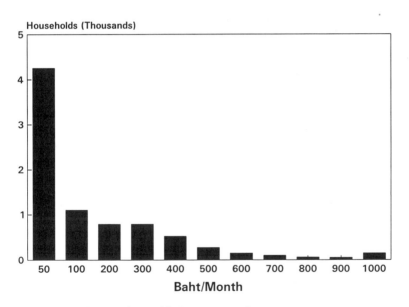

FIGURE 4.4. Reported Monthly Income Distribution

camp situations (see figure 4.3). With improved health services, the infant mortality rate has decreased and life expectancy has increased.
Thus, the costs of maintaining the camp are rising.   63

    A preliminary analysis of the survey suggests that income and class
differences have developed in the camp (see figure 4.4). Centers 8 and 9

are noticeably poorer than the older, originally established centers (1 through 5) as measured by material possessions and income levels. Centers 8 and 9 also house most of the non-Hmong ethnic minorities and lowland Lao and are located outside the main camp boundaries near the sewage treatment area (the least desirable section of the camp) (see figure 4.1). Tou agrees to approach Hmong households in centers 1 to 7 and introduces me to Lee, another parasocial worker from center 9, who will introduce me to households in centers 8 and 9.

The Sisawong Household

The next afternoon, Lee and I, with some randomly chosen addresses in hand, head to centers 8 and 9 at the far end of the camp. I decide to walk and Lee agrees that I need to learn the way. It is a hot afternoon and the main street is crowded. Several Volag vans pass us. One of the drivers stops and offers us a ride. Lee indicates that I should take the ride and he will meet me in center 9. However, we both continue walking. I wonder momentarily if he would have preferred that I ask for a COERR van. Where there are so few vehicles, transportation marks one's affiliation and status. The Volags as a rule provide transportation only to their own staff and workers or to other foreign relief workers in the camp. Occasionally, however, a Hmong passes on a motorcycle. "They are the Resistance leaders," Lee explains.

Lee turns off the main road and takes a back path through the compounds. We pass groups of young Hmong boys playing target games. In one, the boys knock out coins with rubber bands. In another they construct a pile of rubber sandals. Then, taking a sandal, they hurl it with incredible force. Such games in other forms once trained their fathers to hunt wild game. The object is to demolish the pile. Hmong men watch amused. A small child, perhaps two at most, ends up on the bottom of a heap of boys. He protests angrily until one of the older men rescues him.

Hmong women and girls sit on low stools in small groups apart from the men and boys. They are busily sewing *paj ntaub* quilts which they will sell in the Thai markets or through their relatives in the United States. Occasionally, an older woman can be seen batiking blue accordion cloth for a traditional Hmong skirt. Very young girls watch and imitate older girls and women, while babies rest on their mothers' backs.

I am surprised how anonymously we pass. But then, an older woman points me out to a child, who screams and hides in her grandmother's skirt. The old woman threatens the child in Hmong. "What does she say?" I ask Lee to translate. He laughs and replies, "She said, 'She's come to take you to America.' The elders don't want to go to America so they scare the small children."

A ditch appears ahead in our path. Crossing requires balancing on a two by four. An elderly woman walks deftly and quickly across. Lee follows. I take off my high-heeled shoes and, barefoot, inch slowly across, one foot ahead of the next. Below is a green slimy stream of indescribable contents. My head and nose reeling, I try not to panic. Lee laughs at my grim determination and holds out a hand.

Once across we continue up the bank to the next center. An elderly woman squats on the edge and stares blankly across the chasm. She pushes a stick up and down as if she is digging grubs. Nearby, another group of boys play and women and girls sew. Turning the corner we come upon a man squatted over his opium pipe. He seems momentarily startled to see us, but continues to draw on his pipe. Juice drools over the edges of his lips and the smoke encircles his head.

In the afternoon heat, three dimensions become one. I wonder how long it will take me to look beneath the dirt, buzzing flies, dead rats splayed across the road, smoky walls, slimy sewers, and a matted haired child, who stares at me wordlessly. The walk makes me realize that Ban Vinai provides images for the hellish refugee camp existence depicted by the Western press. The beauty of a Hmong mountain village has somehow disappeared in four long and weary years. Or, did it ever exist? Did I want to remember Ban Vinai like that?

Lee asks suddenly, "Do you believe in spirits?" "I don't know," I reply, "Why?" "My uncle was killed by spirits," he relates.[15] "He belonged to the dragon code. Do you know what that is?" "No," I answer. But he does not elaborate.

Instead, he continues: "My uncle was chased out of his village in the mountains. He built a fishing pond. One day he killed a snake, but he had really killed a spirit. The next day he was bitten, but there was no insect bite. The spirit bit him. My uncle swelled up and died."

He speaks mainly in Lao, but translates a few words into English. "What happened to the family?" I ask. He answers: "His wife and sons came to Ban Vinai with us. We couldn't live in Laos. She married a Thai Hmong, a very rich man, so we don't have to support her. She had one child by the man, but that child was killed by spirits, too."

"Are there still spirits in Ban Vinai?" I ask him. "Yes, of course," he replies, "like they say God is everywhere, they are here, too." I ask if he remembers Laos. "Not really," Lee replies, "but I remember my village in the mountains."

After walking for about twenty-five minutes, we cross into center 9, where Lee stops at a room in one of the barracks. Camp addresses are designated by center, quarter, building (barrack), and room numbers. Each refugee has a Ban Vinai (BV) number (except the illegals, who have no identity papers) and a four-figure address. Reaching C9/Q3/B5/R6 where, according to the COERR survey, the Sisawongs live, we stop. From the survey, we know that this lowland Lao household entered the camp in 1981 and that the head of household and wife are highly educated.

On the threshold a woman sits quietly embroidering. As we approach, some young men join her. Lee introduces us. I then explain my interest in having them participate in my research study. The people stare blankly. The formality of the human subject protocols I have carefully written in Lao suddenly seem absurd. I begin describing my work with COERR, a more known entity in the camp. Still, they stare blankly. Finally, a young man informs me. "The Sisawongs? I think you want those people up there." I am at the right address but talking to the wrong household.

At the next address, I begin again. This time a young lowland Lao couple listens intently. As I explain my research plans, their five children and some neighbors gather around us on the bamboo porch (see table 4.1). Having made the necessary inquiries, Lee stands apart from the circle. When he earlier had offered to introduce me to the lowland Lao in his neighborhood, he warned that they may be more receptive to a foreigner than to a Hmong.

When I finish speaking, Khamsai, the man, says, "I would like to help you, but I don't have enough time."

I stare at him in disbelief. His statement seems absurd when everyone appears to be sitting around doing nothing. "Not even an hour a day?" I ask skeptically.

Chanthanom, his wife, says something quietly to him and he disappears into the room. No one speaks.

A few minutes later, Khamsai reemerges with a book. He shows me an old Lao grammar published in France. "Can you bring an English book?" he asks. I nod.

I ask when we should meet. Khamsai opens a composition book. In meticulous Lao, he has blocked out every hour of the day with meetings, lessons, and various community activities. "Between two and three?" he suggests.

66   "Can you come then, too?" I ask Chanthanom. She concurs.

TABLE 4.1.
People of Ban Vinai

Households

1. Sisawong

Ethnicity: Lowland Lao/Khmu
Address: Center 9
Arrival: 1981

Khamsai	Head of household (Lowland Lao), former agricultural extension worker, Volag worker, 35
Chanthanom	Khmu, former teacher, head of women's Catholic group, 34
Boondee	first daughter, 12
Khet	second daughter, 8
Somsai	first son, 10
Choy	second son (thin twin), 2
Tuy	second son (fat twin), 2

2. Thao

Ethnicity: White Hmong
Address: Center one
Arrival: 1975

Seng	Head of household, former soldier, head of hospital workers, 46
Youa	mother ofr Seng, seamstress, 79
Hai	first wife of Seng, seamstress, 38
Moua	second wife, 28
Blia	first daughter, 14
Sri	second daughter, 12
Chia	first son, 10
Mee Lor	third daughter, 5
Vashi	second son, 3
Pao	third son (Moua's son), 3

3. Vang

Ethnicity: Green Hmong
Address: Center 3
Arrival: 1979

Ger	Head of household, former rice farmer, 28
Xiong	female, mother of Ger, shaman, 75
Choua	wife of Ger, seamstress, 25
Pao	first son, 7
Tou	second son, 3
Yia	third son, 1

A
Disciplined
Village

(*continues*) 67

TABLE 4.1. *(Continued)*

Households	
Parasocial workers	
Tou Vang	Hmong, former soldier in Vang Pao's forces, 38
Seng Lee	Hmong, male, 18
Relief workers	
Pere	French, Catholic priest, COERR, 75
Boonchan	Thai, female, social worker, COERR, 23
Anika	Dutch, female, nurse/social worker, COERR, 34
Pierre	French, male, teacher, ESF, 37
Paul	English, male, accountant, COERR, 28
Lynel	American, female, ethnographer, COERR, 33
Ver	Dutch, male, doctor, ZOA, 30

The Thao Household

Locating other households willing to participate in my ethnographic research is more straightforward. Through Pere, I meet the Thaos, a White Hmong household who live in center 1 (see table 1.1). The White Hmong (Hmong: *Hmoob Dawb*) are one of the main subgroups of the Laotian Hmong.[16] Seng Thao, the head of the household, is a well-known camp leader, who directs the hospital workers. He is used to working with foreigners and first met Pere in the mountains of Laos. There, according to Pere, Seng lost his first wife to malaria. Shortly thereafter, Seng married Hai and joined the fighting in the mountains. In the early 1970s, he and Hai were evacuated to refugee settlements around Vientiane, where their first two children, Blia and Sri, were born. In the settlements, they reconnected with Pere, who was also evacuated.

After the war, the family fled again to Ban Vinai. Youa, Seng's mother, fled with them, because Seng's father, who had been a well-known provincial official, had died during the war. In Ban Vinai, Seng met and married Moua, a woman several years younger. He had three more children by Hai and one by Moua. Seng and Moua never officially recorded their marriage (which involved procuring a license from the camp commander). Moua's son, Pao, however, is listed on the Thao UNHCR identity card. Since the youngest two sons were born in the same year, Seng changed the birth date of Hai's youngest son. Seng knew that the immigration rules disallow polygyny and wanted to keep his options open.

Of the three families, the Thaos are the most affluent and, at the

68

same time, very characteristic of the small group of original settlers of Ban Vinai. The Thaos' living space in center 1 is comparatively luxurious. They live in two spacious, concrete-walled rooms. One serves as a sleeping area with a separate latrine, and the other as a living space (kitchen, altar, and dining area), In addition, Seng has built a small bamboo and thatch hut and has hand dug a well.

I ask Seng if I may stay with his household one or two nights a week because, as a leader, Seng can easily negotiate such an arrangement with the Thai guards if he chooses. Seng willingly agrees, but informs me, "I have to put a new roof on the hut first. Then, you can come live with us."

Recognizing the costs he will incur, I offer to contribute. "I'll build it and then I'll let you know, but you are a guest of my family," he informs me.

The Vang Household

Through Tou, I meet the Vangs, the third household. Ger, the head of household, is Tou's cousin and clan brother. The Vangs, a Green Hmong household (Hmong: *Hmoob Ntsuab*), live in center 3. The household includes Ger, his mother, Xiong; his wife, Choua; and their three young sons (see table 4.1). The Vangs have few possessions and very little education or contact with the relief agencies. In Laos, they were swidden rice farmers. Like the majority of Hmong in Ban Vinai, they came from Xieng Khouang province and arrived in the camp in 1979.

When I explain my research to Ger, he initially appears not to show much interest. "You can teach me English and I'll teach you Hmong," he offers. The research cannot easily be explained to other households in the building, nor does it fit Ger's pragmatic sense of time.

"I need to learn English," he explains, "for my life in the future." When I ask if Choua will join us, Ger replies, "Choua can't learn English. She can't read and write Lao." Rather than object to this observation, I decide to wait and learn what lies behind his resistance.

During the first few weeks, I quickly fall into the routine of going into the camp by eight each morning and leaving each evening by five. During the day, I help the parasocial workers analyze the camp-wide survey and regularly visit the three households. In the early morning I often begin with the Vangs since they live nearest to the COERR compound and Ger prefers that I come in the mornings. The afternoons he reserves for his soccer practice.

At first our conversations are very stilted and ritualized. I ask questions about his daily life and experiences as a refugee. He repeats a re-frain I have heard and read so often.[17] "I left Laos because the Commu-nists took over my country. I swam with my family across the Mekong. I am poor because I am a refugee."

I often ask about his future and he answers, "I want to go to the United States, but I can't go because my mother doesn't want to go." Sometimes, I wonder why I have come so far to hear the stories that earn a ticket to the United States.

I eventually stop asking questions about his refugee experience and we begin to talk about our daily lives. I ask Ger about the bags of herbs hanging on his wall. He explains that his mother is a shaman [Lao: *mɔ̌ɔ jaa*; Hmong: *neeb*]. "It is hard to bring her medicines across. We had to make two trips," he claims. "You swam twice?" I ask surprised. "No, we took a boat," he replied. "Whose boat?" I ask. "The Thai. We had to pay them to bring us across. We had to pay to get into the camp, too."

One day Ger surprises me. He begins by telling me about cloth man-ufacturing companies [Lao: *bɔɔli-sát*] he has seen when he visited his clan brothers in Chiang Mai. Ger explains that if he were ever allowed to settle in Thailand, that he hopes to find a job in the manufacturing sector.

"What about farming?" I ask. "There is no land left for the Hmong in Chiang Mai," Ger astutely observes. "What about in the northeast—could the Hmong resettle here?" I ask. "The land is too poor, it is not good farm land," Ger informs me.

As he speaks, Xiong, his mother, slowly enters the room. Her pres-ence fills the small space. I turn my head slightly to acknowledge the staring eyes, but she looks beyond me. We pause in our conversation; no one speaks for a minute. Ger goes on to describe his plans to visit his Thai Hmong cousins.

Xiong slowly lifts a white accordion-pleated skirt off the nail. With her wrinkled and worn hands, she unwraps its layers, then unbuttoning her shirt, slides on another and with it the layers of skirt over her head. Next, she takes her red hood for her shaman's ceremony from the plaid suitcase.

I realize that her ceremonies assuage the grief of homesick people who find relief in familiar whistles and opiated incense. They provide for the family's livelihood in the camp and furnished the life savings that paid the boat journey across the Mekong.

It is for such moments she now prepares. She unrolls her long hair. I watch fascinated as the strands fill the small room. Combing the long, wet strands, she shakes her hair dry and binds it up again in knots. Later, she will cover her head with the red hood which allows her to slip back into the spirit world, to commune with her husband's friendly spirits or to appease another's wrath.

Her knowledge comes from many years of labor, from the pain of losing thirteen children, and of leaving the fourteenth behind in Laos. The fifteenth, her youngest, however, ignores these preparations next to us. Instead, he speaks earnestly of some unspecified departure, of bus routes to Chiang Mai.

She gets ready to leave and clears her throat. But Ger ignores her and continues to talk to me as if she is not there. She knows how to get his attention though when she wants to, taunting and reminding him of his obligation to respect his elders and ancestors. Instead, she asks for the umbrella to shade herself from the noonday sun. Without ceasing to talk to me, Ger hands her one of the family's few material possessions. She places the prized piece over her arm and leaves quickly. The room is quiet and empty without her presence.

Ger turns toward me and asks, "In America is there ever lightning?"

"Yes," I answer. "Why, are you afraid?"

"Yes, because it comes with thunder and when it rains very hard."

"Is lightning bad?" I wonder why he brings up this subject.

He replies: "Yes, because if the person is bad, then he has an angry heart. Lightning—some people die because they are dishonest. Lightning only kills a dishonest person."

"Always?" I ask skeptically.

"Yes."

"But what if lightning strikes me?"

"Then you are dishonest," he replies assuredly.

"What if I don't die, but am struck?"

"Then you have a good heart."

I protest his logic. He counters with an example of a friend, a man about twenty-five or twenty-six.

"While walking this man was struck by lightning, which burned his clothes, but the man did not die because he had a good heart," Ger says. He elaborates, "If I beg lightning to kill you and you are bad, then it will kill you."

To make his point clear, he brings the example back to us. "For example," he begins and then draws two stick figures which he labels "Ger" and "Lynel." He continues, "For example, suppose Ger is not wrong but Lynel is angry. Ger calls lightning down and if he is not wrong, then Lynel dies."

Ger repeats his question about lightning in the United States. Explaining the how but not the why of this phenomena, I describe how certain weather conditions—hot and wet—precipitate lightning. Ger dissatisfied retorts: "Here it usually doesn't come when it is hot unless begged. What do you think?"

Unwilling to attribute intentionality, I reply, "If lightning strikes you, you have bad luck. Do you believe in bad luck?"

"I don't know," he answers.[18]

Ger next asks, "In America do you have deaf people?"

"Yes," I say, "Why, don't you think we do?"

"No, I think you don't," he replies.

Shortly thereafter I leave, but only after Ger has extracted a promise that I will come promptly at ten the following day.

Ger's last question reflects his hopes and fears about the future; his hope that I, a representative of a powerful nation, hear and understand him. The concern with the sudden calamity—the "what if . . . ?" is something he knows well as a refugee. His more immediate concern is to survive, to find ways to trade his wife's cloth outside the camp walls to support the family. Kinship ties to local markets are accessible. In contrast, the third country that I represent, the country of possible re-settlement, is a far-off distant force, a place where Ger cannot be assured that lightning strikes for the same reasons.

The Camp Generation

At four a.m. the sun has not yet risen. At that hour most camp dwellers find their deepest sleep in the coolest part of unending hot days. The Thao children lie sprawled across the bamboo floor on spread out sarongs. A man's snores in the next room do not wake them from their deep sleep. The moon passes behind the hill and a rooster crows the hour of dawn.[1] Then, Sri, the Thaos' second daughter, rises quietly, leaving the other children and woman sleeping. She heads to the upper barracks, where she joins Hai, her mother, and other women preparing the day's food in the kitchen. Sri takes two buckets and leaves to fetch water from the family's hand-dug well.

Chia, the eldest son, stirs and cries out in his sleep. The camp's early morning sounds filter through the bamboo slats: crowing roosters, a barking dog, sloshing water, a crying baby, and revving motorcycle, which Seng Thao, their father, rising early, starts from its hiding place between latrines. In the still hot morning the stench of unwashed bodies and soiled sheets from some infant who wandered across the sleeping forms becomes more oppressive. The dry season's thick dusty haze hides the rising sun, but the heat of its rays saps early morning strength. I swat a mosquito buzzing at my head

73

and realize that Chia, too, has left. In a half waking state, I am not sure when.

Chia appears again at six. He sits and stares until I feel his eyes bore through me with the morning light. He wears his usual attire, a tattered track suit, relic of used-clothes' stores. I pretend to shoot him and he looks worried until I greet him, "*Nyob zoo,*" in Hmong. He smiles, ready to play. Sri brings a bucket of hot water. She walks slowly weighed down by an infant and the heavy pot. Chia watches curiously as I run to assist her. Then, he joins his friends, who are throwing rubber sandals against the latrine. As I disappear into the latrine I hear the rubber resounding against the walls.

The latrine is the coolest and most private place in the compound. Avoiding the dank walls, I carefully balance my clothes and soap on faded sarongs hanging across one wall. I pour pitchers of water cautiously over my back. Each bucket of water represents a trip to a drying well. The bath refreshes, but even as I emerge, red brown dirt streams off my legs. Within minutes, the dusty air mats my hair again.

Pretending to be grown-up, Chia demands that I share some coffee with him. He drinks sugar water slightly flavored with coffee. Vashi, the second son, joins us and stares curiously until I try to clean his nose. "Blow," I command suddenly in English, which of course, he does not understand. He complies anyway, but squirms away in disgust. Like other children in the camp, he suffers from a perpetual upper respiratory infection. Although Hai wipes the phlegm and washes his face several times a day, his nose outruns her efforts.

A woman outside the room screams loudly. In slow motion, I hear the sound of blows and her protests. "Should I intervene?" I wonder. "Would it do any good?" I have witnessed the aftermath of other scenes of family violence in refugee camps.[2] Sometimes, a relief worker's intervention intensified the conflict; other times, they may have saved a life. Feeling sickened and helpless, I ask Chia in Lao, "What's going on?" I know he cannot provide the information I need, but I feel compelled to ask. He shrugs his shoulders. I go to the door.

Hai and several other adults have pulled the couple apart. The woman sits crying soundlessly with her back to the crowd. Neighbors remonstrate with the man who, still evidently angry, glares at his wife. A few minutes later, the woman leaves with Hai to go to the upper porch. Later, Seng explains that she argued with a neighbor over their respective allotments of well water. Her husband, shamed by her behavior, beat her. This is the public version in any case.

Sri appears again in the hut. She is coming from her early morning

Chinese language class. Sri studies Chinese because like many Hmong of her generation, she is fascinated by the land of her ancestors. She plays Chinese tapes, draws pictures of Hmong in China, and dreams of crossing the Laotian mountains to reverse the migration her great-grandparents made.

The largest Hmong population in the world—some five million—live in China.[3] Many children in the camp believe that in China they may again find a homeland. China, in their minds, also represents success and power and has replaced America and Europe as the golden door. They have heard of the hardships and poverty of life in the United States and in other third countries. China, in contrast, an unknown place of stories and myth, provides an image of hope.

Sri studies at the Hmong temple near the compound. The temple has seen better times, but serves as a classroom for Hmong, who hold private language classes. The Hmong temple was built in the late 1970s to house the followers of the late Shong Lue Yang, a messianic leader who represented a Hmong cultural alternative to Vang Pao and the Christian religions.[4] Before he was assassinated by Vang Pao's followers, Leu founded a new faith and writing system (Pahwah Hmong) that in the Hmong syncretic tradition combined elements of Lao Buddhism, Chinese, and traditional Hmong animism.[5]

His ideas enjoyed a brief revival in the camps in the early 1980s when many Hmong began doubting Vang Pao's promise to return them to their homeland and at the height of the proselytizing efforts of the Christian groups. By 1986, interest has waned. The principal followers emigrated to the United States and hopes that this new movement will change the refugees' lives have diminished. The temple grounds have become a soccer field and the buildings have fallen into disrepair. However, an enterprising young Hmong, who works with the Chinese relief agencies, offers early morning Chinese language classes there.

Sri seems unaware of the crowd outside and entering the hut, she asks for my notebook. On a clean page, she writes the Chinese character she learned this morning. I ask her to translate, but looking distracted and uncertain, she writes her favorite character, "love" instead. Underneath she draws a picture of a young Hmong Chinese couple surrounded by flowers. "Not many girls learn Chinese," she proudly tells me.

I hear the sound of Seng's motorcycle coming toward the hut. The bike sputters to a stop and he parks it against the latrine. Chia flies out of the hut in pursuit of his father. I look out the door of the hut and see Seng, trailed by Chia, Vashi, and Pao, his three sons. They stop at several doors to greet the neighbors briefly. At the hut, Seng comes in and reaching inside the bamboo cupboard, pulls out a bottle of homemade Mekong whisky.

"God, I hope he doesn't expect me to drink, too," I think. "It's too early for this." Seng is well-known for his drinking capacities, an indulgence he shares with Pere now and again.

The children watch curiously as he offers me a swig. Seng is evidently displeased when I decline. "Pere ate everything Hmong, drank whisky, too," Seng admonishes. Wondering if he is referring to my refusal to eat the buffalo blood Hai offered the evening before, I protest, "I don't eat blood. I tried it once. But, I don't mind about whisky. I drank whisky at my wedding. Don't Hmong women drink at weddings?"

Knowing that Hmong women rarely drink except at weddings, I try to placate Seng in his own cultural terms. Somehow this ludicrous attempt appeases Seng who admits, "Yes, Hmong women drink at weddings." "Well, I drank at mine," I retort. He nods approvingly and corks the bottle.

To Chia's delight, Seng swoops him up and remounts the bike. They head to market to exchange fish rations for fresh vegetables and other commodities. UNHCR from funding supplied by Western donors, buys food from local producers which is trucked several times a week to the camp. The food is distributed through the center and building leaders to every household with a UNHCR identity card, "BV number." Many Hmong then resell a portion of their food in the local camp market. Like many other Hmong households, the Thaos prefer pork or chicken to fish and use the sales of fish to generate local currency. The exchange also benefits local Thai who buy the subsidized commodity at a lower price.

The surplus of food sold in the camp market suggests that households have other sources of income. At the monthly interagency meeting, the UNHCR field officer protests that the refugees must be eating too well if they can afford to sell their food. "Why don't you provide pork instead?" Boonchan suggests. "Fish prevent goiters," he replies. The field officer proposes cutting back on fish sauce, mung beans, chili peppers, fish, cooking oil, and firewood. He estimates that the cutbacks will result in savings of 21 million baht a year. "We spend one and half million baht a day feeding the camp," he informs the relief workers.

"Wouldn't the savings be more than that?" Paul, a British volunteer, asks. The field officer recalculates and answers, "A half million baht a day." According to the field officer, UNHCR spends $US3.5 million a year for food in Ban Vinai and $US5 million for the total budget. Paul does his own calculations, "If you cut by 21 million baht that represents 42 days of food or one persons' annual share in a family of six." "But, they receive plenty of money from relatives in the United States," the field officer says defending his proposal. "Besides, refugees in Africa are much worse off".[6]

The field officer has served in several countries. "Ban Vinai is not a refugee camp," he argues. "What is it?" I ask surprised. "I think Ban Vinai is in itself a permanent settlement for these people." The field officer in his position deals primarily with the Hmong leaders and the Thai military. He explains, "I do not have any particular problem with refugees. If you have a problem, this is a pyramid society. If you have great difficulty, you should contact refugee leaders. Then no problem."

The camp has many of the demographic and social characteristics of a poor third world country. Like other poor societies, the population in Ban Vinai is predominantly young (see figure 4.3). The vast majority are extremely poor, but there is a comparatively, wealthy minority. Except for a few camp leaders, however, the wealthiest in the camp have fewer possessions than the Thai rural poor.[7] The very wealthy in Ban Vinai may own two sets of clothes, a radio (rather than a television), a watch, an English dictionary (provided by the Volags), a bicycle, and an umbrella. Yet, there is more wealth in the camp than appears in individual households. Ban Vinai is said to be a way station for opium traffic coming from Chiang Mai and Laos to Bangkok and markets beyond.[8]

The Thao family numbers among the upper 10 percent in the camp (see figure 4.4). The wealthy, like Seng, report an average monthly income of 1000 baht (US$40).[9] Seng's wealth is reflected in his ability to take a second wife, the 250 Honda (one of the few in the camp), and a large living space. Since the second wife represents another food ration, the camp's welfare regulations provide some incentive for the wealthy, who can afford the additional cost, to practice polygyny.[10] The Thaos wealth, however, as far as I can tell, is derived primarily from Seng's work with the Volags and remittances from kin in the United States. As leader of the hospital workers, Seng earns 350 Thai baht (about US$14) a month. Hai and his two eldest daughters' earnings from sewing also contribute significantly to the household income. Each quilt nets approximately 500 baht and they sew an average of six a month. In the context of the camp economy, the Thaos live very well and potentially accrue savings. Seng periodically contributes to the Resistance, which further insures the household's security and stature in the camp.[11]

As Seng heads off to the market, Hai takes a stool on the upper porch. I leave with the children who are heading for school. At the bottom of the steps, Mee Lor, the youngest daughter, and another young girl wash each other's hair over a basin of water. Moua emerges from the kitchen. Ignoring us, she and Hai begin arguing heatedly. "What now?" I ask Blia and Sri. "About us," Sri informs me. "Moua hit me." "What did you do?" I ask. "She's lazy," Blia volunteers, "She wanted Sri to work for her." "I hate her!" Sri interrupts. The argument continues until other women with their sewing gather on the porch. Moua, who does not sew, retreats to Seng's brother's compound. This is a pattern with them. Hai and Moua alternate between sharing the common space, but Hai's sewing earns her the upper porch. Unfortunately for Hai, who is pregnant, Moua monopolizes Seng's current affections. Sri and Blia carefully observe and report on these negotiations and movements. But, I often wonder whether being an ethnographer justifies my interest in their gossip.

We head out to the main dirt road. Seng passes us on his motorcycle with Chia astride. Seng waves exuberantly, but Chia ignores us. He seems proud of his newly acquired status as motorcycle rider and is evidently more concerned that his comrades notice him. In the central market, we stop to buy some "poor man's bucket"—pancakes that a young Hmong vendor has franchised from local Thai merchants. The noodle stalls are crowded with people having breakfast. Hmong vendors lay out food rations left over from the previous day. Several smoked fish appear. I head to the Volag offices and the girls continue on to school.

Education

Sri and Blia are in the third and fourth year of school respectively. They study in the camp's primary school system administered by the Thai Ministry of Education. The schools follow the Thai calendar, with a long vacation during the hot season (April and May). The children can study in morning or afternoon classes. Sri, Blia, and Chia, who are old enough to attend school, study in the morning. Each day, they receive two hours of Lao reading and writing, and arithmetic from a Hmong teacher, and one hour of Thai language instruction from a Thai teacher supervisor.

Blia and Sri are exceptional. Most girls drop out after the second year (see table 5.1). Many Hmong prefer that their daughters contribute to household labor—drawing water, child care, cooking, and cleaning, and production—primarily sewing, which constitutes 90 percent of non-black market income.[12] Unlike Hai, many Hmong women are pre-

TABLE 5.1.
Ban Vinai Educational Data

		0–6	7–14	15–24	25–59	60+	Total	Percent
Grade 1	M	180	1313	127	44	2	1666	0.56
	F	114	1000	133	40	0	1287	0.44
	T	294	2313	260	84	2	2953	1.00
Grade 2	M	5	741	324	79	1	1150	0.64
	F	5	467	151	12	0	635	0.36
	T	10	1208	475	91	1	1785	1.00
Grade 3	M	1	400	398	74	3	876	0.74
	F	0	185	114	14	0	313	0.26
	T	1	585	512	88	3	1189	1.00
Grade 4	M	1	246	364	25	0	636	0.80
	F	0	91	72	1	0	164	0.21
	T	1	337	436	26	0	800	1.00
Grade 5	M	0	111	255	25	0	391	0.86
	F	0	33	31	2	0	66	0.14
	T	0	144	286	27	0	457	1.00
Grade 6	M	0	34	210	11	0	255	0.89
	F	0	5	22	3	0	30	0.11
	T	0	39	232	14	0	285	1.00
Other	M	1	11	53	26	0	91	0.34
	F	3	62	67	46	0	178	0.66
	T	4	73	120	72	0	269	1.00
TOTAL	M	188	2856	1731	284	6	5065	0.65
%	M	0.61	0.61	0.75	0.71	1.00	0.65	
	F	122	1843	590	118	0	2673	0.35
%	F	0.39	0.39	0.25	0.29	0.00	0.35	
	T	310	4699	2321	402	6	7738	1.00

SOURCE: COERR 1986a.

literate and those who are literate, are most likely literate in Hmong.[13]
Overall, literacy in Ban Vinai is rapidly increasing, primarily among the
young. The primary school system is having a dramatic impact on the
educational levels in the camp, even though gender differences are evident.

To many relief workers, the Thai government's educational policies

79

appear to contradict their policy that no refugees be allowed to settle in Thailand.[14] The government discourages the Volags from providing training programs. Yet, in replicating the Thai formal school system, the government, in effect, socializes the Hmong children to become more Thai than Lao or Hmong. The children see Thai as the preferred language and are proud of their ability to speak Thai. "You speak Lao very well," I tell Chia and Sri. "No, we speak Thai!" they inform me and consciously employ the Thai: "*Khâ*," "*Khá*" [question] or "*Khráp*" (politeness particles) in their address. In contrast, their parents speak primarily Lao and Hmong, and their grandparents speak only Hmong. The children also eagerly adopt elements of Thai popular culture in their music, dance, and dress (in addition to their enthusiasm for Chinese culture). The more worldly see themselves as part of the new Asia of high technology, wealth, and opportunity.

Asserting that their educational policy does not encourage local settlement, the Thai government prohibits any schooling past the sixth year. The government's rationale is that secondary education will provide an incentive for the refugees to remain in Ban Vinai and that they should not receive more education than the Thai rural poor. The Thai government, however, allows the U.S. State Department to fund American high schools in the processing centers.[15] These schools offer English-as-a-Second Language (ESL), cultural orientation, mathematics and sports classes, and follow an American schedule. The Thai government hopes that the offer of further schooling will encourage more Hmong to resettle in the United States. The Hmong find ways to circumvent this policy by continuing to study in Volag programs and opening private classes. The policy only exacerbates the tensions between those children, who already want to resettle in a third country, and their parents who hope to return to Laos. The children correlate education with their hopes for a future, whereas the elders, see the school as taking their children further away from Laos.

The primary schools, these symbols of the future, are extremely chaotic. The teachers rarely seem to be in control of the class and they teach primarily by the rote and lecture method. I often wonder if Blia, Sri, and Chia learn anything there. Yet, despite the internal chaos, the primary school hours structure the children's time in the camp. The school's daily routine provides a sense of rhythm in their lives with its summer vacations and holidays. During summer breaks, the children complain of boredom. With little to do, but obliged to help their parents, they look forward to the opening of classes again.

Volag Meeting

Leaving Sri and Blia at school, I head to the COERR compound. The parasocial worker staff are holding their weekly meeting. These meetings regulate a relief worker's time and reflect the routines and practices of another world which funds these hours. There are four items on the agenda: 1) update on Htin girls; 2) UNHCR visitor; 3) assessment of parasocial workers; and 4) monthly reports. I offer to take the minutes, which saves recording them in my fieldnotes later.

Update on Htin Girls   Boonchan reported that the UNHCR representative went to Pattaya to collect two refugee prostitutes, Htin girls, eight and ten years. (The Htin are a minority ethnic group that live in Laos and Thailand.) The girls were taken to the hospital and examined by Dr. Ver. One is reported to be pregnant and to have contracted syphilis. Two Thai women in their late 20s were charged, as prostitutes, and spent a night in the Pak Chom jail. They have subsequently been released.

"They probably paid the policeman," Boonchan volunteers. "Or, offered favors!" Paul retorts.

"The girls are being held in the camp jail, but the camp commander may send them to Chiang Kham to ensure their security."

"Hah!" Paul exclaims, "Whose security?"

"The camp commander thinks the discipline is better in Chiang Kham," Boonchan replies.

Boonchan adds that she is visiting the girls periodically in the camp jail.

"What's UNHCR doing?" Pere asks rhetorically.

"Next on the agenda?" Anika asks.

UNHCR Visitor   Paul reported that an American UNHCR representative visited Parasocial Services yesterday and observed that the Hmong have the highest suicide rate of all the camps, despite their supposed/actual strong clan structure. The American also observed that the Vietnamese boat people have the roughest psychological adjustment problems.

"Are we doing anything about these suicides?" Pere asks. "I'm getting the names of the cases from the hospital," Boonchan replies. "Tou Vang visited a family yesterday."

Paul adds, "Suicides often involve conflicts between two wives." Ignoring this observation, Boonchan reports that the majority of the cases seen by Parasocial Services have been young girls.

"Broken hearts," she explains.

Assessment of Parasocial Workers   Anika proposed that the staff use the next month to assess the performance and training outcomes of the parasocial workers.

"How else do we know how they are doing?" she asserts. Boonchan and Paul looked astonished. "We talk every day, the counseling team works very hard," Boonchan suggests. "So does the survey team," Anika replies defending her own group. "But we need to assess each one and determine their training needs. Then, Lynel will know what training they need." "I thought I'd just teach the workers some statistics and interviewing techniques," I offer not wanting my training course to be designed by Anika. "Can I sit in on that class!" Paul jokes.

The staff agreed to assess the Parasocial Workers during the month of April. As per Paul's recommendation, the assessment will involve forty minute interviews with each worker.

"That, at least, will give the workers a chance to practice English and to prepare for JVA interviews," says Paul defending his proposal.

Anika takes responsibility for designing the assessment questionnaire. The staff agrees to forward their comments to her in the next week.

Monthly Reports   Pere reported that COERR complained that Parasocial Services has not been submitting our section of the Bishop's monthly report.

"What do they want?" Paul objects, since he usually writes the reports.

"I have to write a different report for the director, COERR Bangkok, the archdiocese in Illinois, MOI, UNHCR, and my mother. In three languages no less! Boonchan and I spent three hours translating the last one for MOI into Thai. Next you'll say I should send one to Rome! In Latin!"

"Not a bad idea," Pere replies.

Pere recommended that we submit the same report to all constituents with minor revisions as necessary. Paul offered to buy high quality carbon paper on his next trip to Bangkok and Pere will seek funding for a word processor.

"I'll cover the omissions," Pere offers. In his elegant flowing scrawl, he ends each written communication with "Pax Vobiscum." Pere uses his station to remind people that the Lord's spirit, as much as budget deficits, determine such expediencies. "Fine. *Sèt rẙy njāŋ?*" (Finished yet?), asks Paul in Thai. "Finished," Pere replies.

The meeting adjourned at 11:45. LDL, 3/7/86.

The approaching noon sun beats mercilessly down, and sweat drips off our legs, while a fan keeps the black flies away. Thanks to Boonchan, who is in the camp commander's good graces, we have an electrical outlet. I flee to the Vang family's compound, which is dark and cool under the eaves.

Choua invites me to eat in the kitchen. In the heat, she does not bother to open the upper room, where they usually entertain guests. "Where's Xiong?" I ask. "She's doing a ceremony in center 7," Ger replies. We sit on low stools around a wooden table and Choua serves a soup of vegetables and beef. "Eat too," I suggest to Choua. Ger replies, "No, she ate already."

Pao, the eldest son, returns from school. He throws down his books and begs first his mother, then his father, for money. Choua, ignoring him, goes outside to feed the youngest son. When Ger refuses, too, Pao kicks and pounds the floor. Ger calls Choua, but she does not answer.

"I think Lynel doesn't like this food," he says observing that I eat slowly. "No, I don't want to eat too much, I'll get fat." Ger looks surprised. Pao sobs, lying face down on the floor. "What's wrong with fat?" he asks. As Pao subsides, Ger offers his son a chicken bone. "I'm full already," I answer. When we finished the soup, Ger offers Pao five baht to buy some drinks. He cheers up and darts out the door to a nearby stall.

"When your children are grown, what do you want them to do?" I ask Ger. "I want them to study and then find work to support themselves," he replies.

"What do you think of the school?" I ask. Pao, seven years old, is in his second year of the primary school. "He studies Lao, Thai, too. He has a Thai teacher and a Hmong teacher. He still doesn't know letters, not very well," Ger answers, sounding somewhat dissatisfied.

"Did he study before he went to school?" I ask. "No, before he didn't study at home. But, when he comes home, I teach him Lao. Choua does too."

Pao returns with the drinks. Ger is angry when Pao hands him less than a baht. He scolds his son in Hmong and makes Pao count the change again.

"Where's the money?" Ger asks him. Pao shakes his head and runs outside to his mother. "Are you full?" Ger asks as I get up to leave, too. "Fat already!" I reply. He laughs. We go outside.

"What's that?" I ask Ger, noticing some graffiti scrawled in Lao on the wall. "Each person must take care of the cleaning," he reads aloud. "Just a joke," he explains. "Tou wrote it one day after I said it." Choua smiles. I realize that Ger had somehow humorously resolved a neighborhood disagreement.

In the afternoon, Anika leads a discussion with the parasocial workers on procedures for doing community development in the neighborhoods. The heat settles inside the COERR offices. I keep awake by counting trips made to the water cooler. Tou Vang and the other Hmong elders, weary of long hours of listening to English, drift off to sleep. The young male workers shoot rubber bands at each other and at the few female workers in the room. Ten more drinks. Boonchan fills out forms in the corner and Paul disappears to calculate the accounts for the monthly report. "Where are you going?" Anika asks as he stops at the cooler. She is evidently displeased at the absences and inattention, but cannot enlist Pere's support. He sleeps soundly, too.

Lee stands outside and does not participate in the discussion. Since he is usually very active in these meetings, I go outside to see what he is doing. He seems unusually tired and noncommittal. "What's up? Are you ok?" I ask. We speak in English. "Yes," he replies. "You don't look so." "Problems with my father again," he offers. "I wish I could go to the United States."

Anika keeps the other parasocial workers regularly informed on Lee's "psychological problems." He often confides in her. Apparently, Lee lives in a household where the two wives often fight and his own mother is usually the loser.

"Why don't you go to the United States?" I ask. He has hung around relief workers most of his short life and seems sufficiently alienated from his own society to do quite well as an unaccompanied minor. Lee replies, "I signed up for an interview last year but JVA told me I was too young." "What does your father think?" I ask. "He doesn't," Lee replies. "Oh."

I look inside wondering what to say next. There are several people around the cooler. "Did you ever talk to him about this?" Lee replies, "Yes, and after the first time we didn't agree. Then if someone doesn't agree, then you don't talk about it again." I look at him. He looks away and says, "What will my father do, he'll follow what most people do. When the leaders decide."

"But, Lee," I protest, "Many people and many leaders have already left and he didn't follow them. So that's a kind of decision." "Yes," he agrees. "You could go alone," I said. "Maybe I will," he replies.

Inside, the discussion shifts to salaries and hours. The cooler has visibly lowered in my absence. Tou awakes. The older workers debate how many baht should be deducted for an unexcused absence. "Ten baht a day?" Anika proposes. Another worker disagrees. "A hundred (US$4)," he asserts. "Ten is not enough, they won't come if it is only ten." (The increasing penalties appear to correspond with the volume of rubber bands flying around the room.) I object, "100 baht represents a third of a worker's monthly income. Would there be any incentive to return to work after a day's absence?" Anika nods and Pere suddenly awakes in time to leave for afternoon mass. I watch the water cooler nearing empty and wondered whether there will be enough left for the bottle I plan to take to the Thaos that evening. Anika proposes that the workers divide in groups to write different components of a rules manual. I take advantage of the confusion and exit quickly. The water cooler is empty and my bottle, as well.

In the Thao compound, Sri and Blia are sewing on the porch with their mother and other women. The group ranges in age from babies on their mothers' backs to Youa, their grandmother, who uses two pairs of glasses to see her sewing. Mee Lor, the youngest daughter, squats on a stool next to Hai and watches intently. Hai has offered to teach me and I take a stool next to her. She hands me a square already neatly cut and shows me how to fold with one hand as I stitch with the other.

"You want to learn *paj ntaub* [reverse applique]?" Sri asks incredulously. "It's boring." Blia disagrees. She works much more quickly than Sri and produces more finely stitched quilts. Hai is very proud of her eldest daughter's work and recognizing her daughters' different abilities, she encourages Blia more.

Youa, bringing me pieces of cloth, distinguishes *paj ntaub Hmoob* from *paj ntaub Amerika*. *Paj ntaub Hmoob* consists of the intricate collars that the women in Laos would embroider in the evenings and at the end of the harvest for their New Year's dress. That dress reflected the two groups of Laotian Hmong (and their variations): Green (and Striped) Hmong and White Hmong. The White Hmong wore a plain white pleated skirt at New Year's, whereas the Green and Striped dyed theirs blue and decorated them with batik and applique.

Paj ntaub Amerika is a product of camp life and reflects the adaptations the Hmong women have made to the camp economy. In the camp, the women tailor their traditional handicrafts—weaving, batik, embroidery, and applique—to Thai and Western markets. Encouraged by Western missionaries, they embroider story cloths about their past and sewed reverse applique quilts. In embroidered story cloths, they often depict traditional stories and ceremonies, scenes of their lives in Laos, and their refugee experience (war and flight). The women are well aware of their market and often add an American flag or map or depict their flight in biblical motifs. They also ask the relief workers' advice about popular color combinations for the quilts. Although the art form is indigenous to the camp, the stories rarely depict scenes of camp life.

The quilts sell for $US30 in the camp market, $US50 or more in Chiang Mai and Bangkok, and $US200 or more in the United States. The women sell their quilts through subclan kinship connections in Thailand and the United States or through relief agencies and their workers. In these transactions, husbands often act as middlemen in the exchange. While a few elderly women continue to embroider the intricate designs for their ceremonial dress, the art has become a commodity and the camp, a manufacturing plant, with a cheap and large labor supply.

When I have trouble rounding the curve, Hai takes over the square and sews herself. Youa realizes that I am not going to learn to sew this way and assumes the teaching role. She tells me to sit next to her and demonstrates how she holds the cloth in her hand. While we sew, she also teaches me Hmong. In contrast to Hai and her children, Youa prefers I learn Hmong rather than speak Lao and patiently corrects my errors. Youa though refuses to stop a lesson—whether sewing or language—until I have mastered it. When I learned to knit as a child, I was allowed to produce several bad sweaters until over time I eventually improved and knitted one worth wearing. In contrast, Youa removes every bad stitch and returns the square for me to redo. Likewise, she patiently repeats words over and over again until I have the right tone. After three months, I sew a professional square and have mastered several Hmong sewing terms.

Mee Lor is pleased to find someone else at her level. "The American learns *paj ntaub*," she says in Hmong. I agree, "American learns *paj ntaub.*" This exchange is repeated two or three times until our attention is diverted.

Two large women approach. The younger one is crying. Hai brings them some stools and invites them to join the group. We listen, as in Hmong, the older woman tells the younger one's story. "What's going on?" I ask Youa. She listens first and then translates for me in Lao. According to Youa,

The younger woman had become pregnant by a married man with a wife and three children. He refused to offer any dowry for her, but offered to take the baby to his compound. The woman has not seen the baby since the father took it away the day before yesterday. Her mother is wondering what they should do.

The young woman shows the group her swollen breasts. In sympathy, Hai's neighbor offers her own infant to suckle. The seven-month-old infant nurses briefly, but recognizing a different breast, protests loudly. Another woman offers a younger child. He stares curiously at the young woman and then eagerly drinks.

The young woman is surprisingly radical in her willingness to walk away from the husband. Traditionally, sexual relations often precede marriage and most people expect her to move into the man's household. However, the man is also going against social norms by refusing to recognize his obligations of providing the expected bride price. She smiles and looks proudly defiant as Youa translates for me.

The women continue discussing the situation as the young woman nurses. Her crying subsides. Youa explains the various alternatives, "She can move in without a dowry. She can leave the child with the father. She can take the child back into her own family." The women debate for quite awhile. Different women seem to offer suggestions and sympathy.

Eventually, I notice that Youa settles the discussion in an authoritative tone. "What did you tell her to do?" I ask. "I told her to take the child back," she tells me.

Evening in Ban Vinai

Chia, dirty from herding cattle, arrives. He is in a mood to do kung fu and assumes a threatening pose at his younger brothers. His arrival signals the hour of open pumps and van departures. The women put their materials away and head with buckets to the water tanks.

On the road, I pass vans of Volag workers departing for Pak Chom and Chiang Khan. The dust is flying and children and animals scatter in their wake. When the last van disappears, I feel a sense of peace steal over the camp. Gone are the Coca Cola trucks and vans, the noise, the rush. The city turns back into the mountain village. People head to the streets again, kicking soccer balls, gossiping, buying, selling, handing out, hanging out. They stop to say hello. A man with a child on his back translates into Hmong as I buy candy from an elderly woman vendor.

Wanting to be alone, I walk to the far side of the camp. There are winds in the air, a promise of rains to come. But, there have been many false promises. Tomorrow, the heat will again sear the earth. The fires of burning lands around light up the mountains. The brilliant red sun sets over a dump site where smoldering fires throw smoke from the hills to the sky. Naked children swing on ropes across a sewage pond, while their elders search for scraps in charred debris. I walk on further, past boys playing volleyball and women returning home with water on their backs, to the higher hills that shelter the Hmong grave mounds. The mounds stand exposed in the charred earth and children play around them. As the sun sets lower, the fading light casts longer shadows across the land. Shivering, I turn quickly and follow the road back into the camp. En route, I meet Sri and Blia, who are carrying firewood.

As we enter the compound, Chia jumps out from behind a tree. I offer the candy to the children. An argument over just proportions between Chia, Pao, and Vashi ensues. Seng intervenes by giving each child two. Vashi and Pao vie for his attention. When he gives Pao the first piece, Vashi spits furiously in protest. Sri tries to placate her brother with some fruit but he pushes her angrily away. His eyes follow his father intently.

I head with the children to the hut. On the path to the hut, we meet Moua returning from Seng's brother's house. She seems more somber than usual, but greets us. "I'll return to the hut later," she promises. Chia and Mai listen expressionlessly. "Good, come," I say trying to sound friendly.

Inside the hut Mee Lor has found colored pens and draws determinedly in the notebook. Chia takes over, pushes her off the stool, and kicks her in the stomach when she tries to resume her seat. She persists and eventually is given a page to draw her own pictures. Absorbed by the process, she draws several large round shapes. Sri asks Mee Lor who they are. "Is this Chia?" she teases him. "No!" he replies disgustedly, "Mee Lor." Asserting his possession of the notebook, he draws mountains and airplanes. He then loses the book to Sri, who draws mountains with a young couple enclosed in a heart.

Neighborhood children gather at the door looking for an audience. They sing a Hmong version of "Ring Around the Rosy" and all fall down to get our attention. Chia shoos them away. Hai calls the children for dinner and they leave for the upper house.

A few minutes later Sri returns. "Not good to be alone," she explains. Since she evidently wants to talk, I ask if I can interview her. She sits up very straight and replies seriously to my questions:

I was born in Laos on Wednesday. I was born in Ban [village near Vientiane] and came to the camp when I was a year old. I am now twelve. I have lived in Ban Vinai eleven years. I have one older sister, one younger sister, and three younger brothers. I am the second child of the first wife.

"What do you like to do?" I ask. "I like to speak English," she replies immediately. This surprises me because I have never heard her speak English. "What's your name?" I ask in English. "Sri," she says so quietly that I barely hear her. "How are you?" I ask. "Twelve years," she replies.

I recall walking in on a Volag English class taught by a young missionary from Tennessee. He led the children in singing:

> What kinds of trees grow on Mayberry Street?
> Maple and oak and cherry and ash!

(Maybe I should ask about maple trees.)

"What about your future?" I ask instead in Lao.

"My future?" she repeats slowly, surprised. I realize that it is a very American question. She answers, "I would like to go to America. I would like to study lessons, study English."

"Do you want to have children?" I ask. "I don't want to have children. I want to have a husband first!" she corrects me.

"When do you want to marry?" "When I am 18," she replies. "What kind of man do you want to marry?" Sri laughs and answers, "I want someone who can write, who speaks many languages. A teacher or could be a doctor." "Would you marry a man who had another wife?" I ask. "No!" she replies adamantly.

She explains: "If there are two wives, there will be many problems, fighting. If the younger does not do her share of work, making food . . . ,or one wife is better. Young men like many wives, two wives."

This interview is one of the more successful ones with the children. Interviewing children is not a very productive way to learn about their lives. Their drawings, games, songs, alliances, and moods tell much more.[16]

Sri is very self-analytical in comparison to the other children. The other children often comment on her moods. "Sri's in a good mood or she's in a bad mood." Sri seems poised somewhere between childhood and adulthood. In Laos, she would be preparing for marriage; in the camp, she is a school child. Sometimes she plays with the younger children; other times she distances herself from them and their games. Sri is often quiet and prefers to stand apart and observe. She has eyes that look through you sometimes. Unlike the other children, Sri observed me for a few weeks and then one day, decided to befriend me. Since then, she has acted as if my time at the Thao household is hers to claim.

After dinner, the other children arrive. They draw pictures again and sing their usual medley of songs: Hmong New Year songs, Lao school songs, French nursery rhymes, and English hymns. Blia and Sri lead the singing. Hai arrives and prompts them to sing another set. She holds Vashi in her lap and supplies a line when they forget now and again. To everyone's surprise Mee Lor initiates a recitation. She stands up on a chair and recites a Hmong New Year's chant. Chia tries to pull Mee Lor off the chair, but her mother and sisters defend her. The others join in. When she finishes, they clap and cheer.

Hai, leaving with the younger children, leaves her two eldest daughters and me alone in the hut. Sri and Blia discuss the dispute between the Thao women again. Sri observes, "Moua does not do her share of work, making food . . . ,Hai is better." Afraid that someone is listening, they lower their voices. Fortunately, they speak softly because Moua arrives just then with her son.

Moua sits down on the stool. I feel awkward. The girls wait for us to speak. Blia greets Pao. He ignores her. Commanding the space where she sits, Moua discusses in Hmong which deodorants may be bought in the Thai market. "What is she talking about?" I ask Sri. She giggles and translates, but otherwise they appear to listen respectfully. Moua stops speaking in Hmong and asks me in Lao, "How long are you staying?" "I'm leaving tomorrow," I reply. She nods. She then says to the girls in Lao, "Shouldn't you be sleeping now?" Before they can leave, she stands up. "See you later," she says.

After Moua has left, Sri asks Blia, "Moua has nowhere to go?" "Did I take her room?" I ask. "No," they reply emphatically. But, I realize I have. The girls act glad to see her gone.

They resume their gossip. "Mai has taken the boyfriend in center 2?" Sri asks. Blia nods. "The one who can do kung fu?" she asks. Mai, a neighbor, is Sri's best friend. "Yes, she has made house in center 2," Blia admits. "I don't have a boyfriend, have only Mai," Sri says sadly. She claims not to like boys and blames them for the loss of her friend.

I hear noises outside the hut. Sri quickly shuts the door. "What's that?" I ask. They laugh. High-pitched whistles, birdlike sounds, and scratching sounds can be heard on the walls. A particularly harsh sound sends the rats scurrying overhead, and the girls, who claim not to fear rats, tumble into my arms. The traditional courtship sounds of young Hmong men begin again.[17] Sri opens the door slightly to observe two admirers hanging outside. The boys back off toward the latrine shadows as Hai suddenly appears around the corner. Sri and Blia refuse to come out and laugh at the boys through the door.

The girls shut the door. Hai disappears into the inner room. The boys scratch on the bamboo walls and whistle again. Sri and Blia open and slam the door in response. Then, they shut the door for good. Sri assumes a kung fu pose.

At first, I wonder if she is imitating Chia, but her movements take on the quality of a dance. Laughing, Blia becomes the partner and imitates her movements in mirror image. Adopting various warrior poses, they mock the male world and all its pretensions to strength and power. Weaving back and forth, they distort the traditional combat stances of their brothers. The girls dance toward each other, then away, and finally, again, in synchrony. Each attack is followed by a retreat in spasmodic movements that betrays the parody. In the midst of the grace and beauty of the dance, the boys disappear. The movements intensify and then suddenly, Sri stops. Blia follows. The dance begins and ends as spontaneously as clouds pass in the dry season.

SIX

Entrapment

The women in Ban Vinai are luckier than the men, or so I think sometimes. They find many traditional ways to occupy their time. The women have their sewing, house chores, children, and kin to look after. Men have these responsibilities, too, but they appear to count for less in their identity. For the men, there is the Resistance, trading, and a few Volag jobs, but many men spend their time waiting for something to happen. The international relief community calls this problem of nothing to do and nowhere to go, "warehousing." Such language, however, distances the problem of the Vangs, Thaos, Sisawongs, and others who have been locked in this camp for several years—a camp with not enough farm land and where most forms of paid employment are illegal. Such language also treats people as commodities to be shipped from place to place. "Warehousing" implies that the commodities are not moving fast enough and the shipments are stalled in the warehouse.

I am learning about what it means to be trapped in a camp from the Sisawongs. Despite our initial encounter, they talk openly about their camp experiences. Chanthanom and Khamsai, who were educated in the French school system, are used to being around the for-

93

eigners. In contrast to the Hmong households, I become friends with Chanthanom before Khamsai, her husband. Chanthanom and I are almost the same age; she is a year younger. It sometimes amazes me how easily we communicate despite how different the other thirty-two years of our lives have been.

Uprooting

Chanthanom was born in 1953 in a village in the mountains of northern Laos.[1] Indicating with her hand, she describes:

I lived very far up the mountain. In a village like the Hmong villages. There were no roads, first you drive four hours to the bridge at Keun Nam Ngeum and then you climb one day up the mountain. Straight up. You spend the night at a Hmong village on the way. My family were all slash and burn [Lao: *hāj*] rice farmers. It's very hard work, work all the time. But, mountain rice is much better, like American rice.

She asserts the last proudly. "How big was the village?" I ask. "About 100 houses," she replies. Chanthanom is the fourth in a family of six children and one of three daughters.

Initially, Chanthanom does not tell me that she is Khmu, an ethnic Laotian minority, who as some of the earliest known inhabitants of Laos, settled in the upland valleys and lower highlands [Lao: *Láaw thán*]. Chanthanom speaks a very literate Lao and introduces herself and her family as "Lao" (which I interpret as *Láaw lūm*, lowland Lao). The younger French sister, however, who taught Chanthanom in Laos, tells me she is Khmu. Initially, explaining why she left her village, Chanthanom says:

A wealthier man took an interest in me. He sent me to the French sisters' school in the lowlands up to the sixth year (French: *sixième*).

She does not clarify at first how or why she was selected, but implies that it was fate or God's will. Later, she is more explicit:

I left for Savannakhet [the lowlands] when I was eight years old. Pere Bouchard, a French priest, asked the sisters to adopt me since my family was very poor. I studied grades 1 and 2 in my village. I learned to read and write letters but not a letter. When I was eight, the Father and sisters took me away in an airplane. My parents had never seen one before. I remember how afraid I was. All I could do was cry. A sister gave me a cookie but I couldn't eat it. I was crying too hard. I studied with the sisters from eight to fourteen years. I was often homesick. I studied Lao, French, and numbers.

Being adopted by the French sisters radically changed her life. The other members of her family remained in villages in the region. There, despite the war and changes of regime, they work the fields, raise their families, and more or less, continue their traditional village life. War and its aftermath made them poorer and they may have been relieved to have one less person to feed, who at the same time garnered additional resources. For Chanthanom, the airplane ride—like the stories of many refugees airlifted out of the mountains by the Americans—marked the beginning of another way of life, which would lead to her becoming a refugee.

After finishing her studies, Chanthanom decided to return home. She observes that she was more fortunate than her family and she feels obliged to help them.

> After I finished school, I continued living with the sisters from fourteen to seventeen, because my family was too poor and couldn't afford to have me come home again. When I was seventeen, I went to teach at a private Catholic school in Vientiane [the capital]. I taught children eight and nine years old. I taught them French, Lao, and arithmetic, but only one year. My mother and father were very poor so I decided to go home to help them and teach in the countryside. I taught in the countryside for two years. It was very hard.

In the countryside, she met a soldier in the Royal Lao Army who had been sent north to fight against the Pathet Lao, Communist insurgents. She relates:

> I worked about as far away as Loei [a town approximately sixty kilometers from the camp] from my parent's village. I lived with a friend, who worked in a station. I met Khamsai while I was teaching. He came to my school several times. After those two years, I went and helped my parents in the fields for about a year. I married Khamsai after knowing him five months.

Chanthanom is remarkably beautiful and even twelve years later, it is obvious that Khamsai adores her. Being lowland Lao and from the dominant group, predictably he would have had an arranged marriage to another Lao from his region. However, he broke with tradition and married a poor minority of low status. Interethnic marriages were rare and theirs may never have happened in a more peaceful time.

Khamsai, as he tells it, came from a large family who lived in the village of Kongsadok in the province of Pak Chao in central Laos. His family cultivated wet rice. When he finished primary school, he left home and boarded in a larger town to continue his secondary studies. He studied agricultural training to become an extension worker. When he finished his studies, he was conscripted into the Royal Lao forces. He served several years in the war and according to him, "I never had a chance to do my profession so I could be anything now."

I ask Chanthanom why she married Khamsai after only five months. "I thought I was old already so it was time to get married," she replies. "I have spent seven years of my twelve years of marriage in a refugee camp," she reflects. At the end of the war, Khamsai and Chanthanom fled across the border. According to Chanthanom, "Because Khamsai fought for the Royal Lao forces, we had to leave." Their strong connections to the French and interethnic marriage in all likelihood also made life in postwar Laos untenable. Their fates and fortunes had been linked to the Western powers during the war and they saw their future across the border. A man with deep convictions, Khamsai joined the Lao Resistance and the Sisawongs escaped across the Mekong river.

The Sisawongs entered Nong Khai, a refugee camp directly across from Vientiane, in June 1979. Camp life was more difficult than they expected. In Nong Khai, according to Chanthanom:

> We were locked up for several days, months. Locked up in a chicken coop! We sold our watches, belts, everything we had that we could sell to get money for food. Boondi [the oldest daughter] was born in Nong Khai. She was very sick. I thought she would die. There was nothing I could do. There was a Thai doctor there. I persuaded him to give her intravenous injections.

The experience in Nong Khai had a profound impact on her sense of security. She often recalls this experience when discussing possible future plans. After the Nong Khai experience, she has less faith that life will necessarily be better in the future.

After several months in Nong Khai, the Sisawongs traveled by local buses to Ban Vinai. During this period in early 1980, the Thai MOI were moving lowland Lao out of Ban Vinai into Nong Khai and Hmong from Nong Khai into Ban Vinai. (MOI designated Nong Khai and Napho for the lowland Lao and Ban Vinai, Chiang Kham, and the northern camps for the ethnic minorities.) In the comings and goings, it was easy for the Sisawongs to bribe their way out of one camp and into another.[2] Many refugees had heard that Nong Khai was closing (it was eventually closed in 1982) and that Ban Vinai, a Resistance camp, would remain open.

Ironically, the Sisawongs claimed Chanthanom's Khmu ethnicity to gain access to Ban Vinai, which had been designated a highlander camp.

Some neighboring Thai villagers took the Sisawongs in, while they negotiated buying a room inside Ban Vinai. They eventually bought a space in the Khmu neighborhood of center 9 from a Hmong, whose wife was lowland Lao. The Hmong was a member of the Resistance and well connected. He negotiated their entry. He also provided them a space in his front yard. Khamsai built a traditional thatch and bamboo hut and enlisted again in the Resistance.

In Ban Vinai, the Sisawongs reconnected with the French clergy. The younger of the French nuns had been Chanthanom's teacher in Laos. To Chanthanom, the French Catholic clergy represented a kind of security and connection to her childhood. She learned that the sisters had been living in Loei, a town in the northeast, during her stay in Nong Khai. "If only we had known they were nearby in Loei then!" she commented. She saw the Church as one of their protectors in the camp.

In Ban Vinai, Khamsai and Chanthanom had four more children. The last two were twin boys, Choy and Tuy—Thin and Fat, respectively. Both were quite thin, but Choy had tuberculosis at birth and almost died. The Sisawongs had very little money and since Khamsai was often away with the Resistance, Chanthanom had to care for them alone. She described this time as the second-most difficult period in her life. "Choy almost died, we had no money for medicine. Pere helped us." After Choy's illness and three years of coming and going across the border, Khamsai dropped out of the Resistance to help Chanthanom with the five children. Explaining his decision, Chanthanom says, "We were too poor. I needed him here to make some money. The Resistance doesn't pay anything." The Hmong neighbor found a better address in the camp and bequeathed the Sisawongs his room, thereby giving them an official camp address.

In 1981, the Thai MOI formally relocated all the remaining lowland Lao to Napho. Chanthanom and Khamsai, correctly fearing that Napho would be another Nong Khai, did not take advantage of the opportunity to become registered legally as lowland Lao refugees. Chanthanom was also reluctant to leave her Church connections behind. At the same time, the Sisawongs lacked the money to buy their way officially into Ban Vinai and become legally registered as highland refugees. Without an official UNHCR identity card (BV number), they were considered "illegals" and numbered among the camps' 3,000 illegal population. As illegals, they cannot receive food rations or be considered for resettlement in a third country. Khamsai and Chanthanom support their family by working for COERR and other Volags and they periodically receive gifts of rice from Pere and the sisters. Chanthanom, looking back, re-marks bitterly, "If only we had had the money then to buy a number, we wouldn't have these problems today."

Caught between different worlds, different regimes, and different camps, they have somehow slipped through the cracks. Without official refugee status, they are very vulnerable. If they anger a guard or refuse to pay a bribe, they can be shipped back across the border at any moment.

To protect themselves, Chanthanom and Khamsai extend their network of friendships across the camp. Taking advantage of their diverse ethnic backgrounds and experiences, they make friends within the Lao, Khmu, and Hmong communities, with local Thai villagers and the camp administration, and with the foreigners. As lowland Lao they observe the Buddhist ceremonies and as Francophone Lao, attend the Catholic Church. They count on the common roots of the Thai and lowland Lao and know the importance and power of those small gratuitous favors [Thai: *kreeŋcaj*] that socially bind people to one another. To the camp commander and others in power, they act accordingly, which provides them some measure of protection in the camp.

Their main concern is the future. In April, the rumors begin again in the camp that all illegals will have one last chance to register to go to Napho (for the lowland Lao) or Chiang Kham (for the highlanders). Both camps are maximum security camps where life is reportedly harsh, but being registered also means that they can apply for resettlement.

Folksongs

After our initial encounter, I visit the Sisawongs often. In the heat of the dry season, it is a long walk to center 9, where they live. The main bridge to the center has fallen and no one bothers to repair it for several months. This means that all vehicles have to take the long way around either through center 8 or outside the camp and back in through the back gate. To me the fallen bridge symbolizes the status of center 9 in the camp and adds to its sense of remoteness.

Sometimes they are out helping to distribute food rations when I arrive so we miss one another. Boondee, the first daughter, invites me to stay awhile, but the waiting may be hours. UNHCR to save money has instituted a new policy of delivering all rations to a central point rather than directly to the centers. This means that people stand in line for long hours first at the central distribution point and then again in each center. When the refugee leaders objected to this change, they were overruled. "What else do they have to do all day?" asked the UNHCR field officer and several relief workers. Khamsai and Chanthanom often volunteer to help with the distribution. This helps ensure that they have access to the excess which is distributed to the "illegals." Sometimes distributing food takes the better part of a day.

April is the height of the hot season. Each day grows progressively hotter, the dust is thick, and the air heavy and still. The heat hangs in the treeless valley and entering from the outside world, I feel the temperature rise another ten degrees. Anticipating the rains and mud slides to come, the residents plant upturned bottles outside their doors to buttress their thresholds. Occasionally, a brief cloud passes overhead bringing hope of a change in weather, but the fleeting shadows offer no more than momentary shade from the sun's piercing rays. The bare, dry earth appears devoid of life.

Climbing the last hill to their house, which overlooks the dump fires, I see Khamsai above sitting in a squatting position contemplatively appraising the world. He looks like an eagle ready to soar, but seeing me, he descends from their balcony.

"Chanthanom is inside. Thank you for the salary advance," he says very seriously in English. "Don't thank me," I tease, "I didn't give it to you. It's Chanthanom's." Knowing that the children had been ill, I had persuaded the younger nun to advance Chanthanom 300 baht (US$12), her monthly salary.

He rejoins in Lao, "Well, Chanthanom thanks you." Khamsai is very serious. I fear I have offended him.

Chanthanom is resting on the mat with Choy inside the dark room. She has put some herbal medicine with white bandages on what looks like a large boil on his leg. A neighbor sits with her. "The ghosts [Lao: *phǐi*] caused it," the neighbor informs me. Chanthanom laughs, but does not disagree.

There are many flies in the room. "Why not the flies?" I ask. "No, it just came on its own, its the ghosts," the neighbor insists. "Isn't it an infection?" I ask. "Yes," the neighbor agrees. "But the ghosts caused it."

Chanthanom has cooked herbs obtained from the river and then made a poultice. "These plants are in the river beds in Laos, too," she explains. "Are you afraid of ghosts?" I ask Chanthanom. "Not other people's ghosts," she replies.

We go out on the porch. "Lynel, do you have any pills?" she asks complaining of a headache. "Khamsai has a headache, too. He doesn't sleep much these days," she offers.

"Why don't you go to the clinic?" I suggest. "The lines are too long," she complains. "I took Tuy. I saw the Hmong medic who gave me the black pills, but they didn't work. I wanted to see the French doctor but he doesn't come to the clinic."

I offer her the vitamins I happen to carry around in my bag. "Do you have any of the blue pills?" she asks. "No, what are those?" "Vitamin B."

The heat worsens. The next time I go to their place in center 9, Chanthanom is lying with the children on the porch. Khamsai is just leaving for his Volag work as I arrive. He wears a Khmu Family Association T-shirt. The words are written in Lao and English.

"Where did you get that?" I ask. "Chanthanom's friend, a Khmu leader in Texas sent it," he explains. Chanthanom joins us on the porch.

"There are many Khmu families in the U.S., they live in every state," she says, overhearing our conversation. I realized these are their connections to the United States. "Where do you want to live?" I ask. "I don't know, we don't have enough information to decide," she replies. "California?" Most people in the camp have relatives or friends in California. "No, people are unemployed there."

Tuy emerges naked from the room. Khamsai turns back and orders him angrily, "Put some pants on!" The child returns with his sister's knitted pants around his legs. We laugh. Chanthanom helps her son pull the pants on and tucks in his shirt. He pulls the shirt out and retucks it. The pants fall down his legs again. Chanthanom gets up from the mat and helps him again. Tuy tries to climb in her lap. Holding the child, Chanthanom remarks, "He hasn't slept much, has a cold again. Last night, he had more nosebleeds."

Choy joins his brother on the porch. He looks thin and wan. The twins, vying for Chanthanom's attention, fuss. Khet, the second daughter, takes Tuy on her back and lets him ride her like a horse. Boondee is studying. At first she is reluctant to join the game, but then she takes Choy on her back, too. They circle round and round the porch. We stop talking and watch the game. In the heat and circular motion, time suddenly passes very slowly. The observed moment seems endless. I realize I am depressed by my inability to be more than an observer, to make any difference against the suffering I am witnessing.

The neighbor, seeing me on the porch, brings a form to translate. She hands me a public health card. Translating from English to Lao as best I can, I tell her that she has a yeast infection. "It isn't serious," I explain. "Do you have any medicine?" "Yes, but it isn't working," she replies. "Keep taking the medicine," I suggest. "Yes, but it doesn't go away." "Maybe you need to boil your underwear," I tell her. Chanthanom agrees. The neighbor adds that she had a depo-provera injection.

"Could that be the problem?" she asks. "I don't think so, these infections are just difficult," I reply.

When she leaves, Chanthanom comments, "These infections are difficult, very painful, hard to get rid of. It is because the camp is so dirty." "But, you can get them everywhere, every country in the world," I protest. "Yes, but it is very dirty here," she replies.

Choy returns and, leaning against his mother, cries. Tuy joins him. Chanthanom gives them some scraps of paper and a pencil. They grab the pencil back and forth from one another. She asks if I had any more vitamins. "Why do you want them?" I ask surprised that she finished the others so quickly. "Khamsai takes them to sleep," she explains. "A placebo," I realize, handing her three more vitamins. I take the vitamins to overcome the fatigue of long hot days.

Chanthanom yawns. "Are you tired?" I ask. "I'm tired because I didn't sleep last night. Tuy's nosebleed." Perhaps, feeling she complains too much, she changes the topic. "Have you eaten yet?" "No . . . no, I don't want to, I don't want to get fat," I reply, betraying my American middle-class obsessions. It is my excuse for not taking their food. Otherwise she will send her daughter to the market to buy us soft drinks. Chanthanom laughs, "I can always eat, I never get tired of eating."

The neighbor overhears us. "Older women are fatter. When I was young, I was thin like you. Now after three, four children, old women get fatter. When you have lots of children, too."

At that point the sanitation truck arrives. The smell is overpowering. We stop talking, hold our noses. "They have come to pick up the feces," Chanthanom says. "Does this happen every day?" I ask laughing and gagging. "No, not often," Chanthanom replies.

Chanthanom's eldest son accosts his mother. She hands him a baht and he leaves again. Chanthanom explains, "Children won't go to school, you must give them money to buy candy. But, if I give him, I must give the others, too. Five children, three times a day. Fifteen baht. You can't give one without giving the others."

"That's expensive," I reply. "What if you don't give any?"

"Sometimes we have no money to give them. We don't give them anything sometimes but it is difficult when they see what the other children have." Tuy grabs at her pocket. "No, boring," she says trying to dissuade him. I start to leave. She follows. "Stay where you are, boring," I say, trying to dissuade her in her own terms. Chanthanom laughs.

The camp commander announces again that all illegals must register for Napho or Chieng Kham. I wonder if the Sisawongs will register.

The next time I see Chanthanom she is leaning against her house while she watches the children playing. Khamsai has built the twins a seesaw out of bamboo. The twins have a good time as long as their sisters help them operate it. Otherwise, Tuy always ends up on the bottom. Looking wan and tired, Chanthanom tells me she is sick again. This time she has stomach problems. "But, higher up," she explains. "I bought some medicine in the market, but I can't keep food down. This is not a healthy place."

We sit in their bamboo hut. "Lynel," she asks suddenly, "Do you think we should go to Napho?" "Why not?" I reply, hoping that at least they will have a chance to resettle in a third country. Any safe exit out of the camp seems the best option to me. "There might not be enough food in Napho." She explains that Khamsai sent a letter to their kin in Napho and has received word that conditions are severe there. "Maybe our Nong Khai number will let us stay in Ban Vinai," Chanthanom says. We both know it is wishful thinking.

"Do you want to go to the U.S.?" I ask. "I would prefer to go to France. Khamsai wants to go to the U.S., because he speaks English. But, I think the sisters would help us in France."

Khamsai arrives. He must have overheard us because, smiling, he asks, "Do you think we should go to Napho?" I wonder if he is teasing me. "Why not?" I reply. He will do as he wishes in any case. "Maybe we could become Thai," he replies enigmatically and leaves the room. Chanthanom shakes her head.

The neighbor, seeing me, brings a melon. "Are you better?" I ask. "A little, not completely." The melon is big and beautiful. "It's a striped variety," Chanthanom explains. Khamsai returns. I notice that he was eyeing my melon. Hugging the melon to my chest, I say, "This is my striped melon, mine." He stares shocked. The neighbor and Chanthanom laugh. "Lynel is teasing you." He laughs and asks, "Do you know the other melon varieties, too?"

The fresh melon tastes wonderful. It is not chilled—there are no refrigerators in the centers—but the juice flows and the fruit has never seemed so sweet before. I hate watermelon at home; the seeds always get in the way but here, in the heat, the melon is pure bliss.

When Khamsai leaves, I ask Chanthanom, "What does he mean by becoming Thai?" She explains, "He thinks maybe we can buy a place in a village. Buy an identity card from the village head. If only we have enough money." "How much is it?" I ask. "It's about 7,000 baht [US$280]." "Per person?" I ask. She nods. "Couldn't he make you pay again?" I ask, wondering what the word for blackmail is in Lao. "Yes, he could, he could blackmail us," she replies.

The pressure to register continues. "They should go to Chiang Kham or Napho," Pere says when I describe the Sisawongs' situation. The heat persists. "When does the hot season end?" I ask. "After Songkran [the Thai and Lao New Year], when the rains come," I am told.

"Life will get better then," I suggest to Chanthanom the next time I see her. "Perhaps," she replies.

She is teaching the twins the different parts of the body. "Eyes, ears, nose," she says. They repeat. "Fingernails, eyebrows, eyelashes," she adds. These are new words for the twins and they have trouble repeating.

Khamsai is tearing down the sides of their bamboo house to make it into a porch. He listens amused. "Air conditioning," he jokes. Khamsai asks the twins and his younger daughter to hold a piece of bamboo in place as he saws and hammers. A young boy tries to steal some of the bamboo as they work. Khamsai bawls him out and the child runs away. "You sound scary," I tell him. He laughs.

A very bowlegged child passes the house. The children run to look as the child passes. Chanthanom admonishes them, "You must pity him." I am glad the child does not hear. I am equally glad she does not hear the way my own world describes the refugee. But, they both know.

I ask Chanthanom, "Can you teach me some Lao words, too?" She readily agrees. In French, I ask her the words for sexual organs. She translates into Lao. Khamsai overhears and teases us. "This is our lesson," Chanthanom asserts. We speak French instead, which he does not speak well.

The next time I see Chanthanom, she complains of dizziness. She has been sick with a high fever and chills for three days and has violent headaches. "Do you have a backache?" I ask, remembering my own experiences with malaria. She has already thought of malaria and has gone to the public health service for a blood test. Her oldest son also has a high fever.

As we speak on the porch, Tuy and Choy emerge from the room. Hiding under the towel together, wet and naked, they look like a centipede. We laugh, but Chanthanom has to lean against the wall and holds her head. The twins try to put their pants on themselves. I help them pull up their trousers.

I give Chanthanom the Lao dictionary she asked me to buy for her and I show her some photographs I took. "Let me pay you," she says. I decline. She points out different people in the photographs to the twins. "Who's this? What's her name? What's his name?" she asks them. They repeated: "Lynel, Camp Commander, Sister, Father, Mother, etc." "These photographs make me feel better, forget that I am sick," she says.

Khamsai, appearing, asks me to translate the word for poetry [Lao:

khám kɔɔn] versus poem [*khóoŋ kɔɔn*] in English. He is preparing for an English class that he teaches in the early morning. When I ask about Lao poetry, Khamsai describes how in Laos he used to write folksongs [Lao: *lám*] for the *khɛɛn*, a musical instrument.[3]

> I learned to play the *khɛɛn* not very well from an old man. The old men in this camp, some remember how to play — some do, but not the women. I could teach my sons, but I don't play very well. The folksongs sound like the sounds of the *khɛɛn*.

He is more animated than I have ever seen him. "Can you write folksongs?" I ask. "Yes, I could write one for you," he offers. "I'll write you a poem in English," I offer in return. He agrees. "What's your husband's name?" he asks. "Why?" I ask surprised at the apparent change of topic. "I need it for the folksong," Khamsai explains.

"Where did you learn to write folksongs?" I ask. Khamsai replies: "I learned to write at school but some people learn from listening to others at home. Women can speak poetry, but only a few women can write it. People speak poetry and you remember it."

"Is that true?" I ask Chanthanom. "Yes, but I can write poetry, too," she says proudly.

I arrive late the next afternoon. Khamsai has written the folksong and reads it aloud. I listen. "Do you understand it?" he asks. "Yes," I reply, momentarily elsewhere. I am surprised how much he has observed. Khamsai asks Chanthanom to read the song a second time so I can hear the alliteration. I translate the sense for them in English. It goes something like this:

> Dennis, it has been many months since I have seen you.
> How I miss you, my heart is lonely without you,
> I think of nothing but you.
> I live alone, go with no one.
> I think only of you, Oh, Dennis, come soon.

This folksong is considerably longer in Lao and sounds as if I am calling Dennis to me. "You understand it!" Khamsai says surprised at my translation. Such folksongs written to a particular person can project the other person's state of being. I realize that in using the power of the Lao folksong, he has captured my own loneliness. "And your folksong?" he asked. "Tomorrow," I promise.

Sitting on the porch, we watch the children play below. Chanthanom is somewhat better. She shows me her blood test results. "What do you think," she asks. They are all abnormal, but the Hmong medic has summarized in English, "Psychological problems." I translate it for her.

"Did he give you any medicine?" I ask. "Yes, for worms, but the medicine gives me a headache. I have to take five tablets. It's too many. I decided not to take them." "The worm medicine always gives me a bad headache, but you have a worse one if you don't take it," I suggest.

Khamsai concurs. Then, he says that he has not slept well. "Maybe the heat?" I suggest. "I have the same problem, headache, fevers, bad stomach," he replies. It is uncharacteristic of him to complain.

"Look, you eat, sleep, live together—probably hurt together," I conclude. He laughs and agrees as he leaves for another Volag meeting. "He never sleeps anymore," Chanthanom says, "he is worrying too much."

The next day I bring the poem I have written for them. I offer it to them. "No," says Khamsai, giving it back, "Read it aloud." I read in English:

Lonely, passionless dreams
wait out the long waiting
hours until sunrise.
Longing for Laos, a dream long ago
some images
to etch out rats
scurrying in the bamboo shafts.

Today the skies are empty
the sun shines ceaselessly
but not in your heart.

Do you always remember so
longingly of another time?
Is your past more vivid
because the present lies bare
and the future stills the heart?

Long memories of another
land stretch like shadows
over this time
Crying dreams, restless
windless nights
cannot calm the heart
without a future.

The child cries, stirs in the
pain of her father's eyes
which sing yet another folksong

                              mourning the distant land
                              in the nightless days of waiting.

They are both very quiet. I am embarrassed. Have I offended them or do they not understand it? Are my perceptions wrong? I wonder. "Should I translate it?" I ask finally. "Poetry cannot be translated. I understand this poem," Khamsai answers. He translates the lines in Lao, however, for Chanthanom. "I didn't know you could write poetry, too!" she says surprised.[4]

The next time I come, Chanthanom is better. She complains that her arm hurts from where the medic has drawn blood. The French sister once remarked that Chanthanom never complains. "She always keeps busy and cheerful," she observed admiringly. "Chanthanom, you are just sick. Everything hurts you now," I tell her. "That's true," Khamsai agrees. He walks inside the room leaving us on the porch. "I have never been sick so much before," she tells me. "There are good years and bad years." I reply, "You are worrying about a lot about the future now. This has been a difficult year for you." She agrees. Khamsai reemerges on the porch. She repeats our conversation. He nods and goes back into the house.

Returning he brings out a photograph of Chanthanom when she was eighteen. Wearing a straw hat, she looks very romantic, very Audrey Hepburn. "Chanthanom, you were beautiful!" I observe. Khamsai nods approvingly. She looks down but smiles. I look at her and at the photograph again. "You are more beautiful now, your face has more life," I say reflectively. She smiles. I know she understands what I mean and agrees. Khamsai teases, "She has lost many teeth—seven." "Yes, I have," she admits.

Boredom

Chanthanom's health is improving, but the issue of whether to register remains for the Sisawongs. The problem of people being caught in the camp concerns everyone. At the COERR offices, this becomes a topic during the assessment process. Commenting on the issue, Anika observes:

> The main problem is that originally industrious people can fall into the dependency syndrome if they are helped without having to do anything for the help they receive. I would like to see the refugees required to do a certain amount of work to be eligible for their food distribution with the exception, of course, of the handicapped, el-

derly, or children who cannot work. It would have to be an act of the UN. I understand the reason it is not being done now is because of the UN's policy. It would, of course, have to be done in a positive way. Then, the refugees would respond positively to it. I think it would give them a sense of honor, of human dignity, as well as solving the problem of getting work done in the camp.

"Whose honor is at stake here?" I wonder. I think of Chanthanom and Khamsai trying to make a living, their crammed schedules, dual working lives with five children, and perseverance in face of sickness. I want to argue with Anika, but it is pointless. She will say that their situation, as illegal refugees, is unique. I wonder what additional work she expects them to do in the camp. Asking the refugees to run the public health, sanitation, and education programs, and other tasks they already do—without pay—is demeaning. Yet, Anika recognizes the problem of dependency and the contradictions of her own assistance. Like many relief workers, she holds UNHCR rather than distant political powers responsible for solving the problem.

Boonchan vehemently disagrees with Anika. As a Thai, she fears the effects of Western influence. She describes the main problem in the camp, as

the destruction of their culture. During the refugees' stay in Ban Vinai, I'm afraid they lost their own culture. And, they lost identity as Hmong people, lost social customs, social traditions. The young generation is divided into two cultures: those who wish to repatriate, and those who learn English, study, work, and the Western customs—those who are no longer integrated into their own culture, but are not yet ready to be part of the new. I think in every refugee camp, something has changed, especially the Hmong because they are a hill tribe. Before they came here, they could move but now they stay here. I cannot say they can solve this.

Boonchan believes that camp life is dividing families and generations, between those who want to resettle in a third country and those who expect to repatriate. Hopes about the future affect refugees' activities and choices in the camp. Boonchan respects those who are willing to repatriate and fears the enculturation of camp life. I disagree with her assumption that people in the camp have lost their identity as Hmong or Lao. "The refugees have maintained their identity as Hmong or lowland Lao and as, Laotians," I assert. "The difference is that the rest of the world sees them as refugees."

At the end of the assessment process, Boonchan and Anika quarrel. With opposing world views, they often have difficulty communicating. Relief work itself is difficult; not only must relief workers learn to communicate with Hmong, Lao, and other ethnic groups, but they also work with some fifteen or more different nationalities. Their range of experiences and motivations vary widely from fundamentalist missionaries, Vietnam veterans, world travelers, ex-Peace Corps volunteers, social workers, teachers, and others from assorted walks of life and social classes. The hours are long and demands high. Burn-out is common and the relief workers recognize their own "compassion fatigue." Although "compassion fatigue" refers primarily to the unwillingness of international donors to sustain aid, it also describes individuals who can no longer cope with the demands of the job and who are quick to blame the refugees for their distress.

Anika and Boonchan do not speak for several days. Symbolically, they avoid speaking their common language, English. Boonchan asks Paul and me to translate for her from Thai to English, even though she speaks English fluently. Blaming their differences on language makes it easier for Boonchan to accept her own anger. The other Thai workers, noticing her predicament, counsel, "Calm down" [literally "Cool your heart"—Thai: *caj jen jen*]. Anika spends long hours praying. Their different ways of dealing with anger make it even more difficult for them to resolve their differences.

Their quarrel is eventually resolved by time. The rest of us forget what it is about or are no longer willing to listen. Boonchan begins by asking Anika about work-related concerns. In these first conversations, however, she appears very distant and acts as if her thoughts are elsewhere. "Are you still angry?" I ask her. "No, bored," Boonchan explains. "What do you mean?" I ask surprised. She describes Anika's behavior. "She'll never change," she concludes.

Boredom in Boonchan's terms is a response to a persistent and aggravating relationship over which she has no control. Boredom is an endemic state in the camp. In Thai and Lao, however, boredom [*bȳa*] is the negation or absence of emotion. Unlike Thai words for the emotions, *bȳa* lacks the root "heart." The negation or absence, however, is powerful expression of the individual's state of being. In contrast, to negative emotions, which are derived from the word heart—hatred, ignore, jealousy—boredom does not imply the possibility of transcendence.

Boredom is also a by-product of warehousing. Policymakers in Washington and Geneva recognize the problem of boredom in the camps. They believe boredom is symptomatic of a welfare society—a situation that could be resolved by getting refugees off welfare. But, the Hmong in Ban Vinai use the same word to describe war and daily camp life. *Bja* is their typical response to long waits in line for food rations, the camp commander's suspension of their salaries, or the UN field officer's decision to cut food rations.

Entrapment

Ger often complains of being bored, so one day I ask, "Why are you bored in the camp?" Paradoxically denying it, he replies: "No, because I dwell here, I can't go to the fields. If my mother decides to go to America, I will go. I would like to go, but she doesn't want to go." I realize he describes his situation of being caught in the camp.

When I ask Khamsai the same question, he is visibly annoyed. "You should not use that word, it is not polite," he chides. Chanthanom, however, laughs and admits that she sometimes feels bored. Recognizing the problem in general terms is easier to acknowledge than to admit one has reached this state.

Boredom characterizes the expression that outsiders see on people's faces, who have lived in the camps for several years. A Western psychiatrist, visiting the camp briefly, complains about the lack of emotion. The psychiatrist expects the refugees to articulate their distress to an outsider. However, to what avail? They know a doctor cannot cure this condition.

The stresses of camp life in Thailand result in suicides, family violence, and addictions.[5] These reactions, however, are abnormal responses; the pervasive normal reaction is boredom. Boredom may be characteristic of long-term camp situations—the post Second World War camps, Palestinian camps, or the Mozambican camps.[6] In the post Second World War camps, where some 90,000 refugees were warehoused for over a decade, a psychiatrist wrote of the problem of "internment psychosis".[7] Internment psychosis involved two phases. During the first phase, refugees displayed aggressive behavior, expressed in restlessness, projections of hate onto persons and objects, and regressive avoidance reactions, sometimes mass psychoses of flight or mass anxiety. The second phase was marked by apathy [read: boredom], a "desiccation of the ego which is not only a tonic immobility, but a type of self-destruction." From her description, I realize why boredom is such a dangerous state for Ger, Khamsai, and others. Such a state of being is ultimately self-destructive.

The deadlines pass. The Sisawongs never register, but it does not seem to matter. Outwardly everything is calm, normal, routine. Sometimes I fear and hope, "Maybe Ban Vinai will last forever. Maybe, the world will forget these people are here and they can stay forever." The heat is oppressive. These are fantasies of a noon hour, whereas evening clarifies the desperation.

One early morning I go to the Sisawongs again. Seeing me Khamsai asks, "When is JVA coming?" He worries again about whether to register for Napho. I have no idea. He asks again. He refuses to accept that I have no knowledge of when my own compatriots will show up to interview in the camp. Chanthanom looks surprised, too. I realize that she has higher expectations of what I can do for them. Whether to register seems irrelevant, but apparently Khamsai believes the issue is not closed. They look worn, but are healthy, at least. Khamsai is teaching the English class in double shifts and Chanthanom is counseling other women. To entertain them, I relate a dream from the night before.

"I was in some back alleys and canals in Bangkok. I looked over the high walls into a beautiful old wooden house built by an English merchant. It was surrounded by a garden (inside the walls). Two women in the house were drinking tea. I looked into the window at them. They seemed remote and unreachable. I wanted to join the women, but there were high walls all around."

"You must be missing your home and Dennis," Khamsai interprets. "Maybe," I say surprised. The women resemble Anika and the sisters, but the women in the dream are poised and distant. I recall how Anika and Boonchan resolved their conflicts through distancing themselves from one another. Their resolution is like that of government bureaucracies that make decisions about refugees' lives by carefully constructing walls to protect themselves from these situations. Walls preserve rationality and order and suddenly I want in. "Yes, maybe I am missing home," I admit to him.

I ask, "What did you dream about?" Chanthanom replies, "I never dream, I just want to sleep." Khamsai agrees but then reflects a moment and laughs.

"What?" we ask.

"Last night I dreamt . . . ," he begins hesitantly.

"What?" we ask again.

"I dreamt of a cock that shat in a cage." We both burst out laughing. Chanthanom laughs so hard that she can barely speak. "Really?" she asks incredulously. "Yes," he replies.

We laugh again, but suddenly I recognize he is right. The cock caught in a cage cannot escape its own excrement.

SEVEN

Suffering and the Shaman

The hot days continue without abeyance until, one late afternoon, a storm sweeps through Ban Vinai. The rainy season begins, not with a gentle tropical shower, but with a monsoon that pours all the vengeance of hot days on a parched land. The storm starts with dust and winds. The sky darkens and the winds blow stronger. As the storm nears the camp, the skies burst open. Inside huts, barracks, and offices, the water sprays in from all sides leaving no dry corner. The pounding rains strip away the topsoil of the barren land and turn small dried curvatures into swirling mud pools. The dry ground under the bridge becomes a swiftly moving river that engulfs everything in its path. Roads crumble and fall away.

In the space of an hour, the river rises so high that its waves lap over the bridge. Watching the storm from inside the Lao restaurant, I feel chilled to the bone, a strange sensation after so many days of dust stuck to a perspiring body. Shivering I seek a small dry corner in the restaurant and wrap a sarong around my shoulders. The owner brings a cup of coffee and together sipping the hot drink, we watch the progress of the storm outside.

The rains continue in force. The relentless winds and pounding rains drown out other sounds. The water, intensifying, beats down in sheets. The river rises higher and a large plank of the bridge breaks, leaving people stranded on either side. As the waters continue rising, the people draw back. With fear and excitement, we watch as the waters rise to beneath the restaurant porch. On the banks of the river, small naked children unaware of the danger dance in the mud. They celebrate the beginning of the rainy season.

A late van out of camp approaches the river. At the broken bridge, the vehicle stops and the medical team descends. The crowd watches expectantly. After some discussion the driver, guided by the doctors, eases the van slowly across the few remaining planks. The crowd stares as ever so slowly, the team defies the elements. Theirs is an act of both stupidity and daring.

Shortly after the van has left, the storm blows southwest into the hills. The rains lessen. In the dying winds, the crowd's cheering swells. A few elderly men cautiously ford the river. More join them. When the last of the showers ceases, the golden light of dusk filters through the few remaining clouds and illuminates the land and sky. The children cease dancing and hurry home for dinner. Young men strike up music of Hmong and Lao folksongs, Thai love songs, and Western rock with khɛɛn and ghetto blasters. The land smells fresh and clean again. In compounds, people dig up the upturned bottles that are buried in mud. Women hang clothes and bedding out to dry. That night, I huddle with Sri and Blia for warmth. We sleep soundly. In the late evening a full moon comes up over the gully that has become a creek and lights up the hills around the camp.

The next day, I wade through thick, heavy mud to the Sisawongs. Several small gardens planted in the open sewers have washed away. In the compounds, men and women busily dig the mud out of their rooms. Throughout the compounds there are lines of wet clothes and other belongings hanging out to dry. The day is hot and steamy and the rising humidity promises more rains to come.

When I reach the Sisawongs' place, it is ominously still. The children are nowhere to be seen. No one answers when I call out so I climb the steps to the bamboo hut. The darkness of the interior contrasts with the brilliant light outside. It takes several seconds to adjust my eyes. Inside, Chanthanom sits next to a child covered in blankets. At the child's head, someone has lit candles and incense. Drawing nearer, I recognize Boondee, the older daughter. I wonder if she is dead or unconscious until she rasps suddenly in pain. Chanthanom silently motions me to follow her outside. On the porch she explains that Boondee fell into the river during the storm. Chanthanom has called a healer and Khamsai has left for the Catholic church to attend mass. Chanthanom has deep dark circles under her eyes, but her strength has returned. "Boondee will be alright," she tells me firmly, probably reassuring herself as well.

The rainy season brings relief from the heat, but also more sickness and suffering. As the rains continue day after day, an ominous mood permeates the camp. It is difficult to move around outside on the slippery muddy walks and people spend many days indoors. The vegetation grows thick and wild on the hills surrounding the camp.

Each morning two large buses arrive at the central courtyard in front of the UNHCR and MOI buildings. They come to take the "illegals" to Chiang Kham and Napho camps. People load their worldly possessions tied up in plastic bags, rice sacks, and cardboard boxes on top of the buses. The persistent gray drizzle soaks through the belongings even before the buses depart. Friends and kin stand around to bid farewell. The leavetakings are subdued, because no one is certain when or where they might next meet or even of their final destination. These farewells are a striking contrast to the farewells for those departing for processing centers and resettlement countries. Those farewells are filled with great hopes and expectations for the future in the United States.

The political climate in Thailand is worsening for the refugees. UNHCR and the Thai government are not progressing in their negotiations to secure the Laotian government's support for repatriation. The Hmong in Ban Vinai, a known Resistance camp, are least likely to be safely repatriated. Meanwhile, quotas for third- country resettlement are declining. At the annual Volag meeting in late July, Squadron Leader Prasong Soonsiri, secretary general of the National Security Council, warns:

> During the past two to three years an increasing number of displaced persons have been entering Thailand with regularity, particularly from Laos. This takes place while third countries have reduced their intake of refugees. In 1985 only 31,000 refugees were transferred to third countries. This has resulted in the number of refugees left behind in the various centers at the end of 1985 having increased considerably. This situation has caused the Thai authorities to reassess its policies and measures and to finally reach agreement with the United Nations High Commissioner for Refugees on instituting screening measures for Laotians who have fled illegally into Thailand. The process is necessary to screen bona fide refugees from those pretending to be refugees who will have to be sent back to their homeland.[1]

For those already inside Thailand, the Thai government moves to consolidate camps to demonstrate their control over an apparently stymied situation. Such bureaucratic decisions have their intended effect of reminding the refugees that their future is not secure in the camp and their dwellings impermanent. The Ban Vinai residents watch and listen. From their kin in the United States, they receive news of welfare doles and attacks against refugees. Hmong, who would qualify for resettlement, fear to go but also fear to stay.

Illness

The increasing sense of disorder is marked by physical and emotional suffering. The occasional shamanic ceremonies increase during the rainy season. From every corner of the camp, shamans beat their gongs to announce yet another ceremony to appease lost or troubled souls, and souls of the dead, plaguing sick and distressed households. Each morning long lines form around the neighborhood public health clinics. The camp hospital is overcrowded.

Sickness comes to the Vang household, too, but unlike Boondee's which passes quickly, this time it lingers. Yia, the youngest child, has a high fever and bloated stomach. He lies crying in pain in his mother's lap. Although clearly dehydrated, the one-year-old refuses to drink. Choua tries to coax him by offering soft drinks in small plastic bags that Ger buys in the market.

"Have you taken him to the clinic?" I ask. Ger answers, "My mother treated him with herbal medicine. I bought some medicine in the market. Children get these fevers."

"How did you know which medicine to buy?" I ask.

"My neighbor's child has the same fever. He took this medicine," he explains.

"What kind did you buy?" He shows me a liquid antibiotic, that has passed its expiration date. Two children in the camp have recently died from market medicine.

"Give him more fluids," I suggest. "But, he won't drink," Choua replies. She looks exhausted. Ger agrees with my recommendation and sends his eldest son to buy another bag of soft drink.

Despite the child's illness, Ger invites me inside. Choua cradling the child remains under their barracks built on stilts. She sits on a short-legged bamboo table, which she sometimes shares with her friend, another woman her age. I wonder why she stays there. From where she sits, she looks up through to the cobwebbed floorboards above. It is dark and gloomy under the building. The rains and general dampness drive other people inside from their customary nooks. It seems a strange place to care for a sick child, but the place is her domain. Despite the rains and sickness, she must feel more secure there.

Inside their room, Ger asks me, "How many people are there in the U.S.?" "I don't know," I reply, "But, I think there are about 65,000 Hmong." "More than Ban Vinai!" he says surprised.

"Why do Americans hate refugees?" he asks. The question takes me by surprise. "Why do you think that?" I ask. "Some friends told me," he explains. "Your relatives?" I ask thinking that his relatives in Rhode Island may have written him. "No, friends," he replies. "They say it is better to live here, because Americans hate refugees."

He expects me to reassure him otherwise, but my own experiences of working with refugees and immigrants in the United States keeps me silent. His understanding of Americans is based primarily on his relationship to me and our conversations and that worries me at times. "When you go back to America, interview Americans and tell me what they say," he says finally. "Yes," I agree.

"Have you decided to go to the U.S.?" I ask. He replies: "I want to go, but my mother is unwilling. She wants to die in Laos or Thailand. Here, I am very poor. If I go to America, I will not be so poor."

I must look skeptical. A man standing at the window who is listening to our exchange laughs.

"What will you do, if you go to America?" I ask. "I will study for a year and a half. After that, I will work in a company," he replies. "Like Dennis," I say. "No," he answers. "Not the same as Dennis." I realized how naive I am being. "No, not like Dennis. He is an engineer," I amend.

"What will you study?" I ask. He answers, "I will study English and how to make a living." "And Choua?" "She will do the same, but a year and a half will not be enough, because she did not study in the camp." "And, Xiong?" "She won't go. We will have to leave her behind in Ban Vinai."

Ger faces the dilemma that many Hmong in Ban Vinai face in deciding whether to interview for third country resettlement. Like other refugees, he feels the pressure of the Thai government to resettle and is acutely aware of the various shifts in the political climate. He follows the progress of the Thai national elections daily in the local press. "They will determine our future, too," he explains. "I'm afraid the prime minister will be forced to take a harder line against refugees to beat his opposition." He must also deal with the rumors or threats about the conditions under which the refugees will be allowed to remain. "I have heard that only those who join the Resistance will be allowed to stay," he tells me. Resettlement for the Vangs, as in many households, may also mean leaving older people, such as Xiong, behind. For a Hmong son and head of an extended family, that decision has serious social, moral, and psychological implications.

The rains continue, the buses continue to leave, and Yia's condition worsens. Ger obtains some medicine from the public health clinic, but Yia refuses that medicine, too.

After three days, Ger asks his mother to perform a shamanic curing ceremony for the household.[2] Choua remains with Yia under the building, while Ger helps Xiong prepare for the ceremony. Xiong dresses in her traditional dark layered skirt and her red turban. Ger cuts painted paper in intricate patterns. These will become money offerings [joss] to attract and later, appease the spirits. Xiong and Ger arrange the altar inside the kitchen. Over the threshold, Ger hangs strips of spirit paper to announce the ceremony and to alert outsiders to the sickness in the household.

Ger brings Xiong the materials and she arranges them in two small bowls of sand which she sets on the altar.[3] In one bowl, Xiong plants the joss, husked crosses, and incense sticks. In the second, she places two eggs. She lights a candle, which she places on the altar. Sitting on a bench before the altar, she pulls the red turban over her head. The turban veils her eyes, which allows her to achieve a trance state. The bench symbolizes her horse, which takes her to the spirit world. In rhythmic motion, riding the horse, she calls to the spirits by tapping her feet and beating a set of jangles. Her calls sound like bird whistles. She continues deeper into the trance for over an hour. The kitchen is dark, smoky, and hot. I wonder where she summons the energy in the steamy room. Her chanting intensifies.

Ger lights more candles and incense. The chanting continues. After several minutes pass, he draws shapes on the floor to attract the spirits. When Xiong is deep into the trance, he takes his son from Choua and brings him into the room. The child, lifting his head with difficulty, stares wide-eyed at his grandmother's moving back. He buries his head in his father's shoulder. Ger returns Yia to his wife. Returning to his mother, he comments, "My mother calls her [dead] husband and the house spirits to help my son."

Ger brings a Bible that a Protestant missionary once gave him. "Do you want it?" he asks. Puzzled, I briefly hold the book and then give it back. "No, it is yours." "Can you read it?" he asks. I realize he is asking me to contribute my own faith to the ceremony. Together we read a brief passage in Lao.

Outside, Yia, alternating between chills and fever, tosses and turns on the table. Choua continues to offer food and drink, which he refuses. With surprising strength, he knocks over bottles of coke and orange-ade. Choua tries to tempt him to eat, but eventually she eats most of the dinner. Yia cries out in pain. Ger holds him. He carries his son back into the kitchen, but seeing the child's restlessness, carries him outside again.

A helicopter bringing an American congressman and his delegation on a refugee camp tour flies overhead. "See the plane?" Ger asks Yia. When Ger sees the plane, he remembers the war: food supply drops, bombs, airlifts of wounded men, and his own evacuation. Yia, briefly diverted, follows the plane with his eyes. The helicopter lands somewhere in the camp and children leave the compound to find it. Xiong, oblivious to the commotion outside, continues the ceremony. Tou, the second son, sits quietly hammering nails into the dirt. The eldest son returns from school and complains of hunger. Ger brings his elder sons dried smoked fish to eat.

An hour and a half passes. Xiong's pace slows. Ger stands behind her. Taking a fresh piece of silver spirit paper, he cuts an effigy of the child. He lights the effigy and stamps the ashes into the ground at his mother's feet. "Did you see?" he asks. I nod. Xiong slowly emerges from her trance. Ger stands behind ready to support her.

Xiong's ceremony holds the family together in this time of distress. Without Xiong, I wonder who will provide meaning and order out of the changes and confusion in their lives.[4] Her ceremonies create continuity with the past and reaffirm relationships threatened by the uncertainty about the future. She helps her daughter-in-law with the children and comforts her children and grandchildren at night with stories of Laos. She makes the extra money that allows them to live comfortably in the camp, that bought their way into the camp, and that ironically may some day buy their way out again without her.

The Shaman's Past

Before I witness this ceremony, Xiong, like many elders, always avoids me. I represent the foreigner and "Amerika"—the place that threatens to steal her children and grandchildren. Once, however, I have observed her ceremonies, she allows me to interview her about her past and how she became a shaman. She speaks in Hmong and her son translates into Lao.[5] She also agrees to let me tape the interview. Initially, the interview is stilted and, to her, must resemble a JVA [resettlement] interview.

"Where were you born?" I begin. Poking fun at my endeavor, she replies, "I don't know. I asked Mrs. Nou Chou [a friend] and she doesn't know where she was born either."

I try not to laugh and ask her about her family. She answers:

I had four sisters and one brother and they all passed away (and the other lady—Mrs. Nou Chou—do you want to interview her?) I don't remember, I just remember that they all passed away. I was the eldest. The last was my brother and he passed away when he was crawling. My father's second wife had two children, too.

"Did the wives get along?" I ask. "They got along with each other," she replies. "Right now if you take a second wife, what do you think?" Ger repeats in Hmong. She replies, "Now, there would be fighting every day and they would kill one another." She directs the observation at her son, who has had several mistresses [Lao: *miá nɔ̌ɔj*], but never a second wife. Xiong is annoyed by her son's behavior and Choua, distressed. Xiong continues:

She was not my husband's wife, but my father's so what could I do? It was my father's problem, not mine. My father and husband were different so I didn't see any problem, but if my husband had had a second wife, then there would have been problems. In the past, my father, mother, and the second wife all got along.

"How did you earn a living?" I ask.

We were farmers—slash and burn [Lao: *hāj*], dry land farmers. We didn't have wetlands. It's so hot in the wetlands. You need to cultivate earlier in the wetlands, April to June, but in the mountains, June and July.

"Where did you move?" I continue. She does not remember. "Where did you live when you got married?" I ask, thinking that she might remember that village. "When I got married we moved far away. I don't remember. I don't remember how many years." Then, she recalls more precise details of her life (see figure 7.1). She suddenly is more absorbed in the interview and looks directly at me as she speaks.

When I grew up I lived in Nam Ta and then my father passed away. In the mountains, we moved from Nam Ta to Trong So Khua and then

FIGURE 7.1. Map of Laos

to Sa Hea [from North Vietnam to Laos]. I don't remember how long I stayed in any place.

Ger guesses, "Probably about two or three years." She continues:

> I just barely remember—I was probably about four years old when my father died. I don't remember when my mother died.

Ger recalls that his grandmother [father's mother] died in 1970. He adds, "Her mother [i.e., Ger's maternal grandmother] died in 1969." Xiong continues, "Then we moved to Bong Ta." "When?" I ask. "I don't remember." Ger replies, "In 1969." She changes the topic and is visibly agitated. Looking at Ger, she says:

> I'm afraid that she is interviewing me to go to America, but I don't want to go to America. So upset, so sorry, so upset that I don't want to come.

I ask Ger to translate, but he refuses. However, he also knows that I am taping the interview and can have it translated later. Instead, he prompts her to continue the interview.

> All three sisters passed away. My father's wife still has one daughter living. Her child remarried and that child's husband has two more wives. My father remarried later. I had already had two children before he remarried his second wife. My father had three wives. The last one had two children before he married her. He married his brother's widow. Of the three wives, the second is alive in France and the last wife had many children and lives in America.

She corrects herself, "The second wife passed away and the last wife lives in France, but she has remarried." Ger translates, "The second wife lives in France, the third in America." Ger wants to establish the American connection, Xiong does not.

"The second wife," she continues, "remarried twice after my father died, but both [the two husbands] died, too." Later, she remembers that her father died during the First World War in the Guerre des Foux [Lao/Hmong: *Tro Phĭi Baà*] in 1914. Although the Hmong are exogamous (and marry outside their clan and subclan), she also maintained her natal clan ties over the next seventy years.

"Did you ever write to your father's wives?" I ask. Ger answers, "Sent a letter." "No, we never communicated," Xiong disagrees in Hmong. For Ger, however, these relationships provide ties to the resettlement countries.

"How old were you when you married?" I ask trying to return to her own history. Xiong replies, "I don't know how old I was when I married because I cannot read and write. There was nothing down on paper." "About fifteen years old," Ger guesses.

Xiong continues, "I don't remember, but when my husband passed away to the time of the interview was eight years." I am not sure which interview Xiong is talking about—the present one or an interview to enter the camp. She assumes that I know all about the structure of camp life.

Ger and Xiong discuss again in Hmong the issue of whether to resettle in the United States. "Why don't you want to go?" he demands. "I'd like to go, but my heart is not willing. No matter what you tell me, I'm not going to the U.S.," she replied. We stop the interview at that point. She is obviously tired and has another ceremony to do. However, Xiong agrees to continue her history another day.

"Taping? For what?" she asks when we next meet, but she agrees to let me tape the interview again. "I'm from Sam Neua [a province now in North Vietnam, formerly in Laos]. I got married in Sam Neua." "Why did you move from there?" I ask. She explains the Hmong's system of shifting cultivation:

> Because after you farm two or three years, there is no fertilizer left in the soil. The ash is not strong enough to crop. Then, you have to move to a new place.

"Where did you move?" I ask. This time she recalls the precise names of the different villages and hamlets.

> After we moved to Nam Ta, then we went to Trong Xiong, then to Houei Hia [creek that has bamboo], then to Na Lien, Na Mong—Nong Hek [close to the Vietnam border in Xieng Khouang Province]. This only I remember, but I think I moved many times, many towns. After that we moved from Nong Hek to Nong Ouy [Sam Neua], to Nam Khao [Luang Prabang] to Nam Liem [Sam Neua].

"Where did you get married?" I ask. "In Nam Liem." "Did you move again?" I ask. She continues:

> After I married we moved to Kho Ngu, Pha Louang [sharp piece of stone], Ngok Laing, and Phou Nong [villages in the region of Luang Prabang, Sam Neua, and Xieng Khouang]. I moved nine times after I got married. Counting the camp, ten times. Then, we lived in Ban Dang. I don't remember all the places.

She pauses. Ger and she discuss the different villages in which she has lived. With his help, she lists the villages:

We lived in Pha Louang. Then we moved to Phak Boun, Phou Louang, Ban Dang, Pha Noi, Sam Chok, Long Cheng, Pong Ta, Nam Va, Phou San, and then Ban Vinai.

From Phak Boun to Sam Chok, they moved to find more arable lands. Their method of shifting cultivation and resource scarcity primarily motivated these movements. Not until Sam Chok were the Vangs directly involved in the conflict. Sam Chok was about a ten-days' journey by foot from Long Cheng, where Vang Pao's [the Hmong leader supported by the CIA] army was based. Since the Communist Pathet Lao forces controlled the region between Sam Chok and Long Cheng, American pilots airlifted the family out into Long Cheng. The airlift is one of Ger's first memories. He remembers being about five at the time (approximately 1969), but if the year is correct, he was at least eleven. At Long Cheng, they lived on food rations dropped by Air America pilots. By 1973, however, there were too many people in Long Cheng for the food supplies and the air attacks intensified. The Vangs, with many other Hmong, fled to Pong Ta on the other side of the mountain. The attacks continued as the Pathet Lao gained control of the country. The Vangs next descended about 2,000 to 3,000 feet to Nam Va and then moved up the side of another mountain to Phou San. From this point on, they made their way gradually to the Thai border.

After listing the villages, Xiong argues with Ger in Hmong again about going to the United States. She explains:

I won't go to America. I want you to explain to her. I don't want her to misjudge me. If the name comes in and I don't go, I don't want her to misjudge me. I'm afraid she will sponsor me to go to the U.S.

Her son, however, refuses to translate. I continue taping. Instead, he reminds her that they lived in several places between Phou San and Thailand. He was old enough at the time to remember these moves now. With his help, she lists the towns and villages they passed through after the war. "After we escaped from Phou San, we went to Mouang Sao, Vang Vieng, Nam Pi, Nong Pou [near Vientiane], and then Ban Vinai." At Vang Vieng they reached the lowlands and from there, gradually made their way toward Vientiane, the capital of Laos, directly across the river from Thailand.

122   Xiong recalls a total of twenty-nine moves in her life. Like many other Hmong, her life as a refugee began long before her entry into Ban

Vinai. From the mid to late 1960s on, the Vangs moved in response to conflict and ensuing famine. Xiong traveled far from the mountains of North Vietnam and Laos to the lowlands and, finally, to a Thai refugee camp.

When she finishes recounting her moves, I ask about her early life again. "Did you live with your husband's family after marriage?" I ask assuming her family like other Hmong families is patrilocal. She explains:

> If you live with the wife's side, people look down [literally look upside down] on you. It makes your life heavy. If you live close to the husband's side, then they help you.

"Did you choose your husband?" I ask. She laughs and explains, "My husband came to marry me. The woman never goes to marry the man." Xiong's husband paid the obligatory brideprice to her father. Had he not, he might then have been expected to live in his wife's family (to pay the price through work in his father-in-law's fields).

"How did you become a shaman?" I ask. Her shamanism, I soon discover, is at the core of Xiong's identity. Becoming extremely animated, she speaks at length:

> Sickness, I was ill for a long time. Then, I was sent to a diviner [Hmong: *saiv*; Lao: *mɔ̃ɔ du*]. The diviner said, "The spirit of the shaman sits on your body." The diviner put on a hood and then went into a trance. The diviner gave a deadline. "If by this date, you are still ill, you have to find a shaman [Hmong: *ua neeb*; Lao: *mɔ̃ɔ jaa*]. If you heal by that date, you have to become a shaman." The diviner used incense and an egg to divine—rice stick on top of an egg. I had to find a shaman. I found Grandma Cher. I asked her to come and teach me how to do the shamanic practices.

The illness was an initiation, transforming Xiong's world from the profane to the sacred.[6] Although Xiong received her practical and theoretical instructions from a master shaman, Grandma Cher, Xiong could not become a shaman were she not chosen. Her illness was not merely another recurrence of malaria, but an ecstatic experience that transformed her understanding of the world and status within it.[7] Recognizing the importance of this illness (or revelation), Xiong expounds at length about the experience:

> When I was ill, I was very unconscious for many days. I didn't even know my children. I could smell the cooking and they called the

Diviner, as I told you, and the illness healed, so I went to Grandma Cher to help set me up. When I was ill, Grandma Cher came in. They put me in a nice dress and I was still ill. They put me on a seat and they burned incense and played the kongs and she began to shake (and that's what started it all).

After the shaman came, my illness healed so that's why I became a shaman. Before I became a shaman, I was sick nine days and nine nights. If I drank anything, I threw up. I was unconscious for a day and a night. Then I couldn't even feel the shaman and I didn't even know when they made food for me. Grandma Cher was the first shaman, I was the second [in the family].

Being unconscious represents a symbolic death from which Xiong is resurrected in a new higher state of being. The death allows her to dialog with the spirits and souls of dead shamans. Her experience follows the traditional schema of a shamanic initiation ceremony: suffering, (symbolic) death, and resurrection.[8] She explains:

When I was sick, the spirit of the shaman came and I saw a candlelight and many children playing around me. After I became a shaman, I didn't see that anymore. Every time I would close my eyes, I would see many children sitting around the house. After I became a shaman, I didn't see that anymore. Must have been the spirit of the shaman. After I closed my eyes when I was sick, I saw the spirit of the shaman coming in and light a candle. The shaman smoked opium around me and talked to me. Before I became a shaman, I was sick for three years—each year, sick for three months and then I decided to go ahead and become a shaman. I couldn't eat once the spirit of the shaman was in me. I couldn't drink dirty water, eat dirty food. Everything must be clean so the shaman doesn't get ill.

Being a shaman conveys many responsibilities and like any priesthood, involves a radical change in one's way of life. Few women ever become shamans, although beginning in the 1960s, more women found their calling.[9] With the men at war, the Hmong may have been more willing to recognize women shamans and use their services. Xiong reiterates how she resists her calling at first:

The first time I went to the Diviner, I didn't believe what he said and fell ill again. Then, the Diviner drew my name again and I went to the healer [Hmong: *tsawv neeb*], who put me on a bench and played the kongs and started to shake [go into a trance state], and then I felt

high. Few
enatal care
of Xiong's

he fields in
ill for six
veral more
days, some
died and I
and taken

ot natural
r the war],
d into hu-
I was preg-
ave birth at

his natural
the moun-
rest—you

He replies,
l. Evil and
evil there,
haman for

a tape to
it on tape
he United
d. "I don't
tically. She

l causes of
he Vangs to
ed. Xiong,

dirty food. If you draw from someone
. You have to create your own well.

to the camp, my mother couldn't drink
rst. We had to treat her special. But now
shaman, she can eat and drink."

man after many years experience and in-
ught throughout the camp by other kin.
ho find their calling, and works hard to
ive in her progeny with stories and teach-

ng, I return to the subject of her family.
u have?" I ask. She discusses birth and

en died (all except Ger and my daughter,
vo children who died before I became a
haman, three more died.

ondering how she had endured so much
if "you fool, how do you think she felt?"
mpathy behind the question and speaks
vith Hmong]:

o die with the children. I could not make
nyself to die]. Because I felt so badly, I
ln't. After I became a shaman, I helped
of lives and many people asked for my

strength I saw in few other women. She
sonal tragedy and misfortune the insight
She continues:

vas pregnant. We went to farm and I felt
bathroom and I walked to a place where
und and I got scared. When I returned
ame ill. I gave birth to the first child, but
elve days and later, I gave birth to more

traditional beliefs, a miscarriage [i.e., the
occur if the woman: 1) sees a mud- or
he ground and wind, or 3) falls to the

ground.[10] Infant mortality rates in rural Laos were and ar
Hmong in the mountains have access to medical services (p
or immunizations) that they now receive in the camp. Sever
children died in their first year.

> After the first one died, with the second, I went out to
> the lowlands and when I returned home, the child w
> months with a high fever and then died. I gave birth to s
> children after that. Some lived for six days, some for ten
> for twelve days and some for a month and then they a.
> thought that an evil spirit had gotten into my childre
> them all away.[11]

"What kind of evil spirit?" I ask her to clarify. She replies:

> A human evil (transformed), a human evil caused this,
> evil. In Nam Phu [near Vientiane, where she lived aft
> there was human evil. The elderly did not die, but turn
> man evil. The natural evil lives in a big hole [cave]. Wher
> nant, I saw such evil and became ill and had diarrhea and
> eight months and the child died.

Ger interrupts: "In America you probably don't have
kind of evil, because you live in the flatlands, but in Laos i
tains, there is evil. I don't think you have evil in the hole or
can't see it there."

"Would the human evil in America be the same?" I ask
"Wherever human beings live, I think there should be e
human beings cannot separate." Xiong adds, "There must I
because relatives in America have asked people here to
them."

Xiong finishes telling her life history. I offer to give h
record it for her grandchildren. "Why," she asks. "You ha
already." She reiterates her unwillingness to resettle in
States. This time she speaks directly in Lao so that I underst
want to go to the U.S.," she says plaintively. I nod sympath
repeats her statement.

Healing

Xiong assuages the supernatural forces, but the physic
Yia's illness remain to be treated. A week passes. I return to
see how the child is faring. The place looks shut and dese

however, appears at the door. She welcomes me, but looks tired and frail—a contrast to her usual indomitable self. "Where are they?" I ask. She indicates with her hand. A neighbor explains, "They have gone to the hospital, they went late last night." Xiong nods. I tell her that I will go see them. She nods again. She looks extremely sad, as if nothing matters anymore. A child's illness is an experience she knows all too well.

The hospital comprises several long rectangular barracks around a courtyard. As in many poor hospitals, the relatives camp out to care for the patient. In the courtyard, women wash their clothes. Family members wander in and out bringing food and other necessities. The hospital looks like the rest of the camp, except that the buildings are slightly more permanent looking and smell antiseptic. People in Ban Vinai go to the hospital only when they are very ill. The public health clinics in the centers, run by refugee medics, handle most routine health problems.

Zuid-Oost-Azie (ZOA), a Dutch Reformed Protestant Volag, runs the hospital. ZOA has significantly reduced its foreign staff and Dr. Ver, one of the head residents, is proud of their efforts to phase themselves out of work and turn their operations over to the refugees. The hospital has three European doctors and a Burmese dentist. Their primary responsibility is to train refugee medics. The camps' 1-to-15,000 doctor/patient ratio is higher than that of Laos, but lower than the rural areas of Thailand. Extreme and specialized emergencies are handled by Thai hospitals in the region. Although Dr. Ver is training the refugees to take over their own medical system, he doubts that, if his medical team leaves, the camp residents will be able to operate an effective Western medical care system. "If we left," he says, "There would be no Western health care any more. Maybe, if there was still medicine and money and if Hmong leaders appointed real medical leaders, they could still continue at a low level, but gradually it would collapse more and more." Another European doctor observes, "We're training those with less than a fourth-grade education [to be medics] now. The best ones leave for the third countries."

Although ZOA works with the traditional herbalists and midwives, their Dutch Reformed religious beliefs preclude their working with the shamans. Some of the doctors associate shamanism with heathenism and call the shamanic ceremonies a "form of devil worship." The Catholic priests take a more syncretic view. Pere proudly tells me that his first Hmong convert in Laos was a shaman. At the same time, his own view (expressed in French) is that:

The shaman is sort of a fool [French: bouffant], not highly respected, but someone one turns to in times of sickness. Women as well as men can be shamans. They are not necessarily sick, usually poorer, and not the leaders. The shaman offers prayers, mental relief from suffering and if not efficacious, the Hmong will go from one to the next until it works. The shaman comes during and after the illness to make his journey. It works like prayers.

"Is the shaman like the psychiatrist?" I ask. "Maybe something of the psychologist or psychiatrist, maybe a priest," Pere admits. Recognizing the shaman's psychological power, COERR tries to incorporate the shamans into their parasocial services. The shamans, however, rightly resist this incorporation. Their power and effectiveness come from their privileged position within the family and clan and within the household setting. Shamanistic healing, like other forms of healing, is socially constructed and external institutions most likely could not provide the appropriate context that is the source of their power.

I wander through several hospital buildings of sick and dispirited people to find Yia and eventually find him in the children's ward. Ger is trying to amuse his older sons, Pao and Tou, with an empty soda bottle, while Choua holds Yia over the concrete slab that serves as a hospital bed. They have draped cloth over the slab and have placed their food—bowls of rice and stew—at one end. Yia's eyes are half-closed; he tosses and turns in Choua's arms. Once again, she vainly tries to make him drink. "How's he doing?" I ask. Choua shakes her head. Ger asks, "Lynel, what's wrong with him?" "I'll go ask the doctor," I reply.

The doctor is talking to some medics at a table in the center of the ward. "What brings you to our children's ward?" she asks in English. I ask her about the Vangs' case. She calls the medic in charge. "Go examine the child," she instructs. He is a young Hmong man, at most twenty years old, and takes his work very seriously. "We've done a test," he explains looking at Yia's chart. He speaks to me in English, so I ask him to translate for the Vangs. Ger nods when the medic explains in Hmong, but Ger asks me again, "What's wrong with Yia?" The doctor joins us. She exclaims, annoyed: "Look! The child has not finished the [Oral Rehydration] solution. The parents should make him drink. If he doesn't finish it, we'll have to give him an I.V. There's absolutely no reason that this child should have an I.V.!"

"You need to make him drink more," I explain to the Vangs. Choua tries to encourage Yia again, but is unwilling to force him. I help her elevate the child's head and she makes cooing sounds while I offer the child sips. He drinks a little. "You need to do this every five minutes," I explain. She agrees.

The next day I see the doctor at the Lao restaurant. "What happened to the Vangs?" I ask. She replies, "Who? Oh, yes. Your friends. The medic gave the child an I.V. I wouldn't have given him one. I would have made the parents make him drink." She and other doctors at the hospital bemoan the Hmongs' faith in the injection or pill to effect a cure. While funding flows, few relief workers question the refugees' increased dependency on Western, curative medicine. With budget cutbacks, however, ZOA faces the difficult task of persuading people to rely on simpler measures and to practice prevention.

Choua and Yia remain in the hospital for several more days. Once the crisis passes, Ger returns home with his older sons. During my visit to the household, he asks several questions about life in the United States again. "In your village, did anyone ever die from the cold?" "In your village, do you have hospital and shamans?" He is increasingly worried about his household's physical security.

Ger then asks if Xiong can be a shaman in America. I reply, "Why not? There are many shamans in California." I add, "I have met Hmong shamans, too." He persists, "Do Americans hate shamans?" "Why do you ask?" I say surprised. He replies: "I have heard that Americans don't like shamans, because they are too noisy. My brother [clan of the same sublineage] has two houses in Rhode Island. I think she can do her ceremonies there." When Ger states the last proudly, I do not deny the association between ownership of property and the freedom to practice one's traditions.

Ger then asks about life insurance. "What do you want to know?" I ask. "Could I take out a policy on Xiong?" he asks. "You could, but you pay more for older people," I explain. He seems disappointed. After a brief silence, he asks, "Do people play the lottery there?" He likes to play the Thai lottery and hopes the odds are better in America.

Choua returns home with Yia. Two weeks pass and Ger announces that Xiong wants to do another ceremony to enlist the support of her husband's spirit.[12]

"We need to kill one buffalo, one cow, and three pigs," he announces.[13] "One water buffalo!" I exclaim wondering how they can afford this Rolls Royce. He nods.

"Where will you get the money?" I ask, wondering how much he expects from me. "I've been trying to call my brothers in Rhode Island," he explains. "They weren't home so I left a message on their answering machine."

I realize he is serious. Telephoning the United States from the camp is no easy matter. He needs to get permission first to make a call from the booth just outside the camp gates. Then, he must have paid 100 baht (approximately US$4) just to place the call

"What about your family in Chiang Mai [Thailand], couldn't they help?" I ask. "They won't help, not the same mother," he explains (perhaps differentiating those within the same lineage by sublineage and/or affinal alliance)[14].

"What about the hospital medicine?" I ask. Ger replies, "The medicine in the hospital helps and the shaman helps, too."

"Why do you need this ceremony?" I ask. He explains, "If the child is unwell, you don't do this ceremony. If the child is better, then you do it. You need to give gifts to the spirits." Ger is always pragmatic.

"Why was Yia sick?" I ask, expecting a spiritual explanation. "Because I gave him some chicken with hot sauce, he had a bad stomach," Ger explains. He outlines the stages of the child's illness: "First, I bought some medicine in the market. It didn't work. Second, after four days, I did a ceremony to call the spirits, because they had gone away. Then, I took my son to the hospital."

In contrast to ZOA, Ger sees the two forms of healing as different, but compatible. One takes care of the child's physical complaints, the other of the household's spiritual disorders. Healing requires not only treating the symptoms, but also restoring the cosmological order that has been disrupted.

Although the Hmong in Ban Vinai pragmatically try every cure available, they do not necessarily adopt Western beliefs about the causes and origins of illness.[15] As one Hmong medic tells a Volag worker [in English]:

> In contrast to Western medicine, the shaman diagnoses the patient before he or she falls ill. The shaman asks the powerful spirit, "Who will get sick?" Then, the shaman can tell the individual, "You will be the one to get sick." If you don't want to get sick, you should buy a pig (or some other animal offering).

The medic adds, "It is important to do the ceremony before going to the hospital, because otherwise the hospital cure might not work, even if the doctors do everything correctly." This syncretism of beliefs and practices enables many Hmong to maintain an institution that nourishes their spiritual, social, and psychological needs.

As we speak, Xiong enters. She asks Ger in Hmong if he has written to his cousins in Minnesota yet. She looks at me. I realized she is asking for my help, too. "I could give 100 baht," I volunteer. "Is that enough?" Xiong nods approvingly and Ger looks relieved.

As I leave, Ger points out his neighbors. "They have converted to Christianity," he says. "Why?" I ask. He replies: "Because they are poor. They don't have enough money to buy a chicken or a pig for the shaman's ceremonies. For Hmong customs, you need many things, things we don't have and we won't have in the U.S. I think the Christian customs are easier. You only have to go to church. When we go to the U.S., we may have to become Christians."

I disagree, but he is concerned. Neither bound by ascribed status or ideological commitment, he is completely pragmatic in recognizing that religions serve economic as well as spiritual ends. For similar reasons, many Hmong in the United States may willingly adopt Christianity.

Several weeks pass before Xiong performs the second ceremony. Choua kills and prepares a chicken. There are no buffalo or pigs for this ceremony, but there is a chicken. Ger's brothers in Rhode Island never send any money.

As Xiong prepares the altar, he explains: "This ceremony is for the shaman's spirits, spirits of the house and home, not my father's spirit. She is asking her [friendly] spirits to come. She burns the incense and then calls the shaman's spirits. She is friends with these spirits and is now traveling with them. Later she will come back and stop herself. She remembers the journey and what she has seen."

With the child back home from the hospital and well again, Xiong thanks her shaman spirits. The household recognizes that order has been restored and feasts in celebration.

EIGHT

Resistance

In August, the rains pour without abating. The distance between Laos and Thailand increases as the rivers of the Mekong swell. The fishermen leave the river and some days even the farmers stay home. The road to the camp turns to swirling mud and the last hill before the main gate is treacherous. When a van stalls in the mud, relief workers struggle in pouring rain to push it up the hill.

While the rural Thai make their usual seasonal accommodations to the inclement weather, the people of Ban Vinai are further imprisoned and isolated by the elements. They see less of relief workers, who are discouraged from venturing out by the mud. Families huddle together in damp, leaky buildings. Women move their sewing inside, and Khamsai and other men spend many hours sleeping and gambling. They worry about when and if the food trucks will arrive. Disease prevalence rates increase; there are a few outbreaks of cholera and typhoid and many upper respiratory infections. The crying of sick children reverberates through thin plywood walls. Parents look harried and worn and the lines around the health clinics grow daily. These are the worst days of camp life.

The rains further distance the camp from its

133

surroundings and the larger world. Thai villagers come to trade less often and only a few neighborhood stalls remain open. There is little news
from Laos or movement back and forth across the river. The rains also
discourage outside delegations and visitors. The sense of being forgotten pervades.

Despite the increased separation from the outside world, Ger and his
friends avidly follow the upcoming Thai election in the national press.
"Chatichai will have to take a hard line on refugees to get reelected,"
Ger predicts. "The opposition says he will send the Laotians back if
elected." Thai government policies toward refugees, as reported in the
press, do not substantially change, but Ger and his male kin's interpretations do. The upcoming election provokes great concern and they as-
sume the worst. Political instability at the national level increases their
vulnerability, too.

U.S. policies toward refugees are also at a stalemate. Many in Ban
Vinai could apply for U.S. resettlement, but the Hmong leaders tell
them not to go. "Next year, Laos," they promise once again. Events in
Ethiopia and Afghanistan eclipse the problems of a small minority of the
world's refugees waiting in northeast Thailand. Although Congress is on
recess in August, the men in Ban Vinai worry whether the United States
will diminish its quotas. The somber weather increases their sense of
living on the edge and brings out the deepest fears. Their traditional
accommodations to monsoons—visits to neighbors, sewing, fishing—
are limited; the earlier boredom of long hot days is overcome by the
chill of driving winds and rains and a general malaise.

In late August, Hmong Resistance leaders from America on their
summer holidays return to Ban Vinai. Clad in smart, shiny suits and
conveying a sense of extreme purposefulness, they are a marked contrast to their poorer refugee kin. Encountering an American unexpect-
edly in center 3, I know immediately that he does not live in Ban Vinai.
"Where are you from?" I ask in English. "Colorado," he replies with a
very American accent. "What are you doing here?" I ask. "I've come for
meetings—on business," he replies giving me a knowing look. Sharing
the paranoia of the season, I do not pursue the conversation. Like many
other relief workers, I see the Resistance as the enemy—a bunch of
vain old men who have others spend years in refugee camps and die for
their dreams.

The Resistance claims to be funded by semi-religious, right-wing
groups, who periodically convene international meetings of similar
counterrevolutionary groups from around the world—the Khmer Re-

sistance, Afghans, Contras, Karenni, etc. Although many relief workers suspect that these groups are funded by the CIA, the connection is never proven. In the case of the Hmong, it is unclear what strategic interests the CIA has in rural Laos.

More evident is the support of a handful of Vietnam veterans, the diplomatic sympathies of old Asia hands, the humanitarian concerns of relief organizations, and the growing political pressure of Southeast Asian-American interest groups, the Mutual Assistance Associations. A few Vietnam veterans provide military training and participate in periodic Rambo-style forays into Laos. The old Asia hands are a significant group in the State Department. They keep the pressure on to maintain the refugee quotas and disseminate information about human rights violations in the new Communist regime. To raise money for their efforts, relief organizations frame the public debate by portraying the tragic dimensions of being a refugee. Finally, the new Asian-American Mutual Assistance Associations (MAA's) are becoming a significant voting bloc in several Congressional districts. Vang Pao and his followers are the most politically organized and control much of the wealth of the Hmong American community. For the Resistance, whose political power also lies in controlling the resettlement flow between Laos and Thailand, U.S. resettlement policies tacitly, if not directly, support their efforts.

The Dragon's Tale

After encountering the American, I hurry on to the Thao household. The children, enjoying a brief respite from the rain, play in the mud. The rains have lessened temporarily and the weather turns steamy hot punctuated by sudden downpours. Naked toddlers wearing red, blue, and yellow rubber boots provided by some relief agency splash in the puddles and slide up and down mudslicked hills. A sense of exuberance returns briefly in these interludes of clear weather only to be dampened by more long days of rain. Sri returns from drawing water and excitedly announces that a "*zaj*" has been seen in center 9. Not understanding the Hmong word, I ask Blia and Sri to translate into Lao, but they cannot. "Red, white, and blue," Sri describes it.

When Seng arrives home after dark, Blia asks him the Lao word for "*zaj*." Seng, who is eating with the younger children, invites me to join them. His older daughters excitedly describe in Hmong the "*zaj*" that has been seen in center 9. Seng translates the word in Lao for me as

135

"*nỳak*," but I have never heard this word either. "I don't know what the word is in English," Seng admits. "Like a snake," he elaborates in Lao. "Like a cobra?" I clarify. He nods.

I tell him about the American I have just encountered. "I don't go to work this week. They are giving a training. I have many meetings," Seng says in English. "What kind of meetings?" I ask. But, he cannot or will not elaborate.

Returning to the hut to sleep, I draw a picture of the serpent for Seng's elder daughters. "Is this a *nỳak*," I ask in Lao. Sri takes the picture and adds horns to the drawing. Curious, I tell her, "We don't have this kind of serpent in America." "You don't!" she says surprised. "I don't think so," I answer, still uncertain that I comprehend her drawing.

The next morning, forgetting the Lao word, I describe the snake to Chanthanom. "It must be a crocodile or big fish," she replies in Lao. Khamsai disagrees; he has heard stories of this animal and calls his neighbor, another lowland Lao, who knows of the animal to explain. Khamsai translates *nỳak* as "dragon" from his Lao/English dictionary. At the idea of a dragon in center 9, I laugh uproariously. A small crowd gathers, surprised at my reaction—which only increases my laughter. I am completely out of control. Chanthanom and Khamsai, embarrassed by the outburst or out of politeness, laugh too. When our laughter dies, Khamsai says that he doubts anyone has seen a dragon, but the others continue discussing the situation. Chanthanom resumes her sewing.

"Red, white, and blue," the neighbor describes. "What do you think?" I ask. "I don't think it is a dragon, but the ghosts [*phǐi*]," Khamsai explains and elaborates:

"Only the Hmong have seen it. There are dragons in Laos, but I have never seen one. They are mostly ghosts. Dragons eat people. Also, you usually can't see this dragon. The Hmong saw its reflection in the water after ten."

Khamsai is annoyed by talk of ghosts and dragons. "No," he says, shaking his head. Such stories oppose his Christian beliefs; yet, he is enough of a farmer to pay attention to what others observe. In this setting anything can happen.

"Can I see it?" I ask the neighbor. "Yes, you can see it at night," he replies.

"Monday?" I ask more specifically. "They are planning to drain the river to capture the dragon. You should come sooner," he advises.

I ask Khamsai what he thinks. "I don't believe in dragons. The Hmong probably saw a big snake [Lao: *ŋvú*]," he replies.

"But red, white, and blue?" the neighbor objects. "Snakes can be a lot of colors, they probably didn't see clearly," Khamsai counters. The neighbor disagrees.

Khamsai, changing the topic, tells me about his friend who has been jailed for being out of the camp without an official pass. "He's out," Khamsai reports. "How?" I ask. He laughs. The friend's brother, who is a soldier, helped him. It is the usual case of having the right connections and enough money.

Talk of dragons is further laid to rest by the sound of the horn of the International Rescue Committee (IRC) sanitation truck. Since the hill is too muddy for the truck to climb, people carrying baskets of garbage appear from all sides out of their buildings. Khamsai, hearing the blast, gathers up his garbage and leads the throng. Joking and laughing, center 9 residents assist one another through the mud. Children run around the edges picking up the remains. Sewage pickup has become an event in the rainy season.

When the sun sits low in the sky, I start down the hill again. Slipping and sliding I turn and yell back up, "Give my love to the dragon." Khamsai looks briefly astonished and then, shaking his head, laughs. The neighbors appear again to see what is going on and join in the laughter.

Khamsai calls down from the top of the hill, "Heh, Lynel, it's raining. Get out your umbrella." The sun continues radiating through a quiet shower and I wonder if there is a rainbow somewhere in the camp.

That evening the dragon dominates conversation in the van to Chieng Khan. When I announce that a "*nyak*" has been sighted, the Thai van driver wants to know how big it is. "I haven't seen it," I reply. He and the local Thai teachers worry that the stream in center 9 will be drained to find a "*nyak.*"

"Red, white, and blue?" Pierre muses as we discussed "le dragon" in French and English. "It must be the French flag," he decides, worried that the Hmong see the French as dragons. "But the American flag is also red, white, and blue," I object. "Hmmm, JVA!" he nods. Boonchan, reasonable as ever, refuses to let the Americans take the blame. "The Thai flag is also red, white, and blue," she points out and someone else adds that the Laotian flag is red, white, and blue, too.

The next morning I tell Ger that a dragon has been sighted in center 9. He has not heard the news, but says that a dragon is periodically sighted in center 3 near the crossroads when the river is high.

"Have you ever seen a dragon?" I ask. "You can't see a dragon, because they are evil spirits. I have heard of people who have seen them, but I myself have never seen one," he answers.

Not until I return to the United States do I learn that for Thai from regions outside the northeast, the term "nỳak" means "mermaid" [Thai: *nang nỳak*]. Yet, the descriptions and drawings are of a dragon or a mythical sea snake and the Hmong in their own language use *zaj*. Interestingly, however, in Hmong mythology, the dragon and mermaid are connected.[1] When the dragon, who lives in the water, wants to contact human beings, he sends a mermaid to communicate.

Dragons are common in Chinese mythology, but many Thai probably believed that the nyak was a mermaid, about which they have their own tales. In a popular Thai story, for example, Pra Apai Manee, an adventurous playboy, takes a mermaid for a wife.

The Hmong dragon and the lowland Lao sea snake, however, behave in similar ways. They are evil spirits who live in the water and cause drownings.

The various interpretations illustrate the process of communication in the camp. Each nationality translates *zaj* within its own belief system. Different versions of the story for the Lao, Hmong, Thai, Americans, and French alike reflect their own commonsense understandings of the event as well as their relationships to one another. Various interpretations serve different purposes.

"Can you die from seeing a dragon?" I ask Ger. He replies, "No, you don't die from just seeing a dragon." He describes the dragon: "A snake can become a dragon [here he draws a snake and then adds horns to show how it became a dragon]. They live in the water, there are many in Laos. They eat people who fall into the water. If you fell in, the dragons would eat you."

"I doubt we have dragons in the U.S.," I tell him. "Oh, no?" he asks surprised. "Well, maybe," I reply and describe the Loch Ness monster in Scotland. "That's right," he nods in agreement.

"Why are the colors red, white, and blue?" I ask. "Usually dragons are red and green," he answers and elaborates: "You see dragons when it rains a lot; they come out of the water and make a rainbow. The rainbow is the dragon leaving the water. Rainbows don't last very long, maybe only ten minutes. You don't know where it goes then."

Standing up, Ger takes a mirror and refracts its light against the wall and then on his desk. As usual, he counts on empirical evidence to create shared meanings. "Understand?" he asks, recognizing that our interpretations might differ. I nod, recalling a fourth-grade science experiment with prisms.

He continues: "The dragon in center 3 near the restaurant had to leave when there was no water. When there is no water, dragons leave." Sensing my thoughts are elsewhere, he repeats the last statement.

"Where do they go?" I return lamely. "You don't know," he replies. "Where do dragons come from?" I ask, not knowing what else to say. "Large lakes. You can catch a dragon with electricity, on electric wires," he replies.

Resistance

This time I draw a picture of telephone lines to confirm. "Yes, you can catch them on those," he says pointing at my drawing.

"A dragon can become a fish or man or pig!" he adds. "A pig!" I iterate. Ger nods. I try not to laugh and look to see if Ger is amusing himself at my expense. But he seems preoccupied.

"How do you know if he is a man?" I ask, continuing the narrative. "You don't know. He goes inside a person if he wants to eat someone. He could go inside you or me. You wouldn't know."

The "you" is said emphatically and Ger looks at me directly for a moment. The implied personification, however, has little effect on me.

"Would you act crazy?" I ask. "No," he says. "Would your mother know the dragon?" I ask, wondering if shamans interpret such events. Ger nods and explains: "Yes, shamans know because they can see the ghosts. You know if the person has a dragon in him and you go to the water together, then the dragon can come out and eat you from the water."

"Suppose the dragon is interested in eating me?" I ask. Ger replies, "He would go inside someone and bring you to the water. Then when you fell in, he would leave the person and eat you."

"Are there other animals like dragons?" I ask. "Yes, crocodiles, and others, too. Snakes," Ger replies.

"Can I record this?" "No, I don't really know it well enough. There are many legends, but I don't know them well enough for you to record." I continue instead writing in my notebook.

"Would Xiong recognize a dragon inside someone?" I continue. "Yes, a shaman recognizes a dragon in people," Ger replies.

"Do dragons come out in the dry season?" "Yes, there are dragons in the dry and the rainy seasons, but in the dry they must go to the big lakes to live," he explains.

Dragons are the lords of the waters in Hmong mythology.[2] They live underground or in caves, or in rivers, streams, and other bodies of water and they own the fish. Dragons cause rain, which results from the combat and coupling of two monsters, male (yang) and female (yin). As Ger observes, they manifest themselves in rainbows or halos around the moon. Noting the probable Chinese origins of this mythology, Mottin, a missionary and scholar, writes: "These mythical beings had their place

139

in the Chinese calendar. Their holiday fell precisely at the period of the changing of the seasons."³

It is the proper season for the dragon and in nearby Chiang Khan, the farmers are beginning to harvest the rice.

A Resistance Meeting

In the early afternoon, I return to Seng's, where I first heard about the dragon. I tell the children what I have learned, but they have lost interest in the dragon. They are watching Seng, who is preparing for a meeting. To my surprise, he invites me to join him.

"Where are we going?" I ask. "To a party of the leaders," he says mysteriously. I want to ask more but he is busy preparing a speech.

When we finally leave an hour later, the rain is pouring down again. I follow Seng out of the compound and we walk on the main road for several feet when suddenly he takes a turn through another compound. There we begin climbing a hill through a path in center 3 that has turned into a rushing waterfall. The houses on each side of the steep slope are built of thatch and bamboo. "We could be in Laos," I imagine for a moment.

Unused to the slippery steep path, I climb carefully. "This is difficult for you," Seng observes. "Yes," I answer, annoyed that my rubber sandals are sticking to the mud. I step slowly not to slip on the rocks.

When we reach the top, Seng turns into a long house that leans out over the edge of the hill. We walk into a room, where a long banquet table is set. Realizing that I am the only woman in a room of at least fifty Hmong men, I wish I could leave and join the women and a few older girls, who are cooking in the next house.

Seng takes me through the house to an overhanging porch, where some fifteen to twenty men are sitting. He indicates that I should sit on the bench and then disappears. A man in his early twenties addresses me in Lao. Later, I learn that he speaks English. He asks where I work. He tells me that he is a cousin [clan] brother of Seng's from center 3 and has been here since the opening of Ban Vinai in 1975.

"Has it changed?" I ask. "Not really until this year, now it is changing. Life is getting worse. Most Hmong want to go to the U.S."

"What about back to Laos?" I ask. "We can't go back while there is still fighting," he replies.

"And, if the Vietnamese leave, could you go back if the Pathet Lao were there?" He answers: "Yes, if the Vietnamese left we could go back. We speak the same language, we understand one another. But the prob-

lem is Russia. If the Russians would stop helping Vietnam, they would
have to leave. The large countries need to talk to one another. We need
the help of the U.S. to get the Russians to stop the Vietnamese."

The Resistance leaders divide the world by "Free" or "Communist."
This young man, who has spent half of his life in the camp, also has great
faith in the ability of the major powers to shift alignments and the balance of power in the world—to determine those events which will
shape his own life. However, unlike his elders, he questions whether the
Hmong Resistance can influence that balance through force.

"Through fighting?" I ask. "No, we have fought long enough. That
hasn't worked, we need to talk."

"I would like to go to America, join my family in Fresno," he continues. "Why didn't you go before?" I challenge him. "I was waiting,
things were not so bad then in the camp."

"The U.S. government thinks that the Hmong cannot decide," I tell
him. "I know," he replies. "Why can't they decide?" I ask. He enumer-
ates three reasons:

"First, their families in the U.S. aren't working, they are on welfare,
and we don't want to go and have more Hmong on welfare. We know
Americans don't like people on welfare. Second, some have family in
Laos waiting to come out; they are waiting for their families. Third, the
older people are afraid; they don't want to die in the U.S."

These are the same reasons I have heard from Ger and his friends
many times. "Do you think the Thai will keep the camp open?" he asks.
"I don't know," I reply. "Will the Americans help if it becomes dangerous?" he asks. "I don't know," I answer truthfully.

Seng returns and takes me with him into the large room. A number
of middle-aged and elderly men are gathered around a banquet table.
Someone has placed a microphone on the table and a man is recording
the event with a video camera. At the head of the table is a portrait of a
Laotian prince, who is in exile in Paris. When I ask Seng about the portrait, he says, "We hope that he will lead the Hmong someday back to
Laos."

Seng takes a seat at the middle of the table and indicates that I should
sit next to him. As he introduces each person, I suddenly realize that
Seng is master of ceremonies. The Hmong camp leader and several center chiefs sit at the head table. Two Americans are also present: the first,
an elderly man, was the former mayor of a town in Sam Neua, while the
second, a younger man, is addressed as "Doctor." Seng welcomes the
company and announces that we have gathered to celebrate the return
of the mayor.

The mayor confines his greetings to those who speak Hmong, but "Doctor" addresses me in English. "What organization do you work for?" he asks, speaking like Walter Cronkite.

He tells me he studied at an American university before 1975 and after the war ended, he returned to the United States and studied at another American university. He eventually completed his doctorate in business and tells me that he wrote his dissertation on "Success in Southeast Asian Organizations." The dissertation research, he claims, was based on his experiences of founding a local chapter of the Lao Family Association. "I was second in command," he concludes his own history.

"What do you do now?" I ask. "Ask your people," he replies enigmatically.

"Do you think the Resistance can succeed?" I ask. "What do you think?" he returns.

"I'm not sure, I don't really know," I answer, taking the safest course. "You are not sure, you don't really know," he mocks. Then he says vehemently, "If you knew, you would believe."

"I think of people dying and the women and children left behind," I tell him. "Yes, some must die, but it is the only way. You will see."

I decide not to argue the point and ask instead about negotiation. "Ha!" he laughs without humor, "Do you think the Vietnamese will negotiate? If there is no Resistance, they will not negotiate. You cannot trust the Vietnamese, only force will prevail, we are sure."

"Where do you get your money from?" I ask. "From organizations who want to help freedom fighters." "From the U.S. government?" I ask. "They have their consulate in Vientiane, they cannot give to us, at least, not directly, maybe through the organizations," he replies.

As an elder gives the traditional blessings, the men stand. Speeches follow. The guest of honor and other leaders hold platters of food. Each one in his turn holds the microphone and gives a toast while being videotaped. As my turn arrives and the video camera is turned on me, I suddenly feel compromised. Seng reassures me:

"Don't worry I told them all about you and who you are." "What did you say?" I ask curiously. "I told them you come to help the Hmong people and that you work with COERR." "And about my study of Hmong life?" "Yes, that, too," he assures me.

In the manner of a traditional Laotian ceremony, the leaders tie strings on and wish good fortune to each one at the table. The camp and center leaders bless me in Hmong, but "Doctor" says in English, "May

Resistance

142

you keep your pretty smile, may you help our people, and may the Hmong and American people always be smiling together." Despite the implied threat, I continue smiling. I hear only the threat, but later re- member the bitterness and irony.

The meal is a feast of several courses, during which much whisky flows. Seng gives the first toast. He downs two jiggers straight and passes the whisky to the next one. Young men bring a first course of cookies, chips, and hard-boiled eggs. "If the yolk is uneven, one is lucky, the spirits have already eaten it," "Doctor" tells me. All the eggs are uneven. Young men next carry in rice, pig, vegetables. Steaming bowl after steaming bowl arrives. After several rounds Seng, to my surprise, indicates that we should leave. As we get up to leave, younger men and boys come to the table to finish what is left.

I ask "Doctor" for his address. "I'm having new cards made, next time I see you," he says.

At the door, the women are clearing the dishes. We walk home through the rain. Seng refuses my offer of an umbrella, but waits patiently as I pick my way down through the rushing water. It is quite dark when we arrive. Now and then the lights of fires glimmer in the darkness illuminating the rainy night.

Seasons

The rains clear over the next few weeks which, like the Thai elections, pass uneventfully. Khamsai's neighbor announces that the dragon has left the river in center 9. An inhabitant returning from collecting bamboo reports seeing the dragon glide away, up a mountain pass. The neighbor waves his hand in direction of the hills outside the camp. "He headed that way. So now they don't have to empty the river," he says.

One late afternoon, I return to Chiang Khan with Pere in his beat-up, old blue pickup. Despite the vehicle's age, Pere drives at breakneck speeds and honking, passes larger vans at hairpin turns along the river.

"Do you think this war will ever end, that the people in Ban Vinai will ever go home again?" I ask him. We speak in French. Pere ponders for a moment and then replies:

"Remember the Lao in the fourteenth or was it the fifteenth century? I think the fourteenth, were very powerful. They chased the Vietnamese out then. The Shan, Champa, and Angkor, too, were each in their time powerful forces. What seems impossible now can change very quickly. Only ten years ago we thought it would be impossible to

Resistance

143

go to China, that it would always be a closed door. Look at it now. Of course, for the individual who is suffering, waiting, ten years can be a very long time."

"An eternity," I say. "Yes," he agrees.

"Have you ever been to Laos?" he asks. "No, tell me about it," I say.

Pere recalls: "In comparison to Bangkok, Vientiane seemed such a small town. There was only forty kilometers [he indicates the road we are traveling on along the Mekong] of road like this."

"Tarred [French: *goudronne*]?" I clarify. "Yes," he replies and continues:

"The bridges were bombed out so the buses stopped on one side to cross by ferry. That was during the war. After the Pathet Lao took over, the people were happy at first to see the Pathet Lao. They thought now all this war will be over. Even now most Hmong would probably still accept the Pathet Lao if the Vietnamese left."

"What happened to you when the war ended?" I ask. He replies:

"I had left before the war ended. The priests in Vientiane thought for twenty years at any moment they would be kicked out. When they finally were in 1975, they were quite surprised. The Church had withdrawn most of the priests already, only the Italian priests were asked to leave by the government. Of course, when you live twenty years always thinking next year you are going to leave, you live quite differently."

"And here?" I ask. He replies:

"I will stay in Thailand as long as I am asked. But the situation can always change and the Thai may decide that a Thai should do this work. We think we are so important, needed, that the work cannot go on without us, but that is a kind of colonialism."

As he finishes speaking, I look across the river to Laos but its mountains are hidden in thick clouds. When we reach Chiang Khan, the clouds momentarily part and the jagged outline of the peaks appears again. At the old customhouse, which has been closed for many years with the closing of the border, I descend from the van and walk home slowly along the river. The pink and orange light of the fading sun reflects across the waters. I pass two fishermen standing on the banks. One holds up a large silver-scaled fish, which is as long as the man. It scales shimmer and its mouth hangs open revealing rows of teeth. "Will you eat the fish?" I ask. The fishermen shake their heads. The clouds pass over the sun again, shrouding Laos and the darkening river continues its turbulent course.

NINE

The Disinherited

In November winter approaches with its swirling clouds of dust that blanket the earth. Rumors spread throughout the camp that the Joint Voluntary Agency (JVA), the American interviewing team, is coming. Many people who hope to qualify for resettlement prepare their documents for JVA's arrival. Ger, asking for affidavits of sponsorship, sends two letters to his clan brothers in Rhode Island. They respond quickly. When the letters arrive, Ger asks, "Can you read Thai?" and shows me a notice saying that the letters are being held for him at the post office. The next day he asks, "Can you read the postmarks?" Taking out a U.S. map from his language book, he indicates, "Here's Providence. I think it is a long way from California?"

The market women also anticipate JVA's arrival. Embroidered tableaus of tall Paul Bunyan-like characters interviewing short Hmong in traditional black dress suddenly appear for sale. The women seem to capture the camp's power relations in symbolic form, but when suddenly, unannounced, five-foot-ten and six-foot Americans appear in a fleet of vans, I realize the women also represent an empirical reality.

Te laver le visage O mort qu'il soit blanc et doux pour aller au-devant des autres.

From Lemoine's 1983 translation of the Kr'oua Ke.

A rough translation of the epigraph reads: O death which washes the face so that it may be white and soft in preparation for going before the others.

The Americans usher in a new mood throughout the camp. To relief workers, the JVA team conveys a sense of purpose and incorruptibility. To many Ban Vinai residents, their arrival promises alternatives and a possible future.

Yet, their arrival is also unsettling. At the Vangs, Ger and Choua fight again. When I arrive at their place, Choua is sitting under the house. Usually she will stop to talk, but today she barely greets me and immediately offers to find Ger. They arrive a few minutes later and when he asks her for the key to the upstairs room, she throws it at him. He has been spending time with his girlfriend again. Throughout their exchange Xiong intently focuses on her batiking.

Ger, choosing to ignore Choua's anger, talks instead of the camp leaders' plans for the upcoming New Year's celebration. "They are meeting to choose a date," he tells me. "How do they choose the date?" I ask. He replies:

"In Laos it is always the twelfth month, no decision. In Chiang Mai, too, some towns have it the eleventh or twelfth month, each town decides itself, chooses a free time. Thailand and Laos though have a different pace of harvesting rice. New Year's should be four months after the planting."

"And in this camp?" I ask. "Here it can be anytime, no way to decide but they have work in the camp, have to see their work," he says referring to the Resistance and other political activities. Describing New Year's in greater detail, he adds:

"In every house after New Year's there is a party, you go from house to house in one day—go to Chou Thao's, then Ger's, then the Khang's. Yes, we have only one [Hmong] holiday in Ban Vinai. In Laos, too, there was only one but here we celebrate the Lao and Thai people's holidays, too."

"Are there more suicides after Hmong New Year?" I ask him. Some preliminary research I am conducting with other Volag workers suggests that suicide rates (and particularly suicide attempt rates) are extremely high in Ban Vinai and the highest of all the camps in Thailand. The majority of attempts are committed by Hmong teenage girls and young women.[1]

"Yes, there are more then. After the ceremony, new boyfriends and new girlfriends," Ger affirms.

To illustrate, he draws a couple within a circle. Next he draws a second pair outside the circle. Finally he draws the two sets exchanging partners. Indicating the new arrangements on his drawing, he elaborates, "For example, if I saw a beautiful woman with some other man and I wanted her."

"But what about Choua?" I protest. "Yes, Choua would be angry."
"And if she did the same, what then?" I ask. "We would scold and
hit one another afterwards. Men are very angry but women kill
themselves." He suddenly asks, "If I go to America, could Choua divorce me?"

Xiong enters the room and dons her black leg warmers and shaman
accordion skirt with its slips and apron. When she is finished, she wraps
her hair in a woolen scarf, turban style. She says something in Hmong to
Ger as she dresses and looks at me.

"What is she saying?" I ask. "She is going to center 7 to teach another
woman to do the ceremony, so if she goes to America someone can do
it," Ger repeats in Lao for my benefit.

"May I observe and learn, too?" I ask. "Observe, yes, but learn, no.
You don't have spirits," he replies. "Well, maybe you do but I don't
know about that."

Xiong invites me to follow her, but Ger suggests I follow later. He
explains:

"They will kill a pig and chicken, then she does the ceremony. I will
take you to the place so you know where to return around one o'clock.
She will teach a younger woman, maybe forty or fifty."

"When did Xiong become a shaman?" I ask. "She learned when she
was forty, no, maybe younger because she has been a shaman since I was
born, maybe since more than twenty-seven," Ger replies. "How did the
younger woman know she was a shaman?" I ask.

"She had a sickness, a fever, in 1985, about one year ago. She went to
the hospital and nothing worked. She was so sick, she thought she
would die. So my mother did a ceremony and she knew then. The
ceremony worked for her."[2]

"Why now?" Ger, reflecting his own concerns, responds:

"My cousin has a relative in St. Paul, Minnesota, to sponsor him. My
mother is changing her mind, that's why she is teaching the other woman. Maybe, we will go to America, too, but we don't yet have an interview."

He looks suddenly at his watch. "Do we have to go now?" I ask. "Not
yet, at 10:30," he replies. "But, it is already 10:30," I protest. "No,
10:27," he corrects, showing me his watch.

"Can I ask one more question then?" "Yes, you can ask three or
four," he says. "No, only one," I promise.

"At a meeting of the Volags in Bangkok, I heard everyone say that the
Hmong can't decide. That's what people say," I tell him.

"I know," he answers.

"Why do you think people can't decide?"

Ger replies: "It is difficult most of all because of the old people and the Hmong customs. About death. You have to have the *khɛɛn* and the *kongs* [two traditional musical instruments] and do the ceremony in the house."

In their funeral rites, the Hmong sing of death as a voyage to the ancestors.[3] They believe in reincarnation and death is associated with the origins of life. Ger, like many other Hmong, traces his lineage back to a deceased paternal grandfather for whom he has named his son. Observing the death rites is essential, because these traditions protect the lineage in future generations. Xiong therefore worries that they will never again return to the lands of her husband's spirit and of the ancestors.

"In America you have the house to make people die," Ger says.

"What?"

He writes in Lao, "the house to make people die" and repeats in Hmong. He then draws a picture of a house in three dimensions. He says, "No one lives in this house. This house is where you go when you die."

Realizing that he is describing a funeral home, I agree, "Yes, we have those for when they die."

"I understand why you do, but the older people are afraid. They don't have them in Laos. No kong either so when a person dies, you cannot perform the ceremony," Ger says.

I disagree, "You could have a *kong.*" He responds:

"It is too heavy. In the house to make people die you have to do the ceremony for two days, then bury the second day. Hmong people do the ceremony in their own houses for two days. You have to play the *kong*, too."

Autopsies particularly conflict with Hmong beliefs about death. The elderly fear that the person's spirit is being taken and that it will have to revenge the loss. There is little I can say to reassure Ger.

Initiation

Late in the morning, we leave for center 7 by way of back paths. We climb continually through bamboo huts and gardens. Passing two wells, Ger points them out as a landmark. "Do you think you can remember the way?" he asks concerned. We come to a long wooden building with a bamboo porch overhanging the building below. I feel very high up.

A group of women are sewing accordion cloth, one rocks a child in a bamboo cradle. The young men, if they live here, have all departed.

Only the elderly, a few young women, and many young children remain. Ger, explaining that his cousins live here, takes me to Xiong and her friend. Once more he indicates the way to the two wells and then departs.

Xiong's initiation lasts over four hours. I record the following notes:

11:05. We sit on a bench outside waiting for an old man to set the room. The ceremony takes place in two adjacent rooms. One has a door with wooden knives wreathed over it, the second has spirit paper draped across its entrance.[4] The younger woman, the initiate, is graceful and somewhat remote, but less passionate than Xiong. Inside the first room, two altars are set up against the back northern wall. The higher one is suspended from the wall, the second, Xiong's, is set on a bench. The altars are laid identically. (Xiong notices that I am drawing the lay-out and after inspecting my rendition, she nods approvingly.) On the altars are; 1) a cup of rice with several sticks of incense (in the center), 2) a cup of rice with one stick of incense and egg resting inside (to the right as I face it), 3) two piles of puffed rice on each side, 4) buffalo horns on either side of the main cup of rice, each horn split in two, 5) three small cups of herbal or tea water in front of the main rice cup, and 6) joss [spirit paper money] behind the altar and dangling on either side.[5]

An elderly man cuts more spirit paper in circles, which he then places on each side of the altar. He adds three more incense sticks in the rice dishes, first passing the smoking incense over the altar. "There are two altars," he explains in Lao, "one for initiate, one for master." Xiong adds, "the cups of water have medicine in them, the paper is for the spirits, money for them." A large black pot of water is boiling over the fire. Two younger men suddenly appear and stoke the flames.

Meanwhile, the elderly man (dressed in traditional black dress) ties lines across the beams from the door to the back of the upper altar. He strings the line back and forth about five times, creating a kind of net across the eaves.

"These strings attract the spirits, they travel across the strings and then are entrapped in the rice cup (also attracted by the food)," Xiong explains. She sticks her jangles in the ground by the lower altar. She puts her red hood on, pulls it down across her face tightly once, and then pushes it back on her head. She says something to the old man, who lights a small oil lamp and places it on her altar.

Xiong takes up the gong, which she begins beating by her altar.

Next she passes her buffalo horns over the burning incense and throws the horns on the ground.[6] The horns split into four. Squatting down she picks them up in twos and fours several times, reading and rereading them. Then she sets them back on the table.

Playing the gong, she then stands by the high altar. The old man lights a second lamp. Xiong stops, calls the initiate to put her hood on, gestures for her to approach, and indicates that the initiate should sweep the floor in front of her altar. Xiong instructs her to sweep twice to the door and back again.[7]

11:40. Xiong turns back to the altar again, plays the gong, and begins bird whistling sounds and low chanting. Children walk in and out all the while. A young woman boils more water. The elderly man is making some white paste to put around the oil lamps. Smoke fills the room. A young girl brings an opium pipe in, sets it against the wall. An elderly woman walks in. Surprised to see me resting on the side bench, she indicates with one finger, "Are you alone?" The initiate begins preparing food while the master continues to chant. The elderly man places another lamp on the novice's altar. As he lights it, Xiong slows down her bird whistling. She beats the gong turning east, west, south, then north again. Then, she stops.

11:45. Xiong passes a second set of buffalo horns over the incense at the altar, throws them down on the ground, and reads them several times. The novice watches all the while preparing food. "She is reading whether good or bad," a young man, who suddenly reappears, explains in Lao.

The light rays, like falling water, filter through the bamboo roof in the smoky, darkened room . This time the reading takes longer. Xiong turns to the old man and asks about the pig. He ceases smoking his opium pipe and leaves for the back room. He returns with a pair of brown chickens, which are tied together at the feet, and a knife. The chickens squawk. He then brings a second set, a black pair, for Xiong to examine their feet. She sits on the bench by me and examines the birds' backs and feet. She unties one of the black chickens and sets it aside.[8]

Two young men return to assist. The elderly man gives a child two chickens to hold while he kills the first one with one of the young men. They wash first the feet and then the whole bird before killing it. The old man hands the washed bird back to the master before the sacrifice. She passes the bird over the incense in a circular motion and then reads a set of buffalo horns again while holding the bird. Still holding the chicken, she rips off some joss, sets it on fire and burns it to ash on the ground to ward away the evil spirit. "Chicken is used as the spirit of the shaman's wife," explains one of the young men in Lao.[9] As the young men slit the bird's throat, they catch its blood in a pail.

The master, Xiong, goes to the second altar with three chickens. The initiate watches as the master rocks the three chickens and chants facing the altar. The master stops, waves the chickens, east, south, west, and north, and then has the initiate hold the chickens while the master reads the horns again. The master slows her chanting. She picks up more joss for the spirits, burns it on the ground by the chickens, and hands the young men two more chickens to kill.

One of the young men returns with a small, squealing pig tied by string in the back room. The initiate takes the string and hands it to the master to tie to her altar.

12:05. They discuss what kind of string should be used and exchange a cloth string for some plastic ribbon, which the initiate retrieves from a box. The master ties the string again behind the main rice vessel, while the young man steadies the pig. She then beats the gong again and the initiate watches. (Outside the second young man and the old man are killing the two chickens.) The master ends the beating of the gong with a bird whistle, passes a set of buffalo horns over the incense, throws them to the ground, and reads them three times by the squirming pig. She continues chanting. She then takes her buffalo horns to read again. (The men begin plucking the chickens.) The master unties the joss from her own altar, burns it to ash on the ground, and tells the men to remove the pig.

Sitting on the bench together, the two women pause and talk while the men prepare the pig sacrifice. The pig screams horrifically. I retreat from its piercing wail. From her bench, the master nods approvingly at my detailed notes. The men throw the pig across a small stool in front of the altar and slit its throat, while catching the blood in a pail. The master gets up suddenly, takes some joss, and passes it across the blood gushing from the pig's throat. Then, she sets the joss on the ground under her own altar. She takes apart more strips of joss and arranges them around the altar on both sides.

The women rest for almost an hour, while the men skin and clean the sacrifices—three chickens and the pig. The old man adds more joss and the master indicates we should go outside on the bench. She tells me that the spirits are coming to rest in the food: they are leaving the pig's spirit and going to the altar.

As we sit outside in the bright sun, Xiong explains that the elderly man is a younger [clan] brother. One of the young men cleaning the chicken asks me about going to the United States. "Will JVA come again this year?" He stops working and brings some photographs of relatives in Santa Ana. Xiong takes the photographs from me and after she has seen them, hands them back. The slightly out-of-focus photographs show scenes of a Hmong family in their apartment in California and, in one photograph, they are watching a balloon exhibition. The elderly man goes back in the room to smoke his pipe again. Another elderly woman, who suckles a young girl, comes by to talk with Xiong.

1:20. The ceremony recommences slowly. The elderly man takes the last live chicken and places it under a basket by the master's altar. He then puts the bench in front of the initiate's altar and ties a rolled-up blanket across it (to soften the journey by horse). Someone has set the pork on a platter to the side, three chickens are on another platter, and the fourth live one is on the master's altar to the left of the main rice vessel. The old man rings the red stringed jangles briefly and plunges them into the ground by the master's altar.

1:35. The master takes the buffalo horns from her altar, passes them over the burning incense, throws them to the ground, and reads them again several times. The room smells of freshly killed animal and opium. The elderly man is smoking again near the door and a second elderly man briefly joins him. Then, there are only three elderly people in the room—the two women and the old man—and myself. The atmosphere has changed: a quiet ceremonial feeling prevails.

The master directs the initiate to dress. A few minutes later, the initiate emerges in her own accordion skirt and takes a seat on the bed behind to watch. The master takes her own buffalo horns up to the high altar, passes them over the lamp and incense as she quietly chants. She throws the horns down several times. Another elderly man walks in the room and asks her about the reading. She answers in a quiet undertone.

At her own altar, the master passes her hand over the incense sticks in a circular clockwise motion, waving her hand over three times as she holds a small cup of the liquid.[10] With the cup she goes to the open door, chants a few minutes, and drinks from the cup. Spitting out the water, she sprays it through the door three times, stomping her right foot with each spray, and exclaiming, "*Mao.*" She returns to her altar, wets the incense sticks with her fingers, and

drinks the rest in the cup. All the while, she talks to the second elderly man.

At the master's direction, the initiate goes to her own altar and
sits beside the master. The master, taking a drink from the initiate's
cup, spits water on her, stomps her foot again, and exclaims to her
spirits. Then, she hands the glass for the initiate to drink and spit.
The master hands the initiate a red hood to put on and the initiate
pulls the hood over her face. The master makes more chicken
sounds, adds motor sounds, and takes some puffed rice from her
own altar, and throws it across the floor like chicken feed. Dipping
her hand in each cup, she singes the incense. She repeats her actions
at the initiate's altar.

2:00. Both women sit on the bench in front of the main altar with
their hoods in place. The master lifts her hood, picks up some joss,
puts it by the three chickens to the left on a platter, picks up her
jangles in her right hand, and speaks to the second elderly man. The
first beats a gong behind the women, who pull their hoods down
across their faces. The master, followed by the initiate, taps her feet
in time, shakes the jangles, and makes bird whistle sounds. The second man lights his opium pipe, while the first continues beating the
gong and the two women beat time with their feet. The master's
movements are decidedly looser and more expressive than the initiate's.[11]

The gong beating slows and the master begins chanting. The initiate joins in. Their chanting is accompanied by bird whistle and
chicken sounds. The old man brings the pig, draped in joss, on a
platter and sets it on a stool behind the women with its snout facing
the altar. The women continue chanting and then slow briefly for a
long exhalation. Blowing out, they continue.

2:10. The elderly man, taking some incense sticks from the altar,
waves them around the room and places one at the door. The second
man cuts an entrail out of the pig, chops it, and breads it in flour,
while the old man lights some incense and puts it by the pig's ear.
Since I am in a semi-somnambulant state now, my notes are less detailed. The chanting is mesmerizing, the feet stomping hypnotic, the
smells overpowering, and the sweat is pouring down my back.

The master continues to chant without ceasing. The initiate hesitantly joins in from time to time. The master slows 30 seconds at
2:25, but the initiate keeps the pace. The master does a wide arc with
her body and hands leaning forward, more bird sounds.

2:35. The chanting ceases briefly again. I leave for a few minutes and stand outside the door to clear my head.

2:40. The second man takes some joss, burns it by the pig, and says a prayer. The two men approach the women from behind and stand without touching as if to steady them.

2:42: the chanting slows again. The two men are talking, the first holds a knife. Outside a baby screams.

2:45. The elderly man splits open the pig, takes out its entrails, puts them on a plate, and begins cutting up the pig.

2:50. The old man puts the pieces in a pot to cook and spearing the head, toasts it over the fire before adding it to the pot. The women, slowing their chanting, make wide arc motions.

2:56. The master slows again, but the initiate keeps the faster pace. She is now using a jangle and speaks more loudly.

3:05. The master makes bird whistle sounds. The first man steadies her and pounds her back to relax her. She stands up, takes a drink from a cup, dips her hand in water, drops some more puffed rice on the floor, and reads the buffalo horns once again. The initiate follows with bird whistling sounds one to two minutes later. She raises her hood, while the old man pounds her back, too. The men bow their heads two or three times to the floor and one exits. The initiate drops her hands in the water, spreads the puffed rice, wets the incense sticks, and at the master's request, picks up her buffalo horns and throws them to the floor. The master joins her. Spreading their colored skirts around them, they squat over the horns to read them. The master interprets for the initiate. Smiling, she shows the initiate how to throw the horns. At the master's request, the old man places the pig's head and the three chickens on a platter and brings them to the women. The master wipes off the pig's head with her hand.

3:10. The master waves all four sets of buffalo horns over the incense on the upper altar. She throws them on the floor, while the others watch. She interprets the horns as she throws them several times. Then, she returns the horns to the altar and blows out the lamp.

3:15. The ceremony ends, the two women and elderly man in Hmong invite me to eat. In Hmong I reply, "I go to work." They repeat their invitation in Lao. In Lao I explain that I must return before the vans leave and that I am already late. I leave them eating around the fire. Forgetting to turn left at the two wells, I find the main road instead.

The brilliant sun outside is a marked contrast to the darkened, incensed room. It is hard to focus and to bring myself back to the world I know. Descending the hill I realize that Xiong has just passed on her inheritance and that, as an American, I was called to witness.

Processing Interview

Over the next few days, the Americans conduct several more interviews. The leader, an old Asia hand, speaks fluent Thai and has spent many years in Southeast Asia. The men, tall and athletic, wear khaki pants. The women wear make-up, tailored skirts, and cashmere or wool sweaters. Cloistered each evening in Chiang Khan, they keep separate from other relief workers, and each day they work late into the evening. They do not want to be influenced by petitions from relief workers who may want to help a particular refugee. Because their businesslike manner is a marked contrast to other relief workers, one interviewer laughingly reassures us, "JVA is not a profession."

The team sets up their interviewing station in a clinic, which they enclose with a bamboo fence. Each morning, the crowd waits anxiously outside for their names to be called or to petition for interviews. The Volag workers spend long hours discussing America's immigration policies and responding to requests from refugee workers to write letters of assistance in obtaining interviews. Ger's cousin spends the better part of a day typing a letter in English to ask JVA when his interview will be scheduled. After Pere, the Englishman, and I correct several versions, he stands vigil for the next three days at the clinic. He never receives a written reply, but on the fourth day, his name is called.

Obtaining a JVA interview is one of many stages in the resettlement process. Not everyone who crosses the Mekong makes it into a camp. To be admitted officially usually requires paying the local police. The Thai Ministry of Interior (MOI) then screens the Laotian refugees to see if they fit resettlement criteria. MOI determines the family's reason for fleeing to Thailand to distinguish "refugees" from "economic migrants." "Refugees" are former military and government officials (in the Royal Lao government) or persons who have worked for foreigners (embassies, firms, international organizations), who have participated in political and social movements against the Communist government, or who have relatives in a third country.[12] "Economic migrants" are those found to be dissatisfied with the new regime's economic and political policies or are influenced by others (especially Laotian hilltribes) to

155

leave. These tropes (displaced person, economic migrant, or refugee) allow everyone involved—the Americans, the Thai government, and even the refugees themselves—to believe that the flow across the border is being controlled.

Admission to a camp, however, does not guarantee third-country resettlement. The Resistance, too, decides who enters and may demand protection payments. Once the refugee is officially admitted, UNHCR assesses the new arrivals' status and determines which refugees fit various countries' resettlement criteria. UNHCR provides each household with an identity document, which consists of a photograph of the members holding their Ban Vinai (BV) number. After the interview, UNHCR enters the household's biodata into a computer. This information is reported to the UNHCR office in Bangkok. The status of refugee, in contrast to that of the illegal, links the person to a system that confers identity through numbers, computer files, and written documents.

JVA caseworkers act as gatekeepers in a restricted immigration market.[13] Assuming a counselor rather than a law enforcement function, they frame fragmented life histories into resettlement narratives to present each household's case to the U.S. Immigration and Naturalization Service (INS). U.S. resettlement criteria have priorities as follows:

P-1: admission in the national interest or in imminent danger.
P-2: former U.S. government employees.
P-3: with close relatives in the U.S.
P-4a: employed by U.S. businesses or agencies.
P-4b: previously in the civil or armed services of the former governments of Vietnam, Laos, Cambodia.
P-5: with married siblings or grandchildren in the U.S.
P-6: everyone else.

Most Hmong in Ban Vinai claim a P-3 or P-4b status. Once the case is made, INS reviews the file and will often follow up the case with further interviews in the refugee's own language.

The JVA interview is a rite of passage, marking the end of the liminality of camp life and the transition to third-country resettlement.[14] The refugees' changing status is reflected in new languages, relationships, and orientations. Although the JVA interviews add little new information to the UN biodata file, these encounters are symbolically significant. Prior to the interview, many refugees have few encounters with officials. Those they meet speak their own language or Thai and usually only one family member—usually a younger male—negotiates if necessary. JVA, in contrast, conducts interviews in English through interpreters and requires the entire household to come to the hearing process. For many elderly and young, it is their first face-to-face encounter with Westerners and first experience with a Western ritual, the interview.

Inside the clinic, the six JVA caseworkers interview simultaneously. Each averages six cases a day, the team, as a whole, forty. The frenetic pace of the Western world contrasts sharply with the long period of waiting that precedes this moment.

A tall, quiet caseworker from Maine explains JVA's work to me:

> JVA does the anchor research. It's a four-step process. Our interviews are done by American citizens only, six interviewers and our leader. Registrars sign up the families. For that we have three full-time Thai staff and a Thai statistician. Our total staff is 15 to 19 caseworkers, drivers, statistician, registrars, and a Thai field assistant. We work 8 to 5 with half an hour off for lunch. Seven days a week this stint because so many need to be processed. When we work up-country, we usually work a two- week cycle, Monday through Saturday, Sunday off, and then we work through the next Thursday. We'll get some comp time later.

Explaining the timing of their arrival in November, he adds:

> The Volags have trouble resettling Hmong technically approved in December. A certain number are recruited each month to meet the monthly quota. But, the processing centers don't send anyone over Christmas.

In late December, after Christmas, he hopes to take a break.

According to the caseworker, the four steps simplify the process. Step one, the biodata and referrals, is handled by UNHCR. JVA then completes three forms. First, their registrar completes a form, defining family units. JVA next brings in their "form writers."

> Form writers are Hmong writers in the camp who write family trees. Family trees are Form 3. This form documents children in the United States versus the camps.

After several years of working together, the Hmong form writers and JVA caseworkers are experienced in translating the Hmong and other kinship systems into Western terms. The Hmong are also well aware of Western conceptions of the nuclear family—thus, many second wives become "younger sisters."

JVA caseworkers next do Form 2, the "anchor research." The caseworker explains:

Form 2 documents relatives in the United States and other countries. The relatives in other countries include Ban Vinai. The case worker ascertains the family history and why the family qualifies as refugees. We also look at any relationships to military people.

JVA then turns their files over to the Immigration and Naturalization Service (INS), who have the final say.

JVA does not decide the case, INS does. The caseworker prepares the file, just sticks to facts about family composition and the basic reason for being a refugee. An EAO [Ethnic Affairs Officer] will then decide if they were in the military or not, that is, only if they were a former government officer. Then the INS officer interviews. At the INS stage, the family is sworn in and asked, "Do you promise to tell the whole truth and nothing but the truth so help you. . . . " with right hand raised. INS are Justice Department officials and usually ask more pointed questions like, "Why did you leave?" They must prove 101A42. JVA's role is to present the best story for the refugee possible—but no advocacy work.

By the end of the process, the refugee's case has been reviewed by: 1) UNHCR, 2) the JVA registrar, 3) a JVA form writer, 4) a JVA caseworker, 5) an ethnic affairs officer, and 6) INS.

Differentiating JVA work from INS, the caseworker explains:

INS uses its own criteria to see if refugee status is allowed. They're trained officers. INS comes in after JVA sets up but then we come in together. JVA sets the system up, makes up the call list. We are currently preparing for INS's arrival on December 15. They have five officers, handle 50 cases a day. Very good interpreters. Three out-of-camp interpreters, those who have been INS-approved and are bound for the States. They don't live in the camp, because they could be influenced. We take them out of Phanat.

He ceases speaking as several people arrive for an interview. The increased noise level drowns out his quiet voice. The families wear their finest attire; babies in shorts and rubber boots, men in Western pants and sunglasses, and women in Thai sarongs with their umbrellas. Each case sits on a bench facing the interviewer, who sits behind a table stacked high with files. After a few minutes the children take to the floors and mothers nurse infants, while the "head of household" (usually a young male or single female head of household) answers questions.

"Just got a letter that says Sir Jim, sort of like Lord Jim, I think," a female caseworker calls out above the din. With her cashmere sweater and lighted cigarette, she looks more appropriate for a Washington law office than a bamboo dispensary. The leader smiles wryly. It is but one of hundreds of petitions he receives that day.

The Maine caseworker continues:

> Characteristically, the Hmong have the highest "no show" rate. We call 40 to 60 cases a day and 40 would be no shows, but this year it's close to 100 percent [who are showing up]. We didn't expect that coming so close to New Year's.

He pauses and adds:

> JVA hasn't been here since fall, '85. Maybe, we're getting the higher show rate this time because JVA has been gone for fourteen months. People know we are serious.

He says that most Hmong who apply will be accepted for resettlement but wonders whether they will go:

> The Hmong have the highest acceptance rate—100 percent approval in two days in Chieng Kham camp. The Vietnamese know the system better than the Hmong, who are basically very honest. The Vietnamese arrive with all the right documents, right answers. Even the Khmer have more. There is a certain lack of complicity among the Hmong. A primitive people. We approved many in 1984. Then they didn't show. If we called them twice and they were no-show, then they were "recouped." Recouping a case is not an INS function but State Department's. If their original forms have already been microfiched, then they must be written out again. It creates only a bottleneck and lots of paperwork. JVA has no right to refuse a qualified person even if she or he does not show, recouping can only slow down a process. The basic purpose of the U.S. immigration program is family reunification. By definition, those who arrived by 1979, have no problem if they have family in the U.S.

A mother and her four children are waiting for the caseworker to interview them. He stops talking and studies their file for a few minutes. He then retrieves the ex-husband's file from the registrar, because the information in the first file appears to be inconsistent. The woman is a second wife of a husband who divorced her in 1983 to resettle in the United States with his first wife. She claims that her youngest child was born in 1984, after their divorce. The husband, however, has reported the child as being born in 1981. Looking at the children in front of him, the caseworker realizes that the third child of the four is closer to five years old than two and must be the child in question. Taking a bottle of white-out, he corrects the birth date.

The woman's three eldest children crawl on the floor. A young

Hmong male interpreter takes a chair beside the caseworker. The mother nurses the youngest. The caseworker studies the file again for a moment and muses aloud: "Is there an affidavit of relationship? She is claiming relationship to the mother. This guy sent a copy of his Form 1! So I guess I can check and see if it tracks, huh?"

The mother lays down her sleeping infant and places her hands over the form. In the moment of silence, each one seems lost in his or her respective thoughts.

They regard one another again. "How many brothers and sisters does she have in the United States?" asks the caseworker. Repeating the question in Hmong, the young interpreter holds up his fingers in response.[15] The caseworker continues, "What's the second's name? It really is her sister? Same mother, same father?" The interpreter translates, the woman nods. "Does she really want me to add her to the family tree?" The caseworker lists off the names reading down. Brushing his nose and smiling slightly, he adds a new name. The woman and the interpreter watch silently. Realizing suddenly that the same person is listed under two names, the caseworker uses the white-out again.

"Does she have any information about American prisoners of war or Americans missing in action?" the caseworker asks. The interpreter translates and the woman indicates no. This ritualistic, but nevertheless significant question reflects the association many Americans have of the Laotian.

"Was she ever in Nong Khai?" "Yes," the interpreter replies. "Does she know her date of arrival in Nong Khai?" No one replies. "Same date as arrival in Thailand, May '75?" After the interpreter explains, the woman nods.

"Does she know any of the months of date of birth of her children?" This is translated, but the woman does not reply. "How about Yung Sue?" To this translation, she shakes her head. "How about Non?" Again, she gives the same response. "All right, for the rest of them I'm going to assign a day and a month—2/2, 3/3/, 4/4, 5/5," the caseworker replies, listing the dates off again and pointing to each child as he assigns a birth date for future immigration, school, hospital, and refugee assistance forms. The mother watches attentively.

"In 1975 what were you doing?" The interpreter translates, but the woman does not respond. "Do you also do Hmong stitchery?" When this was translated in Hmong, she nods.

"Schooling?" The interpreter indicates that the two eldest children have studied. "Both in camp?" The woman nods in response to the interpreter, who is now translating into Lao (since education is conducted primarily in Lao). "How many years in school?" The translation continues in Lao and the eldest son, who listens to this topic, helps his mother answer. "Two years," the interpreter explains in English. "Finish elementary school?" "No," replies the interpreter, speaking for the child. "English?" "No," he repeats. The infant stirs and the mother nurses him again. An older child grabs her second breast. "Read and write Hmong?" "No," says the interpreter, responding for the woman and her son. "Does anybody speak Lao?" The interpreter repeats the question in Lao. The woman indicates that her older children speak Lao and the two eldest chime in agreement. "How much?" the caseworker asks. Answering the interpreter in Lao, they reply, "Average" [*thámmādaa*].

"Does anybody have two names?" the caseworker asks. There is no response. The caseworker covers the form with more white-out. After correcting several boxes, he looks up again and asks, "Is everybody in good health?" The woman nods yes to the translation.

"Does she have an address for [her former husband]?" "No." "How old was she when her father died?" "Six years ago," the interpreter replies. "Laos or Ban Vinai?" "Laos," he translates. "Occupation before?" "Soldier." The interpreter continues to confirm his responses with the woman in Hmong.

"When did her mother die?" "Seventeen years ago," the interpreter replies. "How old was she when her mother died?" The woman stares without comprehension. "She doesn't know." "Her mother died before Vang Pao left?" the caseworker asks. "Yes," replies the interpreter, after prompting the woman. "Did her family ever adopt anybody?" "No," he translates. "Does she have any idea about when she married Vang Blia [her first husband]?" The woman stares. "No." "How old is she?" "She doesn't know," the interpreter explains. "Doesn't know how old when she got married?" "Doesn't know," he repeats. The caseworker confers with the interpreter and they decide that she must have been about sixteen.

The caseworker asks about her second husband. "What was Khang's occupation when she married him?" "Military," the interpreter replies. "How did he die?" "He was shot by soldier," he continues. "French military?" The woman nods uncertainly. "When did he die—not in Laos, in 1950?" No one speaks as the caseworker confirms aloud. "Did he die before you married Yang?" The woman nods affirmatively to this translation. "Must have died in 1950s, killed by Communists?" the caseworker reiterates. "She doesn't know when, but before married other husband," the interpreter replies.

The Disinherited

161

The caseworker, looking perplexed, says, "This woman is not forty-nine years old!" Speaking more loudly, he asks, "Her first husband's mother, does she know Khang's father's occupation?" The interpreter repeats the question in Thai. When the woman stares blankly back, he quickly switches to Hmong. However, he continues referring to the JVA interviewer with the Thai form of address. "Khang only had one brother?" There is no response. "Is Mou Choua still alive?" The children, who are playing on the floor, yell at one another. The interpreter explains, "He's dead." The infant grabs a book from the desk. The mother pushes the book away and he cries.

"Does she know when her husband married his second wife?" the caseworker asks. "She doesn't know." "How many years after you got married did he take another wife?" The interpreter repeats, "She doesn't know." The caseworker pauses and hands the older child, who is fussing loudly, a pen. "Can you ask her again when her husband divorced her? What year?" The interpreter after a brief discussion with the woman, replies, "Three." "1983?" "Something like that," he translates. "He said '82 so it's probably '82," the caseworker concludes.

"Your daughter is in Laos?" No one replies. "Father of the baby is in Laos?" The interpreter repeats the question in Hmong, "Father?" "Was he in Ban Vinai, then went back to Laos?" The interpreter replies, "Yes." "Does he fight with the Resistance?" Again, he translates, "Yes." "Does he have a BV number?" "No," he translates. The children wander in different directions on the floor. The mother is increasingly distracted by their fussing. "O.K., think I've got everybody figured out," the caseworker concludes.

The caseworker picks up a blank sheet of paper. There is a momentary pause. "Where was she born?" The interpreter replies, "Houay Houy, Mouang Sam Neua." "Not Luang Prabang?" the caseworker asks surprised. The interpreter, tossing his head up and sideways, repeats: "Sam Neua, Houay —Houy, Sam Neua Province." "She wasn't born in Luang Prabang?" the caseworker persists, looking at a map. "Sam Neua was part of Laos. After the fall of Dien Ben Phu, it was controlled by the Pathet Lao," I explain. The caseworker, looking at the map, muses aloud as he locates Sam Neua, "Oh that's what we should have written for the other one."

"Where was she married to [second husband]?" The interpreter starts to explain. "Just village and province." The interpreter writes on a piece of paper: Sapha Kha, Hien, Luang Prabang. There is a momentary pause. "Did she live in her home village until she got married?" The woman replies "No" in Hmong and the interpreter nods negatively.

"Where did she move to when they moved, where did she grow up before she was married?" When this is translated, a long discussion between the woman and interpreter ensues as she describes several places in detail. When they finish, he answers, "She moved from [village in Laos] and she married her first husband in Chua Long." The caseworker records on a clean sheet of paper: "When PA [principal applicant] . . . ." The children crawl closer to their mother. "Did her husband die in Chua Long?" When this is translated, the woman nods. The interpreter, however, repeats his question to her again in Hmong in a louder voice. Staring straight ahead, she nods again. "Did she stay there with her family after her husband died?" The woman nods. "Did your whole family move to Sapha Kha?" The interpreter replies, "Yes." "Where was your father's village in Laos?" The interpreter replies, "Ban [village in Laos]." "Did you remember when he was a village chief?" There is no response. "So she just heard he was?" The interpreter nods affirmatively for the woman. "Did she live in Sapha Kha when Vang Pao left?" The interpreter replies, "Yes, they moved to Houa Suey before they escaped." "O.K.,[pause] just before they came to Thailand?"

"What was Nong [younger brother]? What did he do?" In Hmong, the interpreter gives the woman the choice of farmer or soldier. After she replies, he explains, "Soldier." "Does she know whether PTL, ADC, SGU?" The interpreter pauses and then asks the woman in Hmong, "American?" She shakes her head. "Does she know what his rank was?" The interpreter provides a specific rank. "Are you sure?" The interpreter, after reevaluating his response with the woman, explains, "She didn't say he was, misunderstood." "Where was he based?" The interpreter replies, "Based on the front in the combat troops in Samput." "Was he in the military until '75, until Vang Pao left?" "Yes," he replies again. "Was he always a combat soldier, never did anything?" The interpreter explains, "After he left, free the soldier, he took another job as worker."

The interpreter again asks the woman in Hmong, "What did he do?" Following her response, he elaborates, "He was like Dong say yesterday, náaj kɔɔn [Lao]." The caseworker clarifies, "Vang Pao's special administrative chief?" After a brief pause, he adds, "Village chief but someone under Vang Pao, not under RLG." "So you don't have that in your government?" asks the interpreter. "No," the caseworker replies. He muses aloud, "So why did INS tell me like judicial? Judge?" The interpreter explains, "Yes, you could say that. But, not really because their duty like concerning the Lao." "But they also have responsibility to Vang Pao, wasn't just a civilian?" the caseworker concludes.

There is a pause. The woman has stared ahead impassively throughout this last exchange. "Did you and your husband's other wife all live
together in the same house in Sapha Kha?" the caseworker asks. The
woman nods affirmatively. "Hmmm." "Do you know what your husband's responsibilities were as *náaj kɔɔn* for Vang Pao?" the caseworker
asks, employing the interpreter's term. The interpreter replies, "She
doesn't know." The caseworker writes at length on the form.

"When you came to Thailand, did all of you come together, your
husband with the other wife?" The interpreter explains, "No, she came
first, with her father's wife." "O.K., let's go back a little. When Vang Pao
left, where did she go?" The interpreter replies, "When Vang Pao go she
escape to Nan Suan." "When they went to Nan Suan, did they all go
together?" The interpreter replies, "Her husband stay with her in Sapha
Kha, but they not marry yet." "But they had children, right?" "Yes."
"Where is her husband?" "Ban Nam." "When they were in Nan Suon
were they farming?" "Yes." "When she came to Thailand did she come
with [second husband]?" The interpreter nods affirmatively for the woman. "Did she get married in Ban Vinai?" The interpreter replies, "In Nong
Khai [refugee camp]." "When she came who did she come with in this
group?" "They all came together." The caseworker again reads each name
off the list. The children pull at the mother's back to get her attention.

The caseworker shows the family tree to the interpreter. "Her husband's mother so it's their grandmother?" The interpreter asks for
clarification, "Mother-in-law?" "Yes, mother-in-law." "Her husband
came later, yes?" "Yes." "Are you sure? Sure he didn't come first?"
"Yes," the interpreter repeats.

The caseworker scans the form again. Smiling, he says, "It's not
right. How long did she stay in Nong Khai?" The interpreter replies,
"Doesn't know." "Long time, short time, one month? Are you sure you
were in Nong Khai? Was it more than one night?" the caseworker
smiles. There is no response. The interpreter repeats, "Doesn't know."
"Did she ever sleep in Nong Khai?" the caseworker asks surprised. The
interpreter, after some discussion with the woman, answers, "About
four years, she doesn't know."

He adds, "It says '75 in Ban Vinai, maybe UN made a mistake."

"O.K. Does she have any questions?" the caseworker smiles again.
The woman indicates negatively. "We have to request her son's file from
Bangkok and after we get that file she will, then she will have an INS
interview." The interpreter nods, but does not translate. "If she gets
called to get on the bus, is she ready to go?" When this is translated, the

woman nods. "She's not going to get married, huh?" The interpreter does not translate. The interview ends. Carrying the infant, the woman exits and her children follow.

The caseworker reminisces for a moment with the interpreter after the interview. "What was the story here. Doesn't matter. Most you forget. They always remember where they had their children." Contrasting the Hmong to other ethnic groups, he explains for my benefit.

> They always insist on not knowing. It might be better than the others. One woman told us a story that she was nine years when she got married. She had heard rumors that you won't get taken if you've been married twice or have a big family. Does make it easier to remember if they have a mind to. Vietnamese come with everything, all the necessary documents. They know a lot about our processing. The Khmer have no documents. All have been destroyed. The recent ones we have interviewed, after '79, have some educated Chinese descent. Before we got the farmers. The lowland Lao are educated, pretty much together, lots of military. Hmong, no documents. They don't know dates but they remember their U.S. advisers, they know what they did.

He turns to prepare the next case.

Five months earlier in Washington, D.C., Alan C. Nelson, commissioner of the Immigration and Naturalization Service (INS) testifies in Congress:

> There is growing sentiment within United States refugee program agencies that for certain regions, at least, the current processing priorities are in need of revision. This is particularly the case in Southeast Asia where, 11 years after the fall of allied governments in Vietnam, Cambodia, and Laos, the population reaching first asylum countries is increasingly comprised of persons seeking family reunification and quality of life improvement rather than of persons actually fleeing persecution or fear of persecution.[16]

The domestic climate for refugees is changing. Funding for domestic refugee programs is diminishing and there is considerable discussion of refugees on welfare. In the same hearing, Phillip N. Hawkes, deputy administrator of Health and Human Services, testifies: "The single largest problem in the domestic refugee program is its cost as related to the high percentage of refugees who become dependent on public assistance. Currently over one-half of the refugees who have been in the country less than three years are receiving public assistance."[17]

The Last Bus

Outside the bamboo gates the large crowd keeps its vigil. Wondering why the Vang household is not among them, I go to their compound. A neighbor informs me that they are watching television in the Thai market. Just as I am about to leave, Xiong appears.

"Stay, they are coming," she commands. She has just had some teeth extracted. "Hurts very much, I can't talk or eat yet," she says, speaking as if her mouth is full. She offers me some bananas to eat and refuses to take them back until I eat one.

Her grandson arrives and helps himself to some leftover fried food from the kitchen pot. She breaks a piece off for him. Taking the food, he joins his friend on a mat beneath the porch.

Ger and Choua arrive in high spirits. Ger informs me that he has received a cassette tape announcing that Chia, his brother in Rhode Island, is coming for New Year's. Chia has also informed Ger that the affidavits are insufficient. "This form is no good," Ger informs me in disgust. Describing his clan brother, he adds:

"Chia was first in our family to emigrate to the U.S. A lieutenant of Vang Pao. He arrived in Ban Vinai in 1975 and left for the U.S. in 1977. Chia bought two houses and gave the first to our other cousin. He settled first in Texas but life there was very difficult. When he didn't find work he joined the family in Rhode Island. He makes seven dollars an hour. He bought the first house for $39,000 and the second for $40,000."

" How much does Dennis make an hour? he asks.

I do some quick calculations. Ger prompts, "More than $10 an hour?" When I estimate closer to $20, he is impressed. I tell him how much rent we pay and he is shocked. "No, you don't make so much," he decides.

Ger shows me photographs of Chia and his wife, a portly couple in their late forties who, in Western dress, stand in front of the state capitol in Providence, Rhode Island. Pointing to the wife, Ger says, "She was laid off from her job a few months ago." Chia's two teenage sons are dressed in blue jeans and T-shirts and in one photograph, the younger son sits on the family's Chevy. Impressed by the car, Ger sent a photograph of himself herding a water buffalo. Each side shows its best face.

Ger brings out photographs of himself. One shows a younger Ger in Resistance fatigues taken somewhere in the north. The second is of Ban Vinai in 1979, which I do not recognize. There are many trees and it looks as if the camp was once forested. "There were only five centers and maybe 10,000 in the camp then," Ger explains.

"There are many people in Ban Vinai in the Resistance," he says lowering his voice. "How many?" I ask, surprised at the change of topic. "Maybe one over two," he replies writing a ratio on a piece of paper. Reversing the ratio, he says, "for two who are not, one is." "How many people in this building, for example?" I ask, knowing that the ratio is meant to impress. "Two men. I think next year there will be no camp because they will send many Resistance to the border." "And those who don't go?" "They will all go. I should go to the U.S. That would be best. If you do not go, you must join the Resistance, the Thai say."

Knowing his family connections are limited, I ask, "What if you aren't accepted?" Ger replies, "Maybe I will go back to Laos. Everyone is part of the Resistance, Htin and other ethnic groups. It is much more than you think." I wonder if he is trying to tell me that he has joined too, because he has a new haircut. He assures me otherwise.

"Maybe there will be a convention," Ger says. "What?" He explains that he has heard that there will be an international convention in 1987 about Laos and that after the convention, some refugees will be able to return to Laos.

I had already heard of the idea of a convention from the UNHCR field officer. The field officer was of the opinion that "the Lao government should agree to the repatriation of these people in a big group. We have an office in Vientiane, several projects in Laos for returnees."

"How much are you spending on repatriation," I asked the field officer. He admitted that UNHCR spent only about half a million a year in Laos on repatriation versus twenty million on refugees in Thailand. Then, he said emphatically: "All agencies should withdraw from Ban Vinai and open offices in Vientiane. Should have an international conference between major donor countries, Thai and Lao government. Maybe, next year. MOI says this year, year of resettlement."[18] The idea of a convention is part of camp discourse, but is not heard in international debates about the region.

Worried that he is giving me the wrong impression, Ger says, "Since '75, I have wanted to go to the U.S." "Why didn't you go then?" "I did not go sooner because my mother didn't want to go," he says. After a pause, he asks, "After five years [in the U.S.] could I become a Thai citizen?" "Maybe a temporary visa; it might be easier to repatriate to Laos." He disagrees:

It will be easier to go to Laos, since there are fewer people in Laos. Maybe some want to go back to Laos after the U.S. in the future because you can be a soldier or farmer, but in the U.S., you can only work in a company. It's more comfortable in Laos. In the U.S., though, you can buy a car or house. Very few people have cars in Laos. Only a very few in the U.S. would like to go back because Laos is very poor. I don't think I'll go back myself. The U.S. is best for me.

Xiong returns from a ceremony. She hangs her hood and skirts on the wall and lies exhausted on the bed. Ger reiterates, "This form is no good." He looks at me accusingly, as if I should have known that my government would not accept cousins as sponsors. His final hope rests with Xiong's adopted son. Although she opposes his going, Xiong helps Ger in this claim and nods as he spins out this latest scheme.

"What can you sell for me in the U.S.? You know some get out without relatives, Lynel," he says. "They have lots of money, Ger? You can buy your way out, too?" He replies, "Yes, you must pay a lot to the Thai. Then you will get an interview."

Choua offers us some food. I noticed suddenly she is pregnant. "Four months," she says proudly. "You beat me to it," I tell her. She knows my desire to have a child when I return home. Ger, however, not understanding, explains patiently, "She will have the baby before you, Lynel." He is offended when we laugh. Her pregnancy makes me wonder whether they intend to resettle. Ger often says that a fourth child will make life in the United States more difficult.

One morning shortly thereafter, the JVA fleet no longer comes into the camp. What has been a turning point for some is yet another closed door for the majority. The Vangs never make the list. Forty interviews a day in ten days leaves some 4,600 on the list to go. Those remaining wonder when JVA will return again. "Will it be another fourteen months? Is there enough time? Was this the last bus?" Although JVA has promised to return with INS after Christmas, those who have had their interview no longer lord their newly acquired status over their neighbors, but worry instead, "Will they keep that promise?"

In 1986, the U.S. refugee quota worldwide is 61,000.[19] The Hmong allocation of approximately 7,000 is not met, although JVA approves over 90 percent of those interviewed. Only Xiong appears relieved when JVA no longer comes. Involved with her ceremonies, she is her usual cheerful self. One of these days Ger may buy a ticket on the bus, but the affidavits she feared so much are for naught. Meanwhile, the family prepares for New Year's, as colder mornings signal the approaching festival.

Land of the Ancestors

Pere was sitting in his small office near the chapel when I arrived. He planned to leave again soon to work with Hmong in France. He had lived and worked with Hmong in many places— in Laos, China, France, the United States, and French Guiana. Speaking in French, I asked him how camp life had changed the lives of the Hmong. He replied, "Ban Vinai is a depressing place, their life is narrowing out more and more over time. Before they had a life revolving around the seasons, the planting—here, they cannot really work. When they leave, their life expands again."

He gestured in an hourglass fashion, with his hands widening, narrowing, and then widening again. "I am always depressed when I come to Ban Vinai; I don't like to come any more. Here, people make only dreams."

An elderly Hmong woman walked in and greeted him with great emotion. The woman resembled Xiong, not in her shamanic state but in her daily appearance. She told Pere her troubles in Hmong. He answered in Hmong, paused, and explained in French, "Like this one, only dreams." Others entered and they exchanged stories and tapes, letters for Pere to

TEN

A New Year

From this gateway, Moment, a long, eternal lane leads backward: behind us lies an eternity

Nietzsche, p. 270

169

carry to friends and relatives overseas. When Pere spoke Hmong, his whole appearance changed. He was more animated, more expressive, less ironic, and more elderly.

Pere was as old or older than the oldest man in the room, but I always thought of him as ageless, or at least as young as other relief workers. I realized that he was more aware of death than the rest of us and less afraid. That is why he warned us not to fear things that had not yet happened: another border skirmish, being kicked out of the camp, or pushbacks across the border. But, when the worst events came to pass, he understood them the best. He understood our human frailty, incompleteness, and capacity for evil. Pere's god was not naive.

The others left and we returned to our conversation. A brief shower began. The rain was unusual, an unexpected diversion for this time of year. As the drops clattered on the tin roof, I moved the tape recorder closer to Pere. I asked why he decided to go to Laos and work with the Hmong. Pere looked briefly surprised, then sat back, and replied:

Because I was a priest, you see. The reason. The priests are sent to teach in all nations, you know we are sent to places around the world. Around twelve years old, I knew. It was during a retreat of my first communion. It was at school, we were about fifty boys then. I was going to the school, was already on its grounds. I know the exact place, the moment when I knew, the house we were passing in front of, and from that moment I never changed my mind. Before that they would ask me, 'Do you want to be a priest?' and I would always say "no" but that day, that moment, that second, I decided.

Then, you could be a priest in your own country or overseas. When I did my seminary studies in my country, I studied mission work. When I was fifteen or sixteen I used to think I wanted to be a priest in an Eskimo congregation. But little by little, I changed to Laos. It took a long time. That's another story though.

He paused and continued,

When I finished my studies, I had wanted to be a priest in a mission country. At the end of my studies, I asked the Superior if I might go to Japan, Ceylon, Chad, or Laos. And then, I was given Laos.

I was a professor and I taught Laotian. I worked a day and half; I was impassioned with my work. At the end of my second year, my bishop sent me to Luang Prabang in a mountainous region without precise directives, *without precise directives!* In 1948, no, that was finished . . . in 1948, that was, you see, I went to Laos and in the beginning of 1950 that I took a bicycle and I rode around for a month. There was a road that went. . . . I didn't have a plan, I had no plan! I was looking for where I was going to be a missionary or where I was going to teach the word of God. That was all. No more, that was all. There was no one to say this is how it must be. And, that's how it happened like that.

I was all alone, it was for me to look and decide and thus, there was a road going. The first time I went twenty kilometers down it and got to a village and then returned home. That was a Lao village. Three or four days later, I went further down this road and the second day, the second night, I reached a mountain of 1,400 meters although I didn't know whether there were Hmong there. But, I saw the Hmong along the route and I decided I wanted to spend the night there that evening. We weren't there yet, only the beginning, but there was a village higher up on the summit at 500 meters. And, I waited until the evening when the Hmong returned from their fields and I went to spend the night.

That was my first meeting with the Hmong. I didn't speak their language. I didn't know, I didn't have a plan or any idea to go there, but as in this case, there is a Providence which exists, you see. And that's how it happened like that.

"How did you communicate at first. Did you speak Lao?" I asked. "We spoke Laotian at first in their fashion of speaking Laotian." (He gave examples of the Lao words for "mother" and "father" in the Hmong dialect and repeated them in Hmong.) "It was their fashion of speaking in Luang Prabang."

He continued his story:

In any case, I passed one night and I returned fifteen days later and then, went back and then the third time I moved in. I was nine years in the village on this mountain. In the fourth year I converted my first Christian, the shaman I've told you about before. It was called the mountain of the Buffalo, of the Wild Buffalo. And, it was there that I learned the language, that I transcribed the writing, that I taught my first catechist, my first translation—all alone, all alone with the Hmong.

He paused, remembering those years. I asked him about his plans. We talked about his present work and about the future but I was never certain whether he spoke about himself or the Hmong. He replied: "I must wait here until they are able to overcome their problems. One doesn't have the right to abandon them like that. The ideal would be, for the present, for the Hmong to be in China. But finally, one doesn't know the future."

He laughed and continued, "Perhaps, I, too, will die in China. That wouldn't displease me. I would consider it like a reward." "You want to die in China? Like the Hmong?" I asked. He laughed again and said, "Yes, in the country of the ancestors. In the country of the ancestors."

I saw then how historical events had woven Pere's life history to that of the Hmong's—through peace and war, from Laos to the camp. However, each found their future in the other's past: Pere in his acceptance of the ancestors and the Hmong in the modern nation state.

I realized suddenly that the rain had ceased. The roosters who crowed the end of the rain had also ceased.

Festival of Remembrance

In the ensuing days as New Year's approaches, such conversations are rare. In this week everything changes. Gone is the usual tedium and boredom of daily camp life. Where once New Year's punctuated intense labor and the harsh conditions of life in the mountains, it now revives, transforms, and transports the Ban Vinai residents from their usual state of waiting.[1] The planning and enactment of the events also restore the Hmong's traditional productive cycle again. Men provide and slaughter animals and women prepare feasts. Briefly the daily tensions between men and women dissipate. With each day of planning, the excitement heightens visibly throughout the camp.

Ger bribes his way to Loei, a large market town, to buy new shoes for his cousin's arrival. His Rhode Island relatives, Chia and his wife, have already landed in Bangkok and are trying to obtain camp passes from the Ministry of Interior. Eagerly anticipating their arrival, Ger hopes Chia will find a way to sponsor him to America. I warn Ger not to expect too much, but such warnings are irrelevant in the festivities. The Thaos, too, plan a large feast, which Seng announces will include my farewell. When I protest, he commands, "No, you must come. Everyone has been invited already. We are going to kill a pig." Chanthanom and Khamsai, who as Buddhists celebrate New Year's in April, join in the planning by making special rice cakes to sell at the parade.

New Year's brings Hmong from America, Australia, France, and other parts of Thailand to Ban Vinai. In the costumes and festivities the refugee and alien identities of a dispersed people are forgotten. New Year's in the camp allows them to be Hmong again and keeps their dreams of a homeland alive. But, because this New Year's marks the eleventh year in the camp, a year beyond the decade that the international and Thai community gave for the refugee problem to be solved, there is some foreboding that this may be the last festival in Ban Vinai. As in every renewal, there is also an ending.

The camp commander convenes an interagency meeting. The meeting gives the officials the necessary sense of being in control, but the important events are organized elsewhere within a kinship network that extends across national boundaries. The camp commander announces that in this year's festivities, Ban Vinai will celebrate family planning and opium detoxification. Underlying the opium detoxification theme is the broader concern of both the Volags and the camp administration that the drug trade is increasing and that it accounts for the growing prosperity of a few elite. The camp commander asks the Volags and Hmong leaders to address these issues in the parade and exhibitions.

Pierre objects loudly. He argues that New Year's is a traditional Hmong ceremony that should not be used for Thai political ends. The camp commander nods and turns to the next speaker. Pere protests that the Thai are forcing an involuntary birth control program on the Hmong. The commander smiling replies, "Of course you Catholics would say that." Anika refuses to attend. She thinks that too much fuss is being made about a pagan ceremony and leaves on vacation early. UN-HCR has no comment. The UNHCR field officer is mainly worried that his refugee staff will go on strike if he does not provide marching uniforms. From his perspective, the New Year's comes at an inopportune time. JVA and INS are returning and his staff have new lists to prepare.

Only the Hmong leaders go along with the commander and give him his day. They know that a parade and few exhibits will not affect the world market price for opium or a clan's sense of survival. They have already scheduled the important meetings and ceremonies after the official celebration, when most of the relief staff will have left for vacation but when Hmong from overseas will have arrived.

Looking back later, Pierre and other purists, who nurture dreams of a village New Year's, will claim that this one was not up to par. Pierre fears that the staged and forced events of the first two days foretell the death of Hmong New Year's. But he and other critics bow out before the camp recaptures its village character later in the week.

Opening ceremonies begin late Sunday afternoon. I join Sri, Blia, and others in the crowd at the Catholic church. In the churchyard, Pere, adorned in white robes and a Hmong-embroidered stole, stands with a

Hmong catechist in the middle of a crowd. In the center of the court-yard, parishioners have planted two stakes with a garland of green leaves stretched across them. Pere raises his right arm and we circle the poles four times, twice clockwise and twice counterclockwise. Mean-while, Pere and the catechist spray us with sprigs of leaves dipped in holy water. "This is the traditional Hmong ceremony," explains the French sister proudly. Hai participates with her children, but Seng, since his marriage to Moua, stays away from the church. After ushering out the old and hailing the new, the crowd disperses.

In the Vang neighborhood, a male shaman, dressed in black, incants a traditional New Year's opening. He waves a red-beaked cock in an arc overhead. Again, the crowd circles around laureled posts. Ger carries his infant son, while Choua stands with other women, who watch over a steaming pot. Throughout Hmong neighborhoods and compounds, men, women, and children of all ages usher out the old year and in the new.

After the ceremony, Ger carefully sets aside the whisky I bring for the household's feast. Inside the kitchen, he joins Xiong and Choua, who are plucking white chicken feathers. Although he cannot afford a pig, Ger pays the inflated price for a white cock in the Thai market. The white bring good fortune. As the feathers fly around the room, Ger to no avail tries to organize his sons, who are chasing the feathers. Even-tually, Xiong restores order by giving each child a leg to pluck.

Elsewhere, Seng and his brother are drinking. Seng sets aside the whisky I offer until a crowd of young men approaches. They come bear-ing books commemorating this year's festival. Seng invites them in and they gather inside the kitchen for a second ceremony. Seng with his brother stands at the head of the house altar, while other family mem-bers form a semicircle with the visitors around the altar. Welcoming the group, Seng offers Catholic prayers and traditional greetings to the spir-its. They bless the books and the men toast one another with small cups of whisky. Slightly inebriated and warmed by the whisky, Seng, his brother, and the young men stumble out into the cold twilight air.

Hai cooks her first of many feasts. Blia and Chia talk of nothing but *pov pob* ("play ball"). They suddenly seem very young again. Blia brings out new sarongs and laced white blouses, which Seng has bought in the Thai market. Sri, however, is surprisingly quiet. "What are you wear-ing?" I ask. She replies, "The Hmong dress."

Blia asks excitedly, "Will you play *pov pob* with me, Lynel?" Chia is more reserved about asking, but throws a ball to see if I can catch prop-erly. When they see I cannot, the children demonstrate the proper way to throw a curve underhand and catch overhand while conversing and singing. Since young men and women woo one another in this yearly event, Blia practices more seriously.[2] Sri and Chia tease her about her suitor, but she does not deny the importance of the impending games. Even as we speak, her talcum-faced suitor arrives on his bicycle. Skidding down the hill, he lands in a heap at the door. The children laugh uproariously while he calmly dusts himself off and pays his respects to Hai. Sri, however, disappears until he leaves again.

As we sit talking, Hai's older stepbrother asks if I know Seng has been drinking. "Seng Thao always drinks a lot," he asserts and then asks, "Do you know Seng has a lot of women? I hear he has a new one." Sri and Chia, Seng's children, listen without expression. I am silent. To my embarrassment, Seng appears as the teenager finishes speaking. Seng, showing no expression, thanks me for the whisky and observes approvingly, "Hmong New Year's is a time for drinking." Later, Hai reports, "Seng stays home now." Moua, the second wife, has conveniently disappeared.

As evening falls, the night gets very cold. I wrap layers of cloth around me, but the cold seeps in between the edges. In the morning, I see my breath in the chilled air and there is frost on the ground. "This cold is usual," Sri claims, "Not the coldest, yet."

Vashi wanders into the hut. He speaks excitedly in Hmong, forgetting that I cannot understand him. Sri laughingly translates in Lao, "Your pig is under the house." Seng has tied the animal to the hut's underposts and when the enormous pig bellows, the floor shakes.

As the cold lingers, the official parade, shrouded in the early morning fog, begins. Refugee workers and staff line up by Volag. The staff wear T-shirts proclaiming their agencies' work in slogans such as, "My mystical body is suffering" or "Food for the Hungry." A few borrow traditional dress from Hmong and Mien, which the workers themselves wear. One Volag proudly dons clown-style hats and several Hmong adopt new "turkey" hats imported from the States. Pierre disparages the new styles: "They are being Americanized." When I protest, "A culture is not alive that is not constantly changing," he laughs and says, "You are always so refreshingly optimistic. I look forward to your interpretations."

Primary school children line up by form with their teachers. The children's parents and grandparents have dressed them in traditional skirts, necklaces, turbans, and brocaded and embroidered jackets. Few can afford the traditional heavy silver necklace or silver coined brocade, but tin necklaces and Royal Lao coins bought in Chiang Mai markets provide the same effect. Fathers and sons are dressed in traditional black hats, jackets, and pants. Different groups carry banners in Lao and Hmong proclaiming their agencies' mission. At the head of one, a banner proclaims, "May there be peace in the world for refugees."

The parade, a brilliant profusion of color, weaves through the camp, while bystanders watch and comment on the costumes. The parade resembling elements of a village Buddhist procession and an American half-time is very camp. Periodically, the entire parade halts as someone in the crowd recognizes a friend and takes a photograph or exchanges the traditional greeting, "*Nyob zoo noj tsiab.*" The procession finishes at the soccer field in front of the camp commander's headquarters and the UNHCR Field Office. There, Volags line up in rows facing a bandstand of dignitaries; the provincial governor, camp commander, UNHCR officials, and the Hmong leader. The dignitaries speak and primary school children perform Thai dances. The camp commander releases balloons into the sky to open the "official" New Year's.

Following the ceremonies, dignitaries tour Volag exhibitions on family planning and opium detoxification. COERR has nothing on either topic, but has planned to appease the commander with slides of America. Unfortunately, the electricity fails to function and the dignitaries pass through quickly. By early afternoon many relief workers leave for vacation, while the Ban Vinai residents disperse for family celebrations.

Blia, Sri, and Chia play their first of many days of *pov pob.* These games take place in many compounds throughout the camp. On the first day, they practice for the more formal games and wear ordinary clothes. Boys and girls form two lines on opposite sides and gracefully throw small rubber balls while singing. Since Sri and Chia have not yet come of age, they play with one another and any passerby they can persuade to join them. These first ceremonies allow the younger ones to practice and Blia to show off her skills to her talcum-faced suitor, who aloofly watches with his friends on the sidelines. Vashi and Mee Lor admire nearby and pick up stray balls. Blia pretends not to notice the young man watching her intently, but positions herself appropriately. The children play until dusk when Hai sends word for them to return.

That evening, the children sing in several languages—Hmong, Lao, Thai, English, and finally, "Alouette" in French. They recite chants they have learned for New Year's, at the Thai primary school, and at the Catholic church. Hai joins them and suggests other songs to the children. In the midst of the revelry, Seng reaches in the door and takes Pao off Sri's lap. The singing ceases and the room falls silent. Seng is dressed up with his hair slicked back, Elvis Presley style. Pao protests, but is quickly taken away. Hai asks Chia to follow his father. Folding his arms across his chest, Chia refuses. "Follow him," his sisters plead, but he refuses.

When the sound of Seng's motorcycle fades in the distance, Hai says disapprovingly, "miá nɔ̀ɔj" [Lao: small wife].[3] "Difficult?" I ask. She nods. "I think I would shoot Dennis." She laughs and the remark breaks the tension. "How do you know Dennis doesn't have a miá nɔ̀ɔj?" she asks. "I don't know but I can always divorce him." She listens intently. "It is difficult with the children." "I don't like her!" asserts Sri. "She is not good, too many problems. But, Seng has had many women, she is not the first," observes Hai.

"How long have you been married?" I ask. "Twelve years—we married in Vientiane." Hai, pointing to another child in the room, adds, "Her mother's husband has a miá nɔ̀ɔj, too. And Mai's mother is a miá nɔ̀ɔj. There are many." "Do the women agree?" I ask. "No," Hai replies. "But you make all the money sewing," I protest. "Yes," she asserts proudly, "we do." Her daughters listen carefully except Blia, who has little interest in hearing about conflicts between men and women and waits for her boyfriend. Hai smiles at her innocence and remarks, "I hope she marries this one. He is a good boy."

Blia's suitor arrives and they leave for the films that have been scheduled for New Year's. "I want to go to the U.S. next year," Hai says when her daughter has left. "How will you go?" I ask, wondering if she will divorce Seng. "You won't go!" challenges Sri. "I'll go." "Alone?" I ask. "Yes," Hai nods, "My brother in California will help us." "You won't go!" Sri challenges again but Hai disagrees.

Early the next morning the fog comes in through the slats of the hut. Rolling in waves over and through the mountains, it fills the hollow in which lies the camp. The fog is so thick that it sounds and feels like rain and muffled sounds in the distance bounce off the wall. Seng Thao suddenly appears returning on his motorcycle. Looking like a gecko caught in a corner, he quickly parks the bike and slips quietly into the kitchen.

I leave to visit Chanthanom and Khamsai. When I arrive they are writing letters abroad. Chanthanom writes in French to her godparents, an elderly Lao couple who sent them 400 baht (about $15). She requests sweaters for the children for winter. "What winter?" I ask, but she regards this weather as very cold. "Will it be colder in the U.S.?" she asks concerned. I nod. In the letter she sends two photographs, one of the whole family silhouetted by a painted mountain scene taken in the camp photography store, and the other of the twins with their arms around each other. "You all look sad in these photographs," I comment. Chanthanom agrees, "I know, we must have sad faces. We are refugees."

When she begins a second letter in Lao to their cousin in Georgia, Khamsai protests. Although Khamsai had been the cousin's guardian in the camp, he says: "He has forgotten us and is happy now. He doesn't need us, we shouldn't bother him, but Chanthanom wants to write. I, myself, don't write. If he needed us then I would write."

"My brother paid for his education," Khamsai adds. "Maybe, he will help you?" I say. "No," he replies.

"I think and think about what is happening to my children. There is not enough to eat, I worry about that. We should go to Napho," Khamsai concludes. "Are you worried about the future?" I ask him. "No, about now," he replies. "I worry about the future," I tell him. He laughs and says: "I worry about the present. I cannot think about the future, I know nothing about it. I don't know the third country. I worry about the present, you the future."

Another elderly lowland Lao joins our conversation. "Some people drink whisky to sleep when they can't," he suggests. "I drink wine," I respond. Khamsai laughs again at this and adds, "Some whisky helps but I just keep thinking, worrying." Our conversation ends as he and Chanthanom leave to sell more cakes at the *pov pob* grounds.

The second night of New Year's is colder than the first. The Thao household huddles together in the inner room. Blia, Sri, and Mai fall quickly asleep, exhausted by the games, but Chia and Vashi stay awake for fear that they will miss the pig slaughter. "Go to sleep!" Seng grumbles. At three in the morning, when all are fast asleep, Seng's younger nephew arrives. Vashi and Chia awake instantly and follow their father outside. Stirring, Blia pulls the covers around us to cover the empty spaces left by warm bodies. The noise of muffled voices and of a screeching pig grows louder. As the nephew hauls the animal up the stone steps to the kitchen, the women stir.

Inside the kitchen, Hai directs her daughters to heat pots of water. The steaming water warms the room. The women hang large black pots over the hearth and then join the men outside. The night is so cold that the men's breaths hang in the air as they work. Setting a plastic tarpaulin on the steps, three men lie the pig on its side and tie its feet. The nephew scrapes its neck as others hold the struggling pig. The pig seems to know its end is imminent. As the nephew readies the knife, Vashi with rapt eyes leans over the animal. With a quick plunge, the nephew slits the throat and the pig bellows three times. With each wail, the women catch the blood gushing from its throat in bowls. After a few spasmodic kicks, the life drains out of the animal.

Smelling blood, several dogs come running, but the men kick them away and haul the carcass onto the tarpaulin. The women return with bowls of steaming water, which they pour over the hide. The men deftly skin the pig. Vashi squatting by the men imitates his elder's gestures. Poking at the carcass, he talks about the pig. His comments entertain his elders, but Chia stands back, reserved and embarrassed at his younger brother's nonsensical commentary. Seng, as the eldest present, supervises and leaves the actual labor to the younger men. Despite the chill, the men sweat as they work. Eventually, they build a fire to provide light and warmth until sunrise.

Inside the kitchen, Hai supervises the cooking. The nephew's wife brings her four small children, who lie sleeping in a corner of the room. She does most of the work. Although she is usually cold and reserved, she suddenly asks me as we squat by the boiling pots, "What kind of birth control do you use?" After we discuss various options, she says regretfully, "I once taught primary school for COERR. Now, I sew." I realize she misses her earlier work. "I would like to have a child," I tell her. She agrees and encourages me, "Have one soon." As the youngest child demands her attention, however, she warns, "I am always tired."

When Hai leaves momentarily, Blia and Sri take advantage of her absence to fall asleep on top of each other on a wooden cot by the fire. Youa and I laugh when we see them and she suggests I go back to bed, too. Hai, returning, tries to rouse them to no avail.

The next morning, the women continue cooking pots of pork over the fire. The rich smell of meat permeates the room. The nephew's wife has hung the pig's head on the rafters, and strips of smoking pork dangle from the beams. The warm rays of the sun dispel the morning chill. Inside the hut, Seng and Chia fold invitations to the feast in envelopes, which Seng's nephew distributes by motorcycle throughout the camp. Seng invites camp leaders and kin from every neighborhood. He encourages me to invite my own friends so I go to look for Pierre and Boonchan.

I find them playing *pov pob* with Sri and Blia. Sri wears a traditional white pleated skirt, jacket, silver necklace, and turban. With her hair up, she looks much older. Pierre and Boonchan play together. Blia plays seriously with her suitor. Sri stands on the sideline watching Blia. When Pierre and Boonchan admire her clothes, she does not reply.

Boonchan has borrowed a traditional Hmong dress. She complains that she has received several marriage offers from corpulent Americans, who lord their status and wealth over their camp kin. According to Boonchan, one asked her, "What do you think of Ban Vinai?" She countered, "What do you?" He replied, "It's very dirty, don't you think?" Pierre asks accusingly in French, "Why are Hmong Americans so conceited?" "Most Hmong Americans cannot afford to come to Ban Vinai," I respond.

At the Thaos' place, elderly men, wearing traditional black suits, are already gathered outside the hut. The eldest lights an opium pipe. Inside the kitchen, the women eat together first. When they invite me to join them, I feel honored to be treated as another woman and not as a guest. Hai then carries steaming bowls of pork to the guests who take their place at a long table set up behind the latrines. Pierre and Boonchan join the crowd and Hai and the children stand behind the table on both sides. Standing at the head, Seng asks the eldest man on his left to make offerings to the spirits. Seng follows with Catholic prayers. Next, following a Buddhist tradition Seng and the elders light candles, tie knotted strings on the guests' wrists, and offer blessings.

Placing an egg in my upturned palm, Seng explains: "Lynel has been a part of our family and we hers in Ban Vinai. When she came here, she spoke only a little Lao, but now she speaks very well and can speak a little Hmong. The next time when she returns, she will speak Hmong very well, too. Although we will miss her, we are happy that she has her number and is going to the third country."

The languages symbolize how much I understand, but still have yet to learn about them. The guests laugh and clap approvingly at his last comment. From then on, whenever we speak of my impending departure again, Boonchan says, "You've got your number to go."

Whisky and toasts flow freely. Seng reiterates that in these festivals women drink. Hai and her daughters bring plates of steaming pork, chicken, and vegetables to the table and the eating and drinking continues until the sun is overhead. Noticing my dizziness, Hai pulls me away. The men feast until the late afternoon, when a small number retreat with their pipes and whisky into the hut to discuss politics and their dream of recapturing the mountains.

That night, my last in Ban Vinai, the cold lessens. Seng snores heavily in a deep sleep. Next door, a grandfather quiets a child with a story. Later, I awake to hear a rat nibbling near my head. When I cry out, the children stir. Hai and Seng laugh and reassure me, "Just a rat, don't worry."

Later that night I am awakened by a gunshot or maybe the rats again.

The moonlight streams through the open slats of the still room. Between bamboo walls, I hear a couple arguing softly. A mother quiets a child in the distance. Drawing the mosquito net around me, I try to maintain the illusion that it protects me from falling rats. But, it cannot protect me from the mosquito that has found a hole. Scratching new bites, I turn on the flashlight to hunt for mosquitoes and rats.

Images of thousands of staring, sad, and hungry children's eyes, overflowing latrines that spill sewage in the streets, and streets that lead nowhere but back on themselves, appear. I turn and look at Seng, Hai, and the children, who are sleeping soundly, peacefully in the moonlight. In the distance, the sounds of the stream below us and a slight breeze from the mountains can be heard in the stillness. The couple in the next room cease. Sleep returns.

The next morning, Blia and Sri dress in new sarongs. Hai gathers the younger children and together the household, except Seng, sets out to call on kin and friend. Seng quietly slips away to find Moua.

Throughout the camp children play ball. In the Vang compound, the young sons watch the games of well-dressed young men and women. Ger and Choua are waiting for their relatives to arrive, but he is beginning to doubt whether they will get a pass. Ger has already calculated that he cannot afford the bus ticket to meet them in Chiang Mai. Plotting again how to buy his way out of the camp, Ger hands me a stack of quilts and asks, "Will you sell these quilts for me in America?" Inside the quilts, Ger has wrapped a piece of cloth for Dennis. We discuss how I should send Ger money for the quilts. Fearing that I might not understand money orders, Ger draws an example and demonstrates how I should complete his name and address. As I leave, Ger asks, "Will you remember to write in Lao?" Xiong is nowhere to be seen.

On the main soccer field, crowds of children play *pov pob*. The crowds pass on foot from one feast to the next. The usual official trucks and vans have disappeared. In a corner of the field, Chanthanom sells papaya salad. Khamsai complains, "I don't want her to. I told her to stop but she won't listen to me. She is stubborn." Chanthanom looks exhausted, but tells me she has already made several hundred baht which will pay for winter clothes from the Thai market for the children.

Khamsai asks about my future plans. "What are you going to write about? When will you finish? What will you do next? When will you have children? When will you return?" I am surprised at his sudden interest in the future. He then accuses, "I don't think you will come back here. You will forget us." "Look, Khamsai. I was here before in 1982 and I came back. And I'll come back again." He smiles. "You

181

were?" he says, "I didn't know that!" "You should go to Napho and apply to the United States," I say. He replies, "The going rate to buy Thai citizenship is five hundred dollars. Not much, but more than we have." After a short silence, he adds, "We will go to Napho soon."

Chanthanom reappears with cakes, which Choy and Tuy immediately try to grab. The cakes, covered in sugary white frosting, are slightly stale. The twins lick the sugar, while we drink iced coffee. As she wipes their mouths, Chanthanom pulls a silver bracelet from her sarong and offers it to me. I feel bad that I have no gift for her but she remonstrates, "Just write, don't forget us." Khamsai adds, "Don't just write about us and forget to come back." "I won't," I promise.

That afternoon Seng and his daughters walk me to Crossroads Cafe, where I catch a van out of camp.

A New Cycle

This final section portrays the characteristic depression that follows the New Year's ceremony. It is not based on direct observation in 1987, but on incidents later reported in letters and telephone conversations, and on observations of the camp after the New Year's ceremonies in other years.[4]

In January, the winds blow strong again. A thin sheet of ice spreads across the top of the well. In the morning, the people of Ban Vinai light fires to warm their cold rooms. The young girls shiver as they draw water from the well. In the Vang household, Ger, Choua, and the children huddle against one another for warmth until the youngest son's incessant coughing drives Ger outside.

Ger makes his daily trip to the market to see what he can barter in the early morning. Debris from the New Year's festivities, bits of colored paper, fly about in the wind. They are the only evidence that there ever was a festival. At the gates, the Thai guards are angry and abrupt. They demand to see his identity card. Finding little in the market for sale, Ger quickly returns home. On the way he passes the foreign doctor, who is just returning home, too. The doctor has spent a long night trying to revive a young girl whose boyfriend found another lover at New Year's. "Drank silver polish," she records wearily in a small black notebook.

In the compound, Ger's youngest son comes and sits on his lap. While Ger examines new boils on the child's head, he hears the commander announce over the camp loudspeaker, "From this day on, all refugees must obtain a special pass from my office to market at the gates."

Relief and Refugees

The continuing presence of refugees in camps, such as Ban Vinai, is a reminder that modern wars have long-term human consequences and costs. The devastation from conflict has been enormous. Nearly one million people have died in Afghanistan, more than a million in the Horn of Africa, at least one and half million in South Africa, and several thousands in the continuing conflict in Southeast Asia.[1] The end of the war in Southeast Asia left several million people homeless. Thousands were killed in Laos and more than a tenth of the country's population became refugees.

The refugees of Ban Vinai comprise a small fraction of the world's refugees who currently number some seventeen million (see figure 11.1) and the unenumerated, but countless more displaced internally from civil war. The number of officially counted refugees alone represents a quarter of the voting bloc of the United Nations.[2] Currently, the largest refugee populations come from Afghanistan, the Middle East, the Horn of Africa, and Mozambique, and the majority live in Pakistan, the West Bank, the Horn, and Malawi.[3] Each day hundreds more are displaced by war and conflict and the number of refugee and displaced people continues to grow. In many countries, conflict and famine are endemic.

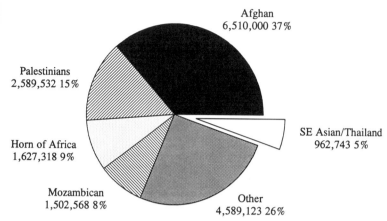

Afghan
6,510,000 37%

Palestinians
2,589,532 15%

SE Asian/Thailand
962,743 5%

Horn of Africa
1,627,318 9%

Mozambican
1,502,568 8%

Other
4,589,123 26%

Total: 17,781,284

FIGURE 11.1. Worldwide Refugee Populations (those accorded asylum), 1991.

Camps such as Ban Vinai, if remembered at all, often become foot-notes in history texts. The refugees themselves are rarely invited to the negotiation table in efforts to resolve such situations. Because many are minorities in some of the poorest countries in the world, governments have little strategic interest in protecting refugees' rights (although they are used to destabilize an opposition). The technological nature and magnitude of modern warfare also makes it increasingly difficult for both outsiders and the participants themselves to register the human impact. Aggressive acts are enumerated in casualties, body counts, or hits. War is waged through television and radar screens. There is an increasing faith in the clean strike, which is said to leave no refugees. The more common form of warfare, the guerrilla war, likewise does not distinguish civilian from combatant. Countless refugee movements go unrecorded, but even refugee movements that become crises fade quickly from the public eye.

   In our social science jargon and statistical reports about refugee situations, we can distance ourselves from the human tragedies and our own involvements. Writing about forms of violence is difficult without dehumanizing both the subject and the writer.[4] In choosing the narra-
184   tive genre, however, I hoped to convey the ordinariness of the refugee camp experience.[5] I also hoped to convey the complexity of the refugee

situation to show why the peace process is not simple or straightforward.

Although the events and interpretations I report are specific to Ban Vinai and other camps in Thailand, this narrative may be important in a larger sense because in many ways these camps established a pattern of relationships and interactions between refugees and the international relief system that is being replicated elsewhere. An understanding of the events in Ban Vinai may also suggest some of the limitations of our current forms of humanitarian assistance. Despite all the humanitarian concern, the people of Ban Vinai remain refugees. How and why is reviewed below.

The Relief Effort

The movements of Lao, Hmong, Khmer, and other Southeast Asians into Thailand after 1975 became a refugee crisis by 1979. Thailand refused to grant more than temporary local asylum and, with the help of international organizations, housed people in refugee camps such as Ban Vinai. In the aftermath of war, the U.S. government had little interest in addressing the political and economic forces underlying these migrations. The current political climate at the time did not allow the United States to support alternatives to resettlement nor did it suit U.S. political purposes.[6] At the same time, American involvement in the war created obligations to former allies, who were now suffering the aftermath. Famine, conflict, and political persecutions continued to generate new waves of refugees. Defining the situation as a refugee crisis suggested the failure of the new socialist regimes but did not permit the in-depth analysis of the particular political economic circumstances that continued to generate refugees. American foreign policy in the region became one of supporting refugee resettlement and the creation of human buffer zones along insecure borders.

For over a decade, resettlement was the only safe passage out of the Southeast Asian camps. American guilt over leaving allies behind and lands destroyed by heavy bombing allowed the Thai government to shift the refugee burden to the resettlement countries and to refuse local integration. Surrounded by poor countries and continuing conflict, the Thai struggled to maintain their own national boundaries and feared that local integration would only bring more refugees.

UNHCR officials concerned about the relative imbalance of funding that favored Southeast Asians over other refugees supported voluntary repatriation. They argued that large-scale resettlement and the camps' feeding programs (i.e., pull factors) drew refugees across the border. While arrival patterns supported their arguments, UNHCR failed or lacked the mandate to respond to the political and economic conditions that generated refugees (i.e., push factors).

Without other sources of support, UNHCR also allowed the Western voluntary agencies and the interests of Western governments to dominate the relief efforts. Although UNHCR continued to support a modest repatriation program and advocated voluntary repatriation and/or local integration, their funding and staffing allocations (a large share of which was paid for by the United States) suggested that they were administering a resettlement program.[7] By 1986, 80 percent of the refugees had been resettled in third countries and the majority in the United States (one million by 1990). According to a Congressional report: "Since 1979 Indochinese resettlement has dominated our refugee program, and that domination continues today with more than three-fourths of all U.S. refugee admissions being allocated to arrivals from Southeast Asia" (p. 1). Of the Laotian refugees, 75 percent of the lowland Lao were resettled (with approximately two-thirds going to the United States) and 50 percent of the Hmong.

During that same decade, a total of 39,821 persons left Ban Vinai for third countries. Although the majority of the Hmong would have qualified for resettlement, many preferred to wait in Ban Vinai. They waited for a variety of reasons: 1) they hoped Vang Pao's Resistance would bring them back to Laos, 2) they heard that life was difficult in the Western countries, and/or 3) they wanted to keep a place open in the camp for kin whose own political and economic future was tenuous in Laos. From 1986 to the present, however, the Hmong and other ethnic groups in Ban Vinai have faced increasing pressure to resettle in the United States. Beginning in 1985, the Thai renewed push-backs across the border for those trying to enter the camp. With growing camp populations (partially due to natural increases), the Thai reiterated that the refugees would not be welcome in Thailand. In 1986, repatriation was no closer in sight. Under mounting pressure from the Thai government, approximately 8,000 Hmong sought resettlement in 1987 and again in 1988. Even as this new cycle of third-country resettlement started again, the Thai government and others worried about the pull factor. Would increased resettlement opportunities bring more refugees?

In June 1989, a decade after the first, a second Conference on Indochinese Refugees was held in Geneva. This second conference unfortunately made little attempt to address the underlying political, economic, and social problems in the region that continued to generate refugees. Conferees proposed yet another set of screening procedures, which have been subsequently implemented with limited success, to distinguish "economic" from "bona fide" refugees. The conference primarily focused on the Vietnamese refugees in the Hong Kong camps and the Laotians once again were mentioned only in passing. What principally emerged from the conference was a recognition on the part of Thailand and other asylum countries in the region that the Western donors were closing their doors to new arrivals.

The international community's failure to achieve a political resolution led to actions by Thailand and other ASEAN countries to resolve the refugee situation themselves. The end of the cold war also paved the way for regional negotiations. The Thai government began negotiating with the Laotian government for the refugees' repatriation. Internally, the government moved to consolidate the camps and to screen out all but 10 percent of the new arrivals. They encouraged people to resettle and moved others to Napho and Chiang Kham camps. In December 1990, the government forcibly repatriated a group of new Hmong arrivals, who had been "screened out."

Tensions also lessened between Thailand and Laos, and trade increased between the two regions. The Australian and Japanese governments financed the construction of a bridge across the Mekong from Nong Khai to Vientiane. (The project is scheduled to be completed in 1992.) During 1988 and 1989, the Vietnamese had also pulled out their 30,000 to 40,000 troops that had been stationed in Laos. With the lessening of the Vietnamese presence, the Thai and Laotian governments were again more willing to reassert their common ethnic and linguistic ties.

In 1992, the Thai government plans to close Ban Vinai and move the remaining 26,000 Hmong to Chiang Khan for their eventual repatriation to Laos. Although UNHCR supports the repatriation program, they have only a small staff in Vientiane. A few Volags have moved their programs to Laos, but the current level of services and infrastructure in rural Laos is far below that of the camp.

Relations between Thailand and Laos have improved and the Thai would prefer to expand their trade with Laos rather than maintain a buffer zone along their border. As early as 1990, the Laotian government began opening its markets to free trade and investment.[8] The World Bank has also provided a loan for the Laotian government to restructure its economy.

The Laotian government has said that it will accept the refugees provided they do not engage in resistance and they encourage those who are willing to invest in Laos to come home. At the national level, at least, there is a willingness to accept most refugees back into Laotian society. However, life continues to be difficult for many Hmong in Laos. The government is encouraging them to settle in the lowlands and to give up opium and swidden farming. Although the government has environmental and political concerns (e.g., in the case of opium, an interest in receiving U.S. aid), crop substitution programs have been largely unsuccessful. There is also evidence that the health and economic status of many Hmong who have been resettled has declined.[9] Thus, how and where the refugees will settle will be critical to the success of the repatriation process.

Despite the favorable political climate, Ban Vinai, like the postwar European camps, is not quickly dismantled. As late as 1991, many people in the camp were not persuaded that life would be better elsewhere or that their security could be assured outside the camp. Although 7,000 Laotians had voluntarily repatriated, only 400 Hmong were among them. Some 54,000 Hmong remained in the Thai camps.[10] UNHCR efforts to persuade the Hmong to repatriate were largely unsuccessful. Many feared to be caught in the crossfire between the Laotian government and the Hmong Resistance again. They also waited for their leaders to decide. Although the Hmong leadership in Ban Vinai was willing to negotiate repatriation, progress was slow. The Resistance continued sporadically in Laos and there was little trust on either side.

Long years of camp life had also changed the lives of the Hmong and lowland Lao. Over 75 percent in Ban Vinai had lived there for more than a decade. Their children had grown up in the camp and had little or no experience of life outside. Experiences of camp life affected their perceptions of the larger world and would affect their eventual acculturation to life in Laos or in third countries.

The Effects of Camp Life

Many of the same processes that occur in refugees' adjustment to life in the United States began in Ban Vinai. As in their adjustment to in the United States, former swidden and rice paddy farmers adapted in the camp to an urban welfare system and Western organizational forms. They depended on UN food rations for their subsistence. Their children received more formal schooling than their elders and lived very different lives. Differences between the generations developed that were reflected in variant aspirations. The youngest generation, who spoke the languages required for work, was more likely to seek and obtain Volag employment. They became translators for their parents, who often had little contact with the relief community. The elders continued familiar routines: looking after grandchildren, smoking opium, telling stories, and carrying out traditional ceremonies.

In the camp's marginal economy, women earned the majority of the household income from sale of their handicrafts. Some men exploited their wives' labor and took second and third wives to enhance their economic status. Tensions between men and women, at times, resulted in wife abuse and in the increased subordination of the woman in the household. Men sat idle and unemployed or in the case of a few, engaged in an underground black market economy of opium trafficking. Men and boys also joined the Resistance, in part out of frustration and powerlessness, to give meaning to their lives. Girls, expected to carry on cultural traditions in face of a rapidly changing and urbanized society, committed or attempted suicide when traditional romantic ideals failed to materialize. The lack of a future for all camp inhabitants engendered anomie and boredom.

Camp life required unique adaptations. The camp's separation from its surroundings divorced the refugees from their traditional patterns of production based on a seasonal cycle. Since the Thai government did not want Ban Vinai and other camps to become permanent asylums, they refused to let the refugees develop new forms of production and opportunities which would have connected them to the larger world to which they now belong.

Without access to a productive life, certain interactions with the international community became critical events for those who inhabited a place where time was no longer punctuated by seasonal cycles. An event, such as the processing interview, punctuated the waiting and allowed for further migrations. In these moments, camp inhabitants assumed new identities as refugees vis-à-vis the outside world, and during the interview, they reconstructed the past in terms accessible to the country of immigration. Resettlement also provided access to new resources and for further migrations. Yet, not all camp inhabitants chose this alternative and while they waited in the camp, they reconstructed familiar routines. New Year's became a critical event marking the passage of camp years and camp inhabitants' attempts to maintain traditional identities.

Institutional interactions with outsiders created new forms of consciousness that affected the sense of self and preservation of traditional identities. These interactions mediated by larger political mandates were subtle and complex. The Thai offered asylum and yet treated camps as human buffer zones. UNHCR administrators offered relief and yet complained that camp inhabitants were becoming welfare dependents. Volag workers identified with the refugees' plight, but took advantage of their vulnerability to proselytize or to assert the Volags' own forms of organization. On their part, camp inhabitants utilized multiple identities to survive. Despite these variant responses, the different actors were nevertheless powerless to affect the larger political and historical forces that created Ban Vinai.

Distancing through refugee consciousness, relief workers often treated the Hmong or lowland Lao as the "other." Despite the desire to provide humanitarian assistance, some relief workers were unwilling to admit that they, too, could be refugees or if they recognized that possibility, feared to acknowledge it and distanced themselves from the situation. However, others came to respect each other's differences and choices. Many relief workers were altruistic and recognized how the circumstances of modern life and a common history had connected the Hmong and lowland Lao across space and time to their own lives.[11]

Hmong and lowland Lao in the camp placed their trust in an institution and in anonymous and distant forces.[12] By so doing, they could easily deny that they were arbiters of their own destinies. Their decision to wait in the camp, however, was a conscious decision as well as their decision to follow one set of leaders as opposed to another. The Hmong who remained in Ban Vinai had choices and chose to remain in the camp. Many elders, in particular, believed that Ban Vinai was the best place—given the circumstances—to maintain their way of life.

Return to Laos

The political situation in Southeast Asia has changed as should America's role in the region. Laotians are still suffering from the aftermath of war but their suffering is of a different kind. Without a Marshall Plan, they are one of the poorest nations in the world. According to observers, many Hmong and Lao living in former war zones lack the livestock and means to initiate new agricultural production.[13] Fields on the Plain of Jars continue to be devastated by antipersonnel bombs, known as "bombis" by the Laotians. Sporadic conflict between the Hmong Resistance and LPDR continues to drive villagers out of their homes to refugee camps or lowland settlements. Although screening programs and the likelihood of repatriation are lessening the flow across the border to Thailand, economic and political conditions in Laos continue to force involuntary migrations.

As a major power the United States can play a constructive role in regional Southeast Asian politics; particularly, in the repatriation of the refugees. The United States should support the current negotiations for the Hmong and Lao's eventual repatriation, but at the same time, ensure that the refugees are well-represented in the negotiation process. The United States can also play an important role in ensuring that repatriation is voluntary. Not every refugee will want to repatriate nor can their safety be assured. Some refugees may not be welcome in Laos. Former Resistance fighters, who have not given up their dreams of recapturing the mountains, cannot easily repatriate. Thus, the United States should continue to offer resettlement for these "former allies" and/or negotiate their eventual integration into Thailand.[14]

Resettlement costs are high and resettling the remaining 54,000 Hmong alone would cost the United States $216 million (at an estimated initial resettlement cost of $4,000 per person). That money could be spent on development assistance to Laos for repatriation. The literacy rate in Laos is around 45 percent and infant mortality rate 109 per 1,000.[15] The country suffers a shortage of trained personnel and a poor infrastructure. Some regions are accessible only by river and it can take several days to travel up-country.

To date, most of U.S. assistance has been for food aid and a very limited amount for medical supplies and prosthetics. As of 1990, U.S. assistance to Laos ($11,425,000) averaged the amount spent for five days of the nine years of bombing during the war.[16] Improving U.S. levels of economic aid and diplomatic relations with Laos and Vietnam could help to alleviate the economic conditions that create refugee movements. The aid program should be expanded to support the government's current efforts to restructure their economy and to develop the rural areas, where many Hmong live. The Hmong American Mutual Assistance Associations (MAAs) and other Volags could also provide assistance to the rural areas (rather than continuing to support Resistance efforts and/or refugee camp programs).

At the international level, the United States and other Western donors should support the United Nations' and regional efforts to resolve refugee conflicts through negotiated political settlements. In taking the lead on resettlement operations, the United States used its resources to dictate its own refugee policies to UNHCR. In contrast, in Africa and other regions, the United States has played an effective advocacy role. However, increasing cutbacks for UNHCR are seriously hampering the organization's ability to respond effectively to new emergencies (see figure 2.1). These cutbacks are occurring, even as the number of refugees worldwide is increasing. The Western donors, justifying the reduced funding levels, blame UNHCR's internal administrative problems. Rather than focusing on the organization's limitations, the United States and other donors should broaden their base of support and ensure that UNHCR acts impartially to represent the world's refugees. With such support, UNHCR is better positioned than either individual governments or Volags to represent the human rights and legal concerns of refugees.

Refugees and displaced persons by their very existence challenge the legitimacy of a nation's claims to sovereignty and representativeness. Through the creation of camps, the international system allows nations to maintain their repressive policies toward minority groups and to expel dissenters. Rather than being forced to recognize the claims of its minority peoples (in some cases, the majority as well), a country such as Laos can continue to reject the Hmong. Likewise, rather than being forced to negotiate their claims with the new regime, the Hmong flee across the border. Although in the initial stages of conflict, refugee camps may protect a people's survival, ultimately long-term camp life ensures their marginalization.

The international relief community is faced with a dilemma: how to make an international system based on the sovereignty of the nation state representative and responsive to the needs of all people. Although international force may be an alternative, in practice, military intervention does not guarantee the protection of human rights. Military interventions also inevitably create more refugees. Unless there are considerable common political and economic interests involved, the international community will also be reluctant to intervene militarily.

More promising are recent attempts to resolve refugee situations at local, national, and regional levels. At the local level, relief workers and refugees themselves often find ways to bring about substantive changes in their lives by creating new means of production and through new relationships, ceremonies, and forms of artistic expression. Certain aspects of camp life, such as increased education, training, and political awareness, may ultimately facilitate a minority peoples access to and acculturation into larger political economies. In some refugee situations, local inhabitants have welcomed refugees into their communities and recognize that refugees are a resource rather than a burden.

Promising negotiations are occurring in southern Africa to resolve civil conflicts at regional and national levels. However, as in the case of the Hmong, regional and national negotiations must also take into account local concerns. Too often refugees, local residents, and relief workers are excluded from debates and negotiations that ultimately affect their lives and work. By involving them more directly in negotiations, refugee and displaced peoples too can become part of the process of making and sustaining peace.

Current domestic debates about refugees often center around distinguishing economic from political refugees. As this narrative suggests, however, such distinctions oversimplify complex social, historical, and political economic processes. Hmong, lowland Lao, and other refugees in Ban Vinai do not fit the neat categories of political or economic refugees. Political refugees are often those who can afford to buy their way out of a camp and have overseas connections. In Ban Vinai, the political elite and the leaders with close ties to the Americans left early on. As in the postwar European camps, the poor, the elderly, the disabled, women, and children remained. As in many refugee situations, Ban Vinai also sheltered a Resistance, who continued the conflict.

The people of Ban Vinai, as this narrative has shown, are not passive victims that the category "refugee" implies. Camp inhabitants exploit national, institutional, and religious differences within the international community to their own political advantage. The mutual construction of a refugee identity by the international community and camp inhabitants is an ideological convenience. For the international community, it bought time in conducting the difficult negotiations, which meant recognizing the new political alignments in the region. For many camp residents, Ban Vinai nourished their dreams of recapturing their homelands and kept generations together. Life in the camp taught them the power of waiting. Meanwhile, they acculturated to a modern, Western institution and its organizational forms. Camp life socialized them to urban poverty and to being a marginalized people, even as it allowed them to resist by waiting.

The continuing presence of camps such as Ban Vinai remind us that peace does not come easily. It often takes years and sometimes generations to create a lasting peace. But, peace will not happen unless all parties have a stake in its outcome. Peace requires political will, but also from a people's standpoint a recognition that the past will be preserved in their children's future.

When I return to Ban Vinai in 1990, Chiang Khan is caught up in the economic boom that sweeps the rest of Thailand.[1] The last stop on the bus line is now listed in the *Lonely Planet Guide* as a popular haunt for world travelers looking for authentic Thailand. Bright neon signs point the way to the military base, post office, and newly renovated customs house. Commercial traffic between Chiang Khan and Loei is increasing. The bus from Bangkok, which often ended its run at Loei because there were not enough passengers to warrant going further, now is fully booked all the way to Chiang Khan. Several new small hotels have sprung up along the river and a room must be reserved several months in advance.

The friendlier relationship between Thailand and Laos is evident. I arrive the day that the border is officially opened and can watch the procession of Thai and Laotians traveling back and forth across the river. Even before the official opening, trade and traffic resume between the two countries. Many Chiang Khan residents visit their Laotian kin and return astonished by the poverty of Laos. The market in Chiang Khan is said to be larger than that of Vientiane. A Thai who journeys across tells stories of gold and gambling in Laos. "Probably from sales of wood or drugs. Even the children are gambling. There is nothing else to do over there," she reports. The Laotians for their part fear being poor cousins to Thai again.

On a hand-drawn tourist map provided by one of the Chiang Khan hotels, Ban Vinai is listed as a local tourist attraction. The camp continues to be inaccessible to all but the most persistent world travelers and most are turned away at the gates. However, I notice driving from Pak Chom to Ban Vinai that the road is now paved. A Volag worker tells me that the Pak Chom–Loei bus stops in front of the camp each day and that the new road is opening up trade for the local villages. Nearing the camp, I notice that the Thai market just outside the gates is considerably expanded.

I bring official camp passes but when I arrive in the COERR truck, the guards nod in recognition and wave us on. I wonder if they know that I have ever left. The new entrance to Ban Vinai is more imposing, but otherwise on first inspection it looks the same. The changes I discover are subtle. The camp is less crowded than in 1986 and there are several vacant, boarded-up rooms. The camp's population has declined to 35,000 and some 15,000 have left for the United States or to one of the two detention camps, Ban Napho or Chieng Kham. The camp streets are very clean, thanks to a new Thai IRC director, who has organized public sanitation teams throughout the camp. The roads are well-graded and the paths neatly demarcated. There is a greater sense of order to the place, but a disquieting sense of permanency.

Many expatriate relief workers have left. Many Thai relief workers I knew in 1986 are also gone, but others have taken their place. The UNHCR field officer now works with refugees in Africa. Several Volags have opened operations in Laos and others talk of phasing out their programs in the camp.

The fates of the three households also reflect the changing times. I learn from a COERR worker that in early 1988, the Sisawongs were rounded up as illegals and forcibly taken to Napho, where Chanthanom and Khamsai were locked up with their five children for several months. Eventually, they were released, but the children were very sick in the interim. "Couldn't you do anything?" I ask Pere. "We didn't know where they were, not until they got out," he explains. "What will happen to them?" "They are waiting to be repatriated." Like others in Napho, their future will eventually be determined by negotiations between Thailand and Laos.

The Thao household, with close ties to the Resistance, has remained in Ban Vinai. Hai, however, tells me of her plans to register for a JVA interview. "I will join my brother in California," she says. Moua also talks of leaving and of divorcing Seng. Seng has taken a third wife and has no plans to leave. "But she [the third wife] has relatives in the U.S. too. Maybe he will come, too." Hai says hopefully.

Her children have grown. Chia talks of joining the Resistance or going to America. "Everyone is in the Resistance," he asserts. One of his friends reports being wounded during a recent foray into Laos and shows me the scar on his leg. "But, I was lucky others were killed. I saw Vang Pao in Laos." The young man adds, "he looked very old." When I do not respond, Chia and his friend ask, "Should we go to the U.S.?"

Blia to Hai's surprise has never married. Her suitor has long since left for the United States. Blia spends her days helping Hai sew *paj ntaub* to sell in the States. Seng, however, arranged Sri's marriage to a Resistance leader, a man in his late forties with two wives. The Resistance leader, hoping to return to Laos, moved the household to Chieng Kham, where shortly thereafter he died. Blia reports that Sri has been adopted into the elder wife's family. Like the Sisawongs, she will eventually be re-patriated to Laos. "At least she isn't the second wife," I respond. Blia laughs and agrees, "Yes, she never wanted to be a second wife."

The Vang household emigrated to the United States. One wintry day in late 1987 I received a telephone call from Ger's relatives in Rhode Island that the Vangs were on their way. The money from the *paj ntaub* I sold for them helped finance their way out of the camp. After that initial phone conversation, months passed and I heard nothing. Ger later called to say that he left Xiong behind in the camp. "I will go see her," I promised when I returned in 1989. We exchanged greetings in Lao; Ger said nothing about his life in the United States. In early fall 1989, my husband, our young daughter, and I visited the household in Rhode Is-land, but Ger was away in Wisconsin looking for work. Choua gave me their new baby daughter to hold and we took turns exchanging daugh-ters and photographing our children. We spoke in Lao, but sometimes I had trouble understanding Choua over the noise of the television, which no one seemed to watch. The children looked very American and asked me to speak English. Only the eldest remembered that we had met first in Ban Vinai.

While I was away in Thailand in spring 1990, Ger visited my husband in Washington, D.C. He came for a rally on Capitol Hill organized by the Hmong Resistance to protest the LPDR's treatment of the Hmong in Laos. Although Ger was still unemployed at the time, a few months later he found work on the third shift in a factory in Rhode Island.

When we visited them again the next fall, he showed me the new house he had bought with his cousins in Providence.

Reflecting on how the lives of the Vangs, Thaos, and Sisawongs have changed over the past four years, I climb the hill to Xiong's place. Although I can no longer draw the route, at each juncture I instinctively follow the familiar turns.

Hmong children play games with rubber bands, a man helps his child push a fluorescent pink plastic car across the road, and women sew in small groups. Occasionally a woman or child looks up and stares, sometimes in recognition, as I pass, but most are absorbed in their sewing and games.

I walk through a semideserted building and stoop low to avoid hitting its overhanging eaves. The place is darker and smaller than I remembered. Several doors are boarded up; one bangs in a late afternoon breeze. In the distance I hear a familiar chant. Otherwise the place is quiet and deserted except for two small dusty children, who shoot pebbles on the earthen floor and a sewing group who guards the entrance to the dark corridor. They look initially suspicious and then recognizing me, smile and wave me on. I follow the long dark passageway to the next to last room. The bird whistles grow louder. An elderly woman standing outside the door motions me into the dark smoky space.

Inside Xiong moves rhythmically back and forth on her horse. She pauses to burn joss and turning in my direction gives a knowing smile. As the joss curls to ash she returns to her bench and begins chanting again. I find a low stool in the corner of the room. The familiar sounds and smells surround me. The chanting grows in intensity. I forget the time that has passed, the loss of distance and reflection, and feel a peace take hold again. The woman on her horse moves faster. Smoke darkens each corner of the room. The horse gallops on and on. The sounds crescendo and then, suddenly cease. The horse slows until Xiong is still again.

I am sorry that she has finished. I want the feeling of that moment to be etched forever in my memory and am not ready to return so soon. But, looking at my watch I realize that it is later than I think and that the van will soon leave.

The elderly woman standing guard enters the room to support Xiong as she returns from her journey. The women speak briefly and then Xiong turns and comes toward me. "What was the ceremony for?" I say asking the familiar question. "For my children in America, that they are well again," she replies.

Endnotes

1. The Road to Ban Vinai

1. The preceding historical analysis of this region is taken from Hafner et al., "River Road to China," pp. 1–11 and "Trade and Transport of the Upper Mekong," pp. 51–74.

2. See Brown and Zasloff, *Apprentice Revolutionaries.*

3. Interviews with various camp leaders and administrators resulted in COERR, *Report of Interviews,* which I co-authored with Chao Thao.

4. See Erikson, "On the Nature of Psycho-Historical Evidence" and Herdt and Stoller, *Intimate Communications,* "Clinical Ethnography," pp. 15–52, for discussion of this approach.

5. Other researchers who have described difficulties of entry and access include Chomsky and Herman, *After the Cataclysm;* Clay and Holcomb, *Politics and the Ethiopian Famine 1984–1985;* Hurlich et al., "Attitudes of Hmong Toward a Medical Research Project."

6. See COERR, *Report of Survey.*

7. This definition of consciousness, which incorporates both its psychological and political economic aspects, is taken from Marx, "Economic and Philosophic Manuscripts," pp. 283–358 and Sartre, *Being and Nothingness.*

8. For this concept of consciousness, see Sartre, *Being and Nothingness.*

9. See Boothby, *The Care and Placement of Unaccompanied Children;* Boothby, *Unaccompanied Children in Emergencies;* Eitinger, "Foreigners in Our Time," pp. 16–26; Ressler et al., *Unaccompanied Children;* Schoenmeier, "Refugee Policy: The Need to Include Psychological Aspects," pp. 66–72; and Zwingmann and Pfister-Ammende, *Uprooting and After.*

10. Boothby, *The Care and Placement of Unaccompanied*

Children; Boothby, *Unaccompanied Children in Emergencies;* Kahnert et al., *Children and War;* Mc-Callum, *Report of a Pilot Study;* Ressler et al., *Unaccompanied Children,* in particular, have focused on the psychological effects of the refugee experience in their work on children of war.

11. UNHCR mental health experts in the postwar European camps, for example, reported how long years of camp life caused personality disorders, asocial behavior, apathy, mistrust, and alcoholism among many refugees (cited in Eitinger, "Foreigners In Our Time," pp. 16–26, and Tabori, *The Anatomy of Exile*). One expert spoke of "camp psychosis" and urged intensive counseling and psychiatric therapy. However, as Pfister-Ammende, *Uprooting and After,* cautioned, the refugee should be defined as a mentally healthy person who, as a consequence of external force and internment, may suffer disorders. She also observed that the "overwhelming majority of persons interviewed retained a sense of inner security and appeared to be rooted" (p. 9).

12. Examples of studies about refugee situations from a sociocultural perspective are: Keller, *Uprooting and Social Change,* on Hindu and Sikh refugees; Boesch, "From Expulsion to Hospitality," on Ethiopian; Grossman, *The Yellow Wind,* on Palestinian; Malkii, "Context and Consciousness," on Hutu; and Harrell-Bond, *Imposing Aid,* on Ugandan.

13. According to Keller, *Uprooting and Social Change,* resettled refugees accept the goals of development and modernization more readily than nonrefugees. Others, Bettelheim, *Surviving;* Erikson, *Life History;* and Frankl, *The Doctor and the Soul,* both in their own experiences and writing, attest to the human capacity for growth from such experiences.

14. The concept of a total institution comes from Goffman's *Asylums,* pp. 1–124.

15. Foucault, *Discipline and Punish.* See also Malkii, "Context and Consciousness," who, in her research on the Hutu refugees in Burundi, likewise identifies the refugee camp as a technology of power (p. 33).

16. Many surveys have been conducted and reports written about the Southeast Asian camps: e.g., CCSDPT, *The CCSDPT Handbook;* UNHCR, *Report on the Status of Refugees: Brief on Ban Vinai;* COERR, *Report of Survey: Report of Interviews;* Bourhis-Nedellac, "Installation et Fonctionnement" and "OHI Programme". Several studies and books from a policy perspective document the relief effort: Levy and Susott, *Years of Horror;* Shawcross, *Quality of Mercy;* Mason and Brown, *Rice, Rivalry, and Politics;* and Tollefson, *Alien Winds,* "Functional Competencies," and "Research on Refugee Resettlement."

17. Marcus and Fisher, *Anthropology as Cultural Critique,* p. 86.

18. See Marcus and Cushman, "Ethnographies as Texts"; Kreiger, "Fiction and Social Science"; and Clifford and Marcus, *Writing Culture,* for discussions of ethnographic conventions, the blurring of the boundaries of social science and fiction, and the genre of experimental ethnography. Marcus and Fisher, *Anthropology as Cultural Critique,* point to the need to ground the narrative in the larger political, economic, and historical context. The idea of reflexivity is based on Giddens, *The Consequences of Modernity,* which is relevant to knowledge created in the refugee camp context.

19. See Rosaldo, "Ideology, Place, and People Without Culture" for discussion of border zones.

20. The concept of liminality is well known in anthropology from Turner's, *Dramas, Fields, and Metaphors* essay on communitas.

21. Erikson, "Identity and Uprootedness," pp. 113–168.

22. In his study, *Imagined Communities,* Anderson analyzes the problematic status of contemporary national boundaries and identities.

2. The Creation of an International Relief System

1. See Tabori, *The Anatomy of Exile,* "The Waves of Exile," pp. 171–273.

2. U.S. Committee for Refugees, *Refugee Protection.*

3. Smyser, *Refugees: A Never Ending Story,* p. 154.

4. Tabori, *The Anatomy of Exile,* p. 276.

5. See Rothkopf's study of *Jean Henri Dunant.*

6. Tabori, *The Anatomy of Exile,* p. 277.

7. Cited in Tabori, *The Anatomy of Exile,* p. 277. Dunant wrote "Un Souvenir de Solferino" as a booklet in Geneva. It was acclaimed by Florence Nightingale and Victor Hugo, but initially attracted little attention. Eventually, Dunant's efforts were recognized and he shared the first Nobel Peace Prize for his humanitarian work.

8. Shawcross, *The Quality of Mercy,* p. 101.

9. Ibid., pp. 101–102.

10. Collins, *A Mandate to Protect and Assist Refugees,* pp. 19–21.

11. Cited in Rothkopf, *Jean Henri Dunant,* p. 64.

12. Arendt, *On Revolution,* p. 5.

13. Kahnert et al., *Children and War,* p. 5.

14. Nansen was a very able diplomat and was very successful in resettling German, Austrian, and Russian prisoners of wars and the Turkish refugees. See Tabori, *Anatomy of Exile,* pp. 279–281.

15. Collins, *A Mandate to Assist and Protect Refugees,* p. 23.

16. Shawcross, *The Quality of Mercy,* p. 46.

17. The history of the IGCR comes primarily from Tabori, *The Anatomy of Exile,* pp. 282–283. Also, reviewed in Collins, *A Mandate to Assist and Protect Refugees,* pp. 25–27.

18. Cited in Collins, *A Mandate to Protect and Assist Refugees,* p. 25.

19. Ibid., p. 25. See also Kitagawa, *American Refugee Policy.*

20. Shawcross, *The Quality of Mercy,* p. 81.

21. Ibid., p. 81.

22. Ibid., p. 81. Also see Tabori, *The Anatomy of Exile,* pp. 283–284.

23. Shawcross, *The Quality of Mercy,* p. 81.

24. U.S. House of Representatives, *Reports on Refugee Aid,* p. 4.

25. Tabori, *The Anatomy of Exile,* p. 289. Tabori further observes that of the seven hundred million, approximately $471 million was financed by the United States with the United Kingdom, Canada, and France paying most of the remaining. Like the other UN relief organizations, UNRWA was established to address immediate needs until a political solution could be obtained.

26. Tabori, *The Anatomy of Exile,* p. 287; also discussed in Collins, *A Mandate to Protect and Assist Refugees,* p. 28.

27. See Smyser, "Refugees: A Never-Ending Story."

28. Tabori, *Anatomy of Exile,* p. 289.

29. For a discussion of Palestinian refugees' situation, see Grossman, *The Yellow Wind* and "Report from Israel."

30. U.S. Committee for Refugees, *World Refugee Survey, 1987 in Review,* p. 3.

31. U.S. House of Representatives, *Reports on Refugee Aid.*

32. Cited in Shawcross, *The Quality of Mercy,* pp. 81–82; Tabori, *The Anatomy of Exile,* p. 24.

33. U.S. House of Representatives, *Reports on Refugee Aid;* also see Pitterman's study, "Determinants of International Refugee Policy."

34. Collins, *A Mandate to Protect and Assist Refugees,* p. 32.

35. Shawcross, *The Quality of Mercy,* p. 82.

36. Hugo "Postwar Refugee Migration"; U.S. House of Representatives, *Reports on Refugee Aid.*

37. Read, *Magna Carta for Refugees.*

38. Pitterman, *Determinants of International Refugee Policy.*

39. Ibid. Pitterman (personal communication 1989) observes that the same conclusion would not be true for the pattern of UNHCR expenditures during the 1980s.

40. See Collins, *A Mandate to Protect and Assist Refugees,* p. 34, and U.S. Committee for Refugees, *World Refugee Survey, 1989,* p. 13, for discussion of asylum under the 1951 Convention.

41. Cited in Simmace, "The Impact of Large-Scale Refugee Movements," p. 9.

42. Henkel, "The International Protection of Refugees."

43. Collins, *A Mandate to Protect and Assist Refugees,* ch. 4. Hereafter cited in text.

44. Tabori, *The Anatomy of Exile,* p. 302.

45. Collins, *A Mandate to Protect and Assist Refugees,* p. 67. Hereafter cited in text.

46. UNHCR Field Officer, Ban Vinai Refugee Camp (interview, 1986). These priorities are also established in several UNHCR policy documents and guidelines.

47. Collins, *A Mandate to Protect and Assist Refugees,* p. 115.

48. Nichols, *The Uneasy Alliance,* provides an extensive history of the increasing role of the religious organizations in relief assistance and their influence on U.S. foreign policy.

49. Holborn, *Refugees: A Problem of Our Time.* Hereafter cited in text.

50. Collins, *A Mandate to Protect and Assist Refugees,* p. 129.

51. Discussed in Ferris, *Refugees and World Politics* and in Melander and Nobel, *African Refugees and the Law.*

52. Holborn, *Refugees: A Problem of Our Time.*

53. Shawcross, *The Quality of Mercy,* pp. 424–425n.

54. See Keely, *Global Refugee Policy.*

55. Holborn, *Refugees: A Problem of Our Time,* p. 754. Hereafter cited in text.

56. Collins, *A Mandate to Protect and Assist Refugees,* p. 103.

57. UNHCR, "Interview with Ken Kragen," p. 40.

58. Shawcross, *The Quality of Mercy,* p. 432.

59. This discussion is primarily based on Arendt's *On Revolution,* ch. 1, observations on the changes in modern warfare.

60. Collins, *A Mandate to Protect and Assist Refugees,* p. 115.

3. Camps in Thailand

1. Coedes, *The Making of Southeast Asia.*

2. Pluvier, *A Handbook and Chart of Southeast Asian History.*

3. See Brown and Zasloff, *Apprentice Revolutionaries,* for a complete description of the historical roots and formation of the Indochinese Communist Party.

4. The decision to use Cambodia versus Kampuchea is based on recent political events. Kamm follows the former Prince Sihanouk's preference for the former. He argues that "Kampuchea" was "imposed on the world by the ultrachauvinist Khmer Rouge regime and is rejected as kowtowing to their views by Cambodians not living under Communist rule (Kamm, "A Broken Country," p. 98). On the other hand, Huffman ("The Ethnolinguistic Background"), a linguist, observes that the official name of the country has for centuries

been "Kampuchea" and that it has been Anglicized to "Cambodia" from the French "Cambodge." This has resulted in the adjectival form "Cambodian," but the word "Cambodia" has no adjectival form in Khmer. According to Huffman, "the people call themselves and their language simply 'Khmer' " (p. 1). Given the strong association of Kampuchea with the disastrous Khmer Rouge government, I use "Cambodia" to refer to the country, but Khmer to the people (the main ethnic group) and their language.

5. See Adams and McCoy, *Laos: War and Revolution;* Branfman, *Voices from the Plain of Jars;* Dommen, *Laos: Keystone of Indochina;* and Karnow, *Vietnam, A History* for a more detailed and complete history of the war.

6. Although called the "Vietnam War," the conflict spread regionally and engulfed Laos and Cambodia. As Shawcross, *Side Show,* observed, the U.S. government treated Laos and Cambodia as a sideshow. However, as events unfolded, each had their own unique histories and experiences that were reflected in the various waves of refugees.

7. Branfman in *Voices from the Plain of Jars* recorded the stories of these refugees, who would have been considered "displaced persons" by UNHCR and other relief organizations since they had not crossed an international boundary.

8. Holborn, *Refugees: A Problem of Our Time.*

9. Cooper, "The Hmong of Laos."

10. Chanda, *Brother Enemy;* Loescher and Scanlan, *Calculated Kindness.*

11. Loescher and Scanlan, *Calculated Kindness;* Montero, *Vietnamese Americans.*

12. Kelly, *From Vietnam to America.*

13. Loescher and Scanlan, *Calculated Kindness;* Montero, *Vietnamese Americans.*

14. Finnan, "Community Influence on Occupational Identity."

15. Loescher and Scanlan, *Calculated Kindness.*

16. See Loescher and Scanlan, ch. 6, for a detailed account.

17. Robinson, "Laotian Refugees in Thailand."

18. Van-es-Beeck, "Refugees from Laos."

19. Robinson, "Laotian Refugees in Thailand."

20. This is based on a conversation with a retired Hmong senior officer in Vang Pao's forces (Thailand, 1986).

21. CCSDPT, *The CCSDPT Handbook.*

22. UNHCR, *Brief on Ban Vinai,* p. 2.

23. Shawcross, *The Quality of Mercy;* Van-es-Beeck, "Refugees from Laos."

24. Shawcross, *The Quality of Mercy,* pp. 82–83.

25. CCSDPT, *The CCSDPT Handbook.*

26. Robinson, "Laotian Refugees in Thailand."

27. Loescher and Scanlan, *Calculated Kindness,* p. 122.

28. CCSDPT, *The CCSDPT Handbook.*

29. Loescher and Scanlan, *Calculated Kindness,* p. 127.

30. Chanda, *Brother Enemy,* p. 408.

31. CCSDPT, *The CCSDPT Handbook.*

32. "Push" and "pull" factors were common terminology used by relief officials and workers to suggest motivations for refugee migrations. Such terms ignored the complex socioeconomic and political circumstances underlying these migrations.

33. Cooper, "The Hmong of Laos."

34. Brown and Zasloff, *Apprentice Revolutionaries;* Van-es-Beeck, "Refugees from Laos"; informal interviews in the Philippines Refugee Processing Center (1981).

35. Loescher and Scanlan, *Calculated Kindness.*

36. Age Investigation, *The Boat People*.

37. Ibid.; Loescher and Scanlan, *Calculated Kindness*.

38. Chiou, "China's Policy Towards Laos."

39. Chanda, *Brother Enemy*.

40. CCSDPT, *The CCSDPT Handbook*.

41. The sequence of events cited are reported in Shawcross, *The Quality of Mercy*.

42. Ibid.; informal interviews in the Philippines Refugee Processing Center (1981).

43. Informal interview in the Philippines Refugee Processing Center (1981).

44. Shawcross, *The Quality of Mercy*, p. 91.

45. Ibid.

46. Loescher and Scanlan, *Calculated Kindness;* UNHCR, *Report on the Status of Refugees*.

47. Levy and Susott, *Years of Horror;* Shawcross, *The Quality of Mercy*.

48. Loescher and Scanlan, *Calculated Kindness*.

49. Discussions with relief officials, Philippines Refugee Processing Center (1980).

50. Age Investigation, *The Boat People*.

51. Shawcross, *Side Show*.

52. Chomsky and Herman, *After the Cataclysm*.

53. Cooper, "The Hmong of Laos."

54. Robinson, "Laotian Refugees in Thailand."

55. CCSDPT, *The CCSDPT Handbook*.

56. Robinson, "Laotian Refugees in Thailand."

57. CCSDPT, *The CCSDPT Handbook*, p. 3.

58. See Mason and Brown, *Rice, Rivalry, and Politics*, for a description and analysis of the border operation.

59. Shawcross, *The Quality of Mercy*.

60. Levy and Susott, *Years of Horror*.

61. Shawcross, *The Quality of Mercy*.

62 Ibid.

63. Brown and Zasloff, *Apprentice Revolutionaries*.

64. Chanda, "Economic Changes in Laos."

65. Burley, "Foreign Aid to the Lao People's Democratic Republic."

66. Chanda, *Brother Enemy*.

67. Stuart-Fox, "Foreign Policy of the Lao People's Democratic Republic."

68. Burley, "Foreign Aid to the Lao People's Democratic Republic."

69. Brown and Zasloff, *Apprentice Revolutionaries*.

70. This was reported by Wendy Bateson, who had been the American Friends Service Committee (AFSC) Representative in Laos at the time (Interview).

71. CCSDPT, *The CCSDPT Handbook*, pp. 9–10.

72. Loescher and Scanlan, *Calculated Kindness*, p. 180.

73. U.S. Senate, *Refugee Problems in Southeast Asia*, p. 33.

74. Interviews with relief workers, who had worked in Ban Nam Yao in 1982 (Ban Vinai Refugee Camp, 1986).

75. Chanda, *Brother Enemy*, p. 402.

76. CCSDPT, *The CCSDPT Handbook*.

77. Interviews in Site 2, 1986; Crossette, "After the Killing Fields."

78. Brown and Zasloff, *Apprentice Revolutionaries*.

79. Ranard, "Thailand: The Last Bus."

80. Brown and Zasloff, *Apprentice Revolutionaries*.

81. Ibid.; CCSDPT, *The CCSDPT Handbook.*
82. Cooper, "The Hmong of Laos," p. 38.
83. Brown and Zasloff, *Apprentice Revolutionaries.*
84. Cerquone, "Refugees from Laos"; CCSDPT, *The CCSDPT Handbook.*
85. CCSDPT, *The CCSDPT Handbook,* pp. 13, 14.
86. Ibid., p. 19.
87. COERR, *Report of Survey.* Estimated data for Site 2 were reported by Chris Elias, COERR medical coordinator in Site 2 (1986).
88. COERR Survey (1986b).
89. Robinson, "Laotian Refugees in Thailand."
90. USCR, *World Refugee Survey, 1986;* interviews in Chieng Kham Camp, 1986.
91. Speech at CCSDPT Annual Meeting, July 11, 1986, Bangkok, Thailand.
92. Informal interview with Janet Lim, UNHCR Social Services Officer, Bangkok, Thailand, 1986.
93. Speech at CCSDPT Annual Meeting, July 11, 1986, Bangkok, Thailand.

4. A Disciplined Village

1. The concept of civil inattention, characteristic of modern urban life, is taken from Goffman, *Behavior in Public Places.* Giddens, *The Consequences of Modernity,* referencing Goffman, also discusses this aspect of modern life.

2. The Thai Ministry of Education provided primary education in Ban Vinai. Until 1990, classes were taught in Thai and Lao. Thai teachers supervised Hmong teachers. Several relief workers pointed out that offering education in Thai was counter to the government's policy of encouraging the Hmong to repatriate. In 1990, as the likelihood of repatriation increased, the UNHCR Ban Vinai field officer instituted a reform that gave control of the educational system to the Hmong, themselves, and made the language of instruction, Lao.

3. These observations come from fieldnotes I recorded during 1982 when I first worked in Ban Vinai with the public health workers.

4. Robinson, "Laotian Refugees in Thailand."

5. Tinker, personal communication, 1989.

6. This is based on my 1982 fieldnotes.

7. For an analysis of the yellow rain controversy see Marshall, "Yellow Rain Evidence" and Bazell, "Bees Did It."

8. UNHCR, *Report on the Status of Refugees.*

9. Finck, "Secondary Migration."

10. Different ethnic groups in Laos occupied different ecological niches and, correspondingly, practiced different forms of cultivation. The Lao Loum [*láaw lum*] (or lowland Lao) numbered about 1.7 million, but minority peoples constituted approximately half of the population of Laos (Dommen, *Laos*). The Lao Soung [*láaw sung*] (highlanders), Hmong, and Yao generally settled above 3,000 feet, where opium grew well. They practiced primarily *hǎj* (swidden or slash and burn) agriculture. The Lao Theung [*láaw thá̌ŋ*] (uplanders) settled on the mountain sides. They included the numerous indigenous peoples—Khmu, Lamet, and other Mon-Khmer (formerly known as "*Kha,*"or slaves)—settled between the highland Hmong and lowland Lao (Westermeyer, *Poppies, Pipes, and People*). These peoples were materially poorer than the lowland Lao and Hmong and some became a labor pool for nearby Hmong villages (Westermeyer 1982:32). The Lao Loum (lowland Lao) settled in the lowlands and river deltas, where they generally practiced

na (wet rice) agriculture. However, Halpern, *The Natural Economy,* observes that: "swidden agriculture as practiced by the Meo [Hmong] in Laos seems to be a cultural adaptation that may not have a very great time depth."

Within their ecological niche, many Laotian and Thai Hmong practiced a rotational and shifting system of swidden cultivation (Lemoine, *Un village Hmong vert;* Geddes, *Migrants of the Mountains;* Cooper, *Resource Scarcity and the Hmong Response*). Cooper, however, shows that these patterns were not fixed or determinate nor is one single economic system applicable to all tribal societies. Cooper, in *Resource Scarcity and the Hmong Response,* observes that Hmong villages in northern Thailand differ on patterns of production. He observes a transition from swidden rice and cooperation to swidden opium and paid labor to irrigated rice and labor exchange—as a kind of continuum or evolution. The Thai Hmong respond not only to resource scarcity and changing capitalist relations, but the changing social structure also reflects the particular sets of social relationships that constitute that structure and there is no set pattern of change.

Cooper's *Resource Scarcity and the Hmong Response,* which looks at resource availability and methods of resource exploitation with reference to forms of work organization, provides a useful framework for interpreting why Hmong households differed in their decisions to stay or leave Ban Vinai. Such decisions most likely reflect particular household structures and relationships, as well as the opportunities and resources available in each situation.

11. Cooper, "The Hmong of Laos."

12. I observed this gender disparity during interviews with the voluntary agencies (see COERR, *Report of Interviews*).

13. For a compelling analysis of relief worker/refugee relationships and the differing agenda, see Harrell-Bond, *Imposing Aid.* Although her study is of the Ugandan relief operation in southern Sudan, her conclusions are widely applicable to other relief situations.

14. The statistics that follow are taken from COERR, *Report of Survey* and UNHCR, *Brief on Ban Vinai.*

15. The Hmong believe in ancestral spirits, who continue to interact with living descendants (Yang, personal communication; Conquergood, "Establishing the World"). The natural world is inhabited by spirits, which may be evil or good. The shaman has the expertise to move between the human and the spirit world.

16. The Hmong divide themselves into different cultural groupings that are not based on kinship structure or economic function (Cooper, *Resource Scarcity and the Hmong Response;* fieldnotes). In Laos and Thailand, Hmong refer to two divisions: Green or Blue Hmong (*Hmoob Ntsuab*) and White Hmong (*Hmoob Dawb*). In the camp, Hmong further distinguished themselves as belonging to a third group, the Striped Hmong. According to Cooper, the latter classification is not made by the Hmong in their language, but is made in Thai or northern Thai dialect. This term was also reported to me in the northern Thai dialect.

In the camp, differences between White and Green Hmong are seen in men's and women's dress, dialects, and interactions (fieldnotes). Although Green and White Hmong might live in the same barracks, each group tends to interact primarily with members from their same cultural group. Intermarriage occurs, but is not likely. These groupings, however, do not affect the Hmong's overall identification with other Hmong. One's clan rather than one's cultural grouping is also more salient for Hmong in their decisions about their future and in their self-identification.

17. I use "refrain" in the same sense that Goffman, in *Asylums,* characterizes the asylum inmate's lamentation, a story designed to arouse compassion for one's situation.

18. This situation is analogous to how the Azande interpret a house falling on someone. I borrow from Evans-Pritchard's, *Witchcraft, Oracles, and Magic,* classic account to explain why my "scientific" explanation is insufficient.

5. The Camp Generation

1. Hmong in their villages in Laos marked the first hour of the day by the crowing of the rooster (Lemoine, *Un village Hmong vert*). This was also the case in the camp.

2. During 1980–1981 I witnessed several incidents of family violence in the processing center in the Philippines. Mental health workers in the processing center observed that the incidents appeared to increase prior to a departure for the United States and that transitions from one camp to the next augmented the stress. This particular incident was one of a few that I witnessed in Ban Vinai during 1986. That these incidents were not the norm (or that wife abuse was condoned) was evident in the neighbors' reactions and their attempts to separate the couple.

Camp life in Thailand, in contrast to village or refugee camp life in Laos, introduced new social and psychological stresses. As Westermeyer in "Mental Health of Southeast Asian Refugees" observes, there was a discontinuity of political and social organization when the Hmong moved to the camps in Thailand. Westermeyer reports: "Extended families broke off from larger groups to husband food and resources for themselves. Even nuclear families sometimes broke off from extended families to provide for their own youth and elderly. Isolation, suspiciousness, and projection of hostile intent onto others began in this context" (p. 70).

The pressure to decide whether to emigrate to Laos or to resettle in the United States further split extended families and created new pressures for the Hmong. In this context, a small inconvenience, such as the camp's limited water supply, could come to symbolize these larger worries and concerns.

3. Bertrais estimates that some five million Hmong remain in China (personal communication, 1986). According to Schein, "The Miao in Contemporary China," the vast majority of the more than five million Hmong and Miao scattered throughout the world still live in south and southwest China. As Shein observes, "From the perspective of Hmong in other parts of the world, this region has been regarded as a remote ancestral homeland, a repository of archaic cultural forms" (p. 73).

4. Lemoine, "Shamanism in the Context of Hmong Resettlement."

5. A Hmong student, who took me to the temple, described Pahwah Hmong as a mixture of Lao Buddhism, Chinese, and traditional Hmong religion. Smalley et al., *Mother of Writing,* likewise observes that the shapes of the characters bear resemblance to letters in the Roman, Tai-language, and Russian alphabets. However, Smalley et al. provide evidence that Shong Lue independently invented the Pahwah Hmong writing system and that the characters were not modeled after the writing systems of the region.

Smalley et al. describe how center 3 became the primary Pahwah Hmong area of the camp (pp. 110–111). In 1976, several followers of the late Shong Lue Yang settled in center 3. Colonel Soua Yang, the center leader, had spread the word that anyone who knew Pahawh Hmong, or was sympathetic to it, could settle there. After Chia Koua and Gnia Yee, two leaders of the movement, emigrated to the United States in 1978, there may have been a leadership vacuum. However, interest in the movement continued through the early 1980s, in part, because it represented an alternative to Vang Pao and his organization.

6. This is objectively true when measured in terms of international expenditures for refugees in Southeast Asia versus those in Africa. African refugees (estimated at more than five million) also far outnumber the Southeast Asian refugees (less than half a million). However, in terms of reception, many African governments and communities with far fewer resources have also allowed refugees to integrate in local villages and often to their own detriment, they have generously shared their own resources with the refugees.

7. COERR, *Report of Survey.*

8. This observation is based on informal discussions with Thai relief workers, UNHCR staff, and refugees. The information, however, was not documented by anyone who claimed to have directly witnessed the trafficking.

9. COERR, *Report of Survey.*

10. As noted earlier, only the wealthy in the camp could afford polygyny, which in turn often enhanced their wealth (since women earned 90 percent of the nonblack market income). Less wealthy Hmong men often followed the Thai custom of taking a "*mia noi,*" lesser or small wife, who was often treated as a mistress.

11. During my fieldwork in Ban Vinai, I witnessed several occasions when households were asked to contribute to the Resistance. Often, people gave voluntarily. At times, they were exhorted to give.

12. COERR, *Report of Survey.*

13. Long, "Literacy Acquisition of Hmong Refugees."

14. This issue was raised at the Annual CCSDPT Meeting, 1986, in Bangkok by a group of Volag representatives, who worked in Ban Vinai.

15. The processing centers offered six months of English as a second language (ESL) and cultural orientation classes, which were funded by the U.S. State Department and organized by U.S. Volags (fieldnotes, 1981; Tollefson, *Alien Winds;* "Functional Competencies"; "Research on Refugee Resettlement"). For almost a decade (1980–1990), there were three centers: Galang (Indonesia), Bataan (Philippines), and Panat Nikhom (Thailand). Hmong who resettled in the United States went either to Phanat Nikhom or Bataan.

16. The majority of my data about children were collected through direct observation of their games or through drawings, which they would then describe to me. This individual interview was unusual.

17. Descriptions of Hmong courtship may be found in Cooper, *Resource Scarcity and the Hmong Response,* pp. 143–146, and Lemoine, *Un village Hmong vert,* pp. 170–171. Most Hmong marriages are arranged between the fathers after the girl and boy have entered into a relationship. As in this case, the girl's mother may be the first to notice that a relationship has begun. Sometimes, the boy and his male kin kidnap the girl (marriage by capture) if the girl's father objects to the relationship. Kidnapping, however, became less common in the camp, because the girl's father could go to the Thai authorities and threaten to bring legal action against the kidnappers.

6. Entrapment

1. The life history of Chanthanom is primarily based on two interviews. The first interview was conducted during one of my early meetings with Chanthanom. She initiated the interview and I listened and asked questions only to clarify meaning. The second interview held a few months later was at my request. This time I taped the interview and transcribed the passages that I quote. Again, I asked questions primarily to clarify. During the second interview, however, I noticed that she spoke more about her childhood, whereas in the first she spoke primarily about her own and her family's refugee camp experiences.

The life history methodology in anthropology has been well documented (Agar, *The Professional Stranger;* Langness and Frank, *Lives;* Ferrarotti, *Histoire et histoires de vie*). In interpreting and reporting on the interviews, I adopted the novelist's realism (to the extent that my translation skills allowed) by transcribing certain passages verbatim (Rosaldo, "Ilongot Hunting as Story and Experience"). I also maintained her narrative sequence within each section. (The second interview began with her childhood and the first with her entry into the camp.) I include my own questions, as I have throughout this text, to show how I, at times, structured the flow of our conversation (see Herdt and Stoller, *Intimate Communications,* for relevance of this approach).

Later, in interpreting the refugee women's histories, I realized the similarities of Chanthanom's history to Western autobiography as opposed to Xiong's life history, which did not follow a Western chronological sequence. Chanthanom, as her history suggests, had spent many years living with and near Westerners. The refugee experience had also made her more conscious of her Western audience and such interviews were common events in camp life. At the same time, in contrast to many Western autobiographies, Chanthanom uses events to demonstrate our interconnectedness and to establish the historical ties and relationships that bind us together.

2. This detail of how the Sisawongs went from one camp to the next came out of a later conversation. Several refugees told me about how they had bribed their way into the camps after they had known me several months. Chanthanom was one of the first to share such information. She treated it as a confidence. In contrast, Ger and others provided such details in casual conversation, as we came to know one another.

3. According to Chamberlain, "The Literature of Laos," the *lám* may be a full-blown theatrical performance with musical instruments (such as the khɛɛn) or a single performance and may last all night. *Lám,* such as this one, may also involve only a few people.

4. After returning to the United States, I received a *lam* from Chanthanom and Khamsai. In this folksong, they wrote about what they thought had happened to me in the United States

5. In this chapter and the next, I report on some behaviors that Western medical care practitioners might recognize as symptoms of depression. I prefer, however, to use the term "boredom," which the lowland Lao and Hmong used, which also captures the institutional effects of the refugee experience. The distinction, however, is subtle and the term "boredom" itself has multiple meanings. Chanthanom, Khamsai, and other Lao somatize boredom. Ger and other Hmong describe it as an unending state of aggravation. In the most profound sense of the term, they describe war as "boring." Boonchan, a Thai, in her argument with Anika, uses the term to describe a state that cannot be transcended.

As Lutz, in "Depression and the Translation of Emotional Worlds," observes, "the extent to which the person is seen as a body-with-a-mind or a mind-with-a-body, rather than as a unified system with mental and physical elements more freely intermingling, will play a fundamental role in structuring the way in which illness is described" (p. 69). As these narratives suggest, both Hmong and lowland Lao in the camp portray illness as a unified system with physical, social, and mental elements combined. Thus, the term "boredom" is broader than "depression" in that it characterizes complaints about camp bureaucracy and physical symptoms as well.

6. Similar observations are made by Boesch, "From Expulsion to Hospitality," about the Ethiopian refugees, and by Zwingman and Pfister-Ammende, *Uprooting and After,* about the postwar European refugees. Grossman, *The Yellow Wind,* summarizing

6. Entrapment

the findings of a long detailed study of the dreams of 11- to 13-year-old children in different parts of Israel and the West Bank, observes: "The dreams offer neither escape nor relief . . . This conflict, from which there is no escape even in dreams" (p. 33).

7. Zwingmann and Pfister-Ammende, *Uprooting and After*.

7. Suffering and the Shaman

1. CCCSDPT Annual Meeting. Keynote Speech by Squadron Leader Prasong Soonsiri. July 11, 1986, p. 3.

2. What follows from my fieldnotes is an example of an *Ua Neeb*, which is performed by a shaman when a person is sick (Thao, "Hmong Perceptions of Illness," pp. 375–376). In the ritual, the shaman travels to the spirit world to search for a lost or kidnapped soul. The Hmong believe that illness may be of natural or organic causes or of supernatural, spirit, or magical causes (p. 367). The primary case is the loss of the soul. Every person is believed to have a soul that lives in and governs the body. However, the soul will leave when a person is frightened or lonely and in other highly emotional circumstances.

3. Xiong, as a shaman, was a person with a "neeb" or healing spirit. As Thao observes, "A person whose body hosts a 'neng' [neeb] or healing spirit, is probably considered the Hmong diagnostician with the greatest abilities. He or she is also a healer" (p. 357).

The shamans I observed differed to some extent on the particular aspects of a given ritual, but each had a characteristic form. In this particular ceremony, *Ua Neeb Sai*, Xiong determines the cause of illness and propitiates the spirits, as necessary. Xiong explained that the joss, husked crosses, and incense are used to attract the spirits. According to Thao, the position of the eggs allows the shaman to determine when the soul has returned.

4. Lemoine, "Shamanism in the Context of Hmong Resettlement," also observes that "Hmong shamanism is generally a positive therapy to counteract anxiety and other psychic and psychosomatic disorders" (p. 345).

5. This life history is based on an extensive taped interview which was conducted over two sessions. I translated as much as I could at the time based on Ger's simultaneous translation into Lao. Later, Long Yang, a Hmong businessman, provided a more detailed translation of these tapes from Hmong into English. He pointed out several observations that Ger had neglected or was unwilling to translate, because of Ger's own emotional involvement and stake in the discussion. In this section, I provide both Xiong's own words and Ger's translation.

6. This contrast between two worlds as demarcated through certain distinguishing events in which ordinary life is transformed is taken from Durkheim 1915. The illness itself is an initiatory sickness that changes the religious status of the "chosen " person (Eliade, *Shamanism*, p. 33).

7. For a more detailed description of Hmong shamanic initiation, see Lemoine, "Shamanism in the Context of Hmong Resettlement," pp. 340–342. Lemoine explains that a dead shaman when he or she thinks the time is appropriate sends two of his/her troops, the Inspiring Spirit and the Spirit of the Trance, to the chosen heir. These spirits will not leave the chosen one alone until he or she begins calling them regularly with the help of a consultant shaman. The consultant then becomes the master, who instructs the novice. The training period may last as long as two or three years.

8. Eliade, *Shamanism*.

9. Lemoine observes that female shamans are much less common and that the Hmong would say that a male soul has been reincarnated in a woman's body (p. 342). Bertrais also

observes that female shamans are rare, but suggests the circumstances of the war may have provided an opportunity for more women to become shamans (personal communication, 1986).

10. Long Yang explained these beliefs when translating this part of the interview (personal commmunication, 1990).

11. Several of the deaths may have been from neonatal tetanus. Neonatal tetanus was also the primary cause of infant mortality in Ban Vinai.

12. This second ceremony is most likely a curing ceremony (*ua neeb khu*), which is performed after the patient is better to propitiate the spirits (Lemoine, "Shamanism in the Context of Hmong Resettlement").

13. Thao ("Hmong Perceptions of Illness") observes that animal sacrifices may be performed when the shaman determines that the soul has gone too far or has been transformed into another form of life. Thao explains, "The Hmong believe the animal's soul will replace the person's soul" (p. 369).

14. The Hmong's social system is based on agnatic descent. At the classificatory level, Hmong belong to exogamous patriclans (*xeem*), which determine a Hmong's legal identity (Cooper, *Resource Scarcity and the Hmong Response*, p. 35). Within the clan, Hmong recognize lineage or blood relationships. Those belonging to the same lineage recognize a common historical male ancestor within recent history (three or four generations) and from whom a direct, living descendant can usually be traced. Within lineages, Dunnigan, in "Segmentary Kinship in an Urban Society," observes that American Hmong further form sublineages, which are tightly organized groups for collective action (p. 128). Sublineages were formed in Laos when households from the same lineage broke off to settle a new area. Dunnigan observes that such segmentation also occurs in the United States, often for economic reasons. Sublineages are further embedded in a network of marriage alliances with kinship groups across clans (p. 130).

Sublineages are composed of extended families whose members may be physically separated (and live in different households). In the camp, Hmong households included either extended or nuclear families. However, in the United States, the traditional joint household combining several nuclear families is common (p. 129).

Given this kinship structure, Ger's comment suggests that his relationship to those in Chiang Mai was of a different order than that of his relationship to those in Rhode Island. However, it is surprising that he distinguishes the relationship through his mother rather than a common male ancestor or father. I may have misunderstood him or he may be implying that he can only borrow from those from the same nuclear family or from where there is an affinal relationship as well.

15. Lemoine, "Shamanism in the Context of Hmong Resettlement."

8. *Resistance*

1. See Mottin, *Allons faire le tour*. These observations were further confirmed and interpreted by Long Yang (personal communication, 1989). Lemoine in "Shamanism in the Context of Hmong Resettlement," observes that when a shaman is about to die, s/he summons his/her progeny to drink the contents of his magic water. The bowl represents the dragon pond, the place where the dragon who rules thunder and lightning comes to rest (pp. 340–341).

2. Ibid.

3. "Ces êtres mythiques avaient leur place dans le calendrier chinois. Leur fête tombait précisément, à l'époque des changements de moissons." Mottin, *Allons faire le tour*, p. 273.

1. During 1986, Robert Mather, Nipa Thorudomsak, and I collected data from the chief medical officer of each camp on suicide incidents and attempts. Ban Vinai was reported to have the highest incidence of all the camps in Thailand and Ban Napho, the lowland Lao camp, the lowest (almost none). The suicide incidence in Ban Vinai was an estimated 0.9/1000 in 1985 (n=41,974) and this estimate may have been low given that it reflected only those who were sent to the hospital (COERR, *Report of Survey*). The vast majority of those who committed (or attempted) suicide in Ban Vinai were young women (16 to 35 years of age).

We hypothesized that camp differences reflected each group's religious beliefs about afterlife and the extent to which shame was associated with the practice (as in the case of many lowland Lao Buddhists). For the Hmong, suicide was traditionally accepted as a response to a failed romance and there are several references to the practice in the ethnographic literature (Bernatzik, *Akha and Miao*; Cooper, *Resource Scarcity and the Hmong Response*; Geddes, *Migrants of the Mountains*; Kunstadter, *Health of Hmong in Thailand*; Lemoine, *Un village Hmong vert*; Westermeyer, "Use of Alcohol and Opium"; Williams and Westermeyer, *Psychiatric Problems Among Hmong Adolescents*). However, in the past, there seemed to be more diversity in the kinds of suicide reported (and corresponding terms) and suicide may have been less gender specific. Although there is no direct statistical evidence, it may also be that camp life intensifies the practice.

2. The dead shaman sends his/her spirits to "importune" a son (or daughter) (Bernatzik, *Akha and Miao*; Chindarsi, "Hmong Shamanism"; Lemoine, *Shamanism in the Context of Hmong Resettlement*). In some cases, a shaman who is about to die may also designate his or her successor (Bernatzik, *Akha and Miao*). The spirits make the son or daughter sick until s/he calls for a shaman to diagnose the illness as a vocation or calling (otherwise the sickness cannot be cured). The experienced shaman summons his/her spirit helpers and if there is relief, this proves the calling. The spirits then come to reside in the patient's house in a specially constructed altar (Chindarsi, "Hmong Shamanism," p. 188).

3. Lemoine, *L'initiation du mort*, provides a detailed description of Hmong funeral rites in an translation of the Kr'oua Ke, the funeral chant for the initiation of death. According to Bernatzik, *Akha and Miao*, the Hmong believe that if a person dies, his or her soul is born in the next child of the family or sibling.

4. The wooden knives, also translated as swords, are used to exorcise evil spirits (Bernatzik, *Akha and Miao*) and in cases of sickness, serve to warn others of their presence in a household (fieldnotes 1986).

5. According to Bernatzik, *Akha and Miao*, the gongs are beaten until the shaman believes the spirits are present. The objects used in this ceremony—the spirit paper, incense candles for the teacher's spirit and assistant spirits, small bowls of tea and rice—are characteristic of many shaman ceremonies (Bernatzik, *Akha and Miao*; fieldnotes 1986). Thao likewise describes how the egg, rice, and animal sacrifices are used in healing ceremonies to appease or banish the spirits.

I did not ask Xiong to interpret the symbolic significance of each practice or object used in the initiation ceremony since that was not the focus of my research at the time (nor would she necessarily have been willing to do so). Later, upon analyzing these fieldnotes, however, I believe that the timing of the ceremony and Xiong's willingness to allow me to witness this event were significant in terms of other impending events (i.e., the JVA interview and the Vang household's eventual departure).

6. The buffalo horns are oracle horns, which allow the shaman to know the presence, relative power, and location of the good and evil spirits (Bernatzik, *Akha and Miao*). Male shamans generally use two oracle horns and female shamans four. The shaman may throw the oracle horns several times, as in this case Xiong does, to avert an unfavorable outcome. If the oracle is not propitious, it means that the evil spirit is more powerful than the good one and that the shaman cannot avert the misfortune.

7. As part of the preparation for such a ceremony, the house is typically swept clean (Bernatzik, *Akha and Miao*).

8. The number four, which is considered an auspicious number, is repeated several times in this ceremony (i.e., the bowls of rice, sticks of incense, horns, and two sets of chickens).

9. The animals are typically sacrificed to appease the evil spirits when they have captured the soul of the person (in this case the initiate's).

10. This happens when evil spirits have entered and must be driven away. Uneven numbers, in this case the three, are regarded as unfavorable and used in driving away evil (Bernatzik, *Akha and Miao*).

11. At this point in the ceremony, they are traveling to the spirit world.

12. Robinson, "Laotian Refugees in Thailand," provides a detailed description of the screening program.

13. The concept of the gatekeeping function of counselors comes from Erickson and Shultz, *The Counselor as Gatekeeper*.

14. Turner, *Drama, Fields, and Metaphors*, pp. 231–232, distinguishes three phases in a transition rite: separation, margin, and reaggregation. Such distinctions are useful for understanding the phases of camp life and the camp experience as a transition rite. During the first UNHCR interview and upon entering the camp, the refugee is separated from an earlier established set of cultural conditions. The second phase is the time spent in the camp— the liminal period. The JVA interview marks the end of the liminal period, at which time the refugee reenters the social structure, not necessarily at a higher status level.

15. In these passages the Hmong interpreter translates the caseworker's questions into Hmong for the woman and then, her response into English unless otherwise indicated. Where I understand the Hmong, I indicate those parts where his translation differed from the caseworker's question. Because these are official and confidential interviews, I was allowed to observe with the understanding that I would only hand record (and not tape) the interview. I have changed or deleted the names and places mentioned in the interview to preserve confidentiality.

16. U.S. Congress. Senate, *Midyear Consultation*, p. 29.

17. Ibid., p. 39.

18. COERR, *Report of Interviews*, p. 42.

19. U.S. Congress. Senate, *U.S. Refugee Program.*

10. A New Year

1. The Hmong New Year may be compared to the corroborri, as described by Durkheim, *The Elementary Forms of Religious Life,* pp. 245–251. As the corroborri, Hmong New Year demarcates the sacred from the profane. The desire for control over aspects of the festival on the part of the Thai camp administration, the Catholic Church, and the other religious groups attests to the sacred character and importance of this ceremony in the camp cycle.

2. This ball courting game is also played by the Hmong in the villages in Laos and Thailand.

3. Polygyny, although traditionally practiced, may act in the camp context as a form of social control on the part of men over women. The practice was traditionally practiced among many Hmong in Laos and Thailand, although Bertrais argues that it was practiced in fewer than 10 percent of the households (personal communication, 1986). According to Lemoine, *Un village Hmong vert,* however, men were more likely in a conjugal household to take a second wife, because she added to the productive life of the household (p. 168). Polygyny was also practiced when the woman was infertile or when a man married his brother's widow (levirate). However, several observers also report that women objected to the practice and that in the villages, as well, it was a source of marital tension (Geddes, *Migrants of the Mountains,* p. 84; Bertrais, personal communication, 1986).

In the camp, there are also economic incentives for taking a second wife: she and her household represent additional food rations and sewing income. At the same time, from the woman's standpoint, she risks being divorced and left behind when the family resettles,because Western laws disallow polygyny. The first wife in a polygamous household is likewise vulnerable and many women strongly object to the practice. First wives may try to treat the second wife as a mistress rather than admit her into the household. Given these ramifications, men use both the threat as well as the practice of polygyny to diminish women's social status.

4. This last section, which I have fictionalized, is based on telephone conversations and letters with several people in the camp, but not on direct observation. It is also based on my knowledge of people's daily lives and activities and observations during other visits to Ban Vinai during January.

The incidence of suicide increases after the New Year's festivities. In January 1987, the camp commander also decided to terminate refugee workers' salaries and to require market passes. These actions further demoralized the camp.

11. Relief and Refugees

1. Lake, *After the Wars,* p. 4.

2. Long, *Language and Literacy Shifts,* p. 1.

3. Reported by Roger Winter, director, U.S. Committee for Refugees, in a speech to the Overseas Development Council, January 1992. Dallas, in "Two Many Refugees," December 1991, p. 89, estimates twenty million refugees worldwide. The data presented in figure 11 come from the U.S. Committee for Refugees, *World Refugee Survey,* 1990, and U.S. Department of State, *World Refugee Report,* 1992.

4. Malkii, *Context and Consciousness,* raises this issue based on her own research of the Hutu refugees.

5. In Arendt's terms, the "banality of evil" (Arendt, *Eichmann in Jerusalem*).

6. Loescher and Scanlan, *Calculated Kindness.*

7. U.S. Congress. Senate, *U.S. Refugee Program,* p. 30.

8. Sesser, "A Reporter At Large."

9. Luche, *Socio-economic Analysis of the Lao;* Women's Commission for Refugee Women and Children, *Repatriation and Reintegration.*

10. Women's Commision for Refugee Women and Children, *Repatriation and Reintegration,* pp. 2 and 7.

11. See Giddens, *The Consequences of Modernity,* for discussion of how modernity extends relationships across space and time.

12. Giddens, in *The Consequences of Modernity,* describes the role of trust in such modern institutions, as money and professional expertise. Similarly, by becoming a refugee, the person trusts that asylum will be provided and maintained.

13. Cerquone, "Refugees from Laos"; Bateson (interview, 1988).

14. Local integration for a limited number of Hmong is proposed by Robinson, "Laotian Refugees in Thailand."

15. Sesser, "A Reporter At Large," p. 44.

16. Sesser, "A Reporter At Large," p. 66. Also cited in the Women's Commission for Refugee Women and Children, *Repatriation and Reintegration.*

Epilogue

1. I returned to Ban Vinai in 1989 and 1990. Each time I spent one to two weeks in the camp primarily to conduct follow-up interviews with the households and to collect further data on suicides.

Bibliography

Adams, Nina S. and Alfred W. McCoy. *Laos: War and Revolution*. New York: Harper & Row, 1970.

Agar, Michael H. *The Professional Stranger: An Informal Introduction to Ethnography*. New York: Academic Press, 1980.

Age Investigation. *The Boat People: An "Age" Investigation with Bruce Grant*. England and Australia: Penguin Books, 1979.

Anderson, Benedict. *Imagined Communities: Reflections on the Origin and Spread of Nationalism*. London: Verso, 1983.

Arendt, Hannah. *The Origins of Totalitarianism*. Cleveland and New York: World Publishing, 1969.

—— *On Revolution*. New York: Viking Press, 1965.

—— *Eichmann in Jerusalem; A Report on the Banality of Evil*. New York: Viking Press, 1964.

Bazell, R. "Bees Did It." *The New Republic*. February 2, 1987, 196:9–10.

Bernatzik, Hugo Adolph. *Akha and Miao: Problems of Applied Ethnography In Farther India*. Translated from the German by Alois Nagler. New Haven: Human Relations Area Files, 1970.

Bettelheim, Bruno. *Surviving and Other Essays*. New York: Vintage Books, 1979.

Boesch, Ernst E. "From Expulsion to Hospitality: A Psychologist's Look at the Refugee Problem." In Ernst E. Boesch and Armin M. F. Goldschmidt, eds., *Refugees and Development,* pp. 53–74. Baden-Baden: Nomos Verlagsgesellschaft, 1983.

Boothby, Neil. "The Care and Placement of Unaccompanied Children in Emergencies." Ph.D. dissertation, Harvard University, 1984.

—— "Unaccompanied Children in Emergencies: A Psychological Perspective." Qualifying paper, Harvard Graduate School of Education, Cambridge, 1982.

217

Bourhis-Nedellec, Marie Helene. "OHI Ban Kae (Chieng Kham): Installation et Fonctionnement d'un Programme." Operation Handicap International, Thailand, 1988.

—— "OHI Programme de Ban Vinai: Activites, Problemes, Projets." Operation Handicap International, Thailand, 1986.

Branfman, Fredric R. *Voices from the Plain of Jars: Life Under an Air War.* New York: Harper & Row, 1973.

Brown, MacAlister and Joseph J. Zasloff. *Apprentice Revolutionaries: The Communist Movement in Laos, 1930–1985.* Histories of Ruling Communist Parties. Stanford, Calif.: Hoover Institution Press, 1986.

Bruner, Edward M. "Ethnography as Narrative." In Victor W. Turner and Edward M. Brunner, eds., *The Anthropology of Experience,* pp. 139–158. Urbana and Chicago,: University of Illinois Press, 1986.

Burley, T.M. "Foreign Aid to the Lao People's Democratic Republic." In Martin Stuart-Fox, ed., *Contemporary Laos: Studies in the Politics and Society of the Lao People's Democratic Republic,* pp. 129–147. St. Lucia: University of Queensland Press, 1982.

Catholic Office for Emergency Relief and Refugees, *see under* COERR.

Cerquone, Joseph. *Refugees from Laos: In Harm's Way.* Washington, D.C.: U.S. Committee for Refugees Issue Paper, American Council for Nationalities Service, 1986.

Chamberlain, James. "The Literature of Laos." In John K. Whitmore, ed., *An Introduction to Indochinese History, Culture, and Life,* pp. 58–64. Ann Arbor: University of Michigan Press, 1979.

Chanda, Nayan. *Brother Enemy: The War After the War.* New York: Collier Books, Macmillan, 1986.

—— "Economic Changes in Laos, 1975–1980." In Martin Stuart-Fox, ed., *Contemporary Laos: Studies in the Politics and Society of the Lao People's Democratic Republic,* pp. 116–128. St. Lucia: University of Queensland Press, 1982.

Chindarsi, Nusit. "Hmong Shamanism." In John McKinnon and Wanat Bhruksasri, eds., *Highlanders of Thailand,* pp. 187–194. Kuala Lumpur: Oxford University Press, 1983.

Chiou, C.L. "China's Policy Towards Laos: Politics of Neutralization." In Martin Stuart-Fox, ed., *Contemporary Laos: Contemporary Studies in the Politics and Society of the Lao People's Democratic Republic,* pp. 291–305. St. Lucia: University of Queensland Press, 1982.

Chomsky, Noam and Edward S. Herman. *After the Cataclysm: Postwar Indochina and the Reconstruction of Imperial Ideology.* Volume 2 in *The Political Economy of Human Rights.* Boston: South End Press, 1979.

Clay, Jason W. and Bonnie K. Holcomb. *Politics and the Ethiopian Famine, 1984–1985.* Cambridge, Mass.: Cultural Survival, 1986.

Clifford, James and George E. Marcus. *Writing Culture: The Poetics and Politics of Ethnography.* Berkeley: University of California Press, 1986.

Coedes, G. *The Making of South East Asia.* Translated by H. M. Wright. Berkeley: University of California Press, 1962.

COERR (Catholic Office for Emergency Relief and Refugees). *Report of Survey of Refugee Needs and Problems in Ben Vinai Refugee Camp, Thailand, 1985–1986.* 1986a.

COERR. *Report of Interviews of Voluntary Agencies in Ban Vinai Refugee Camp, Thailand, 1986.* 1986b.

Collins, Peter. *A Mandate to Protect and Assist Refugees; 20 Years of Service in the Cause of Refugees, 1951–1971.* Geneva: United Nations High Commissioner for Refugees, 1971.

Committee for Coordination of Services to Displaced Persons in Thailand (CCSDPT). *The CCSDPT Handbook: Refugee Services in Thailand.* Bangkok: 1986.

Conquergood, Dwight. "Establishing the World: Hmong Shamans." *Southeast Asian Refugee Studies Newsletter* (Summer 1989), 9:5–10.

Cooper, Robert. "The Hmong of Laos: Economic Factors in the Refugee Exodus and Return." In Glenn L. Hendricks, Bruce T. Downing, and Amos S. Deinard, eds., *The Hmong in Transition,* pp. 23–40. Center for Migration Studies of New York, and the Southeast Asian Refugee Studies Project of the University of Minnesota, 1986.

—— *Resource Scarcity and the Hmong Response: Patterns of Settlement and Economy in Transition.* Singapore: Singapore University Press, 1984.

—— "Sexual Inequality Among the Hmong." In John McKinnon and Wanat Bhruksasri, eds., *Highlanders of Thailand,* pp. 174–186. Kuala Lumpur: Oxford University Press, 1983.

Crapanzano, Vincent. *Waiting: The Whites of South Africa.* New York: Vintage Books, Random House, 1986.

Crossette, Barbara. "After the Killing Fields: Cambodia's Forgotten Refugees." *New York Times Magazine,* June 26, 1988, pp. 16ff.

Dallas, Roland. "Too Many Refugees." *The World in 1992.* Economist Publications, London, December 1991, pp. 89–90.

Dommen, Arthur J. *Laos: Keystone of Indochina.* Boulder, Colo.: Westview Press, 1985.

Dunnigan, Timothy. "Segmentary Kinship in an Urban Society: The Hmong of St. Paul–Minneapolis." *Anthropological Quarterly* (1982), 55:126–134.

Durkheim, Emile. *Suicide.* Translated by John A. Spaulding and George Simpson. New York: Free Press, 1951.

—— *The Elementary Forms of the Religious Life.* Translated by Joseph Ward Swain. New York: Free Press. By arrangement with George Allen and Unwin (1915), 1965.

Eitinger, Leo. "Foreigners in Our Time: Historical Survey on Psychiatry's Approach to Migration and Refugee Status." In *Strangers in the World,* pp. 16–26. Bern/Stuttgart: Hans Huber, 1981.

Eliade, Mircea. *Shamanism: Archaic Techniques of Ecstasy.* Translated by Willard R. Trask. Princeton, N.J.: Princeton University Press, 1964.

Erickson, Frederick and Jeffrey Shultz. *The Counselor as Gatekeeper: Social Interaction in Interviews.* New York: Academic Press, 1982.

Erikson, Erik H. "On the Nature of Psycho-Historical Evidence." In *Life History and the Historical Moment: Diverse Presentations,* pp. 113–168. New York: Norton, 1975.

—— "Identity and Uprootedness in Our Time." In *Insight and Responsibility.* New York: Norton, 1964.

Evans-Pritchard, E. E. *Witchcraft, Oracles, and Magic Among the Azande.* Oxford: Oxford University Press, 1976.

Ferrarotti, Franco. *Histoire et histoires de vie: La methode biographique dans les sciences sociales.* Paris: Librairie des Meridiens, 1983.

Ferris, Elizabeth G. Overview: "Refugees and World Politics." In *Refugees and World Politics,* pp. 1–25. New York: Praeger, 1985.

Finck, John. "Secondary Migration to California's Central Valley." In Glenn L. Hendricks. Bruce T. Downing, and Amos S. Deinard, eds., *The Hmong in Transition,* pp. 184–187. Center for Migration Studies of New York, and the Southeast Asian Refugee Studies of the University of Minnesota, 1986.

Finnan, Christine. "Community Influence on Occupational Identity Development:

Vietnamese Refugees and Job Training." Presented at the Annual Meeting of the American Anthropological Association, Washington, D.C., December 1980.

Ford Foundation Working Paper. *Refugees and Migrants: Problems and Program Responses.* New York: Office of Reports, Ford Foundation, 1983.

Foucault, Michel. *Discipline and Punish: The Birth of the Prison.* New York: Vintage Books, 1979.

Frankl, Viktor E. *The Doctor and the Soul: From Psychotherapy to Logotherapy.* Translated by Richard and Clara Winston. New York: Vintage Books, Random House, 1965.

Gallagher, Dennis. "Community Participation: Now you see it, now you don't." *UNICEF News,* 1986, 124:21–23.

Geddes, William Robert. *Migrants of the Mountains: The Cultural Ecology of the Blue Miao (Hmong Njua) of Thailand.* Oxford: Clarendon Press, 1976.

Geertz, Clifford. "Blurred Genres: The Refiguration of Social Thought." In *Local Knowledge,* pp. 19–36. New York: Basic Books, 1983.

—— "The Integrative Revolution: Primordial Sentiments and Civil Politics in the New States." In *The Interpretation of Cultures,* pp. 255–318. New York: Basic Books, 1973.

Gide, Andre. *Les caves du Vatican.* Paris: Editions Gallimard, 1922.

Giddens, Anthony. *The Consequences of Modernity.* Stanford, Calif: Stanford University Press, 1990.

Goldschmidt, Armin M. F. and Ernst E. Boesch. "The World Refugee Problem: Refugees and Development." In *Refugees and Development,* pp. 15–52. Baden-Baden: Nomos Verlagsgesellschaft, 1983.

Goffman, Erving. *Behavior in Public Places.* New York: Free Press, 1963.

—— "On the Characteristics of Total Institutions." In *Asylums; Essays on the Social Situation of Mental Patients and Other Inmates,* pp. 1–124. New York: Doubleday Anchor Books, 1961.

Grossman, David. "Report from Israel." *The New Yorker,* February 8, 1988, part 1, pp. 41–66 and February 15, 1988, part 2, pp. 58–74. Translated by Haim Watzman.

—— *The Yellow Wind.* Translated by Haim Watzman. New York: Delta, 1988.

Hafner, James A. "Trade and Transport of the Upper Mekong." In Hafner, Halpern, and Kerewsky-Halpern, eds., *River Road Through Laos,* pp. 51–74.

Hafner, James A., Joel M. Halpern, and Barbara Kerewsky, "River Road to China: The Mekong River, Explorations of the 19th Century." In Hafner, Halpern, and Kerewsky-Halpern, eds., *River Road Through Laos,* pp. 1–11.

Hafner, James A., Joel M. Halpern, and Barbara Kerewsky-Halpern, eds., *River Road Through Laos: Reflections of the Mekong.* Asian Studies Occasional Papers, no. 10, International Areas Studies Program. Amherst: University of Massachusetts, 1983.

Halpern, Joel M. "Demographic Data." In *Laos Project: Paper No. 3.* Department of Anthropology, University of California, Los Angeles, 1961.

—— "Economic Data." In *Laos Project: Paper No. 11.* Department of Anthropology, University of California, Los Angeles, 1961.

—— "Geographic, Demographic, and Ethnic Background on Lao." In *Laos Project: Paper No. 4.* Department of Anthropology, University of California, Los Angeles, 1961.

—— "The Natural Economy of Laos." In *Laos Project: Paper No. 17.* Department of
Anthropology, University of California, Los Angeles, 1961.

Hammer, Ellen J. *The Struggle for Indochina, 1940–1955.* Stanford, Calif.: Stanford University Press, 1966.

Harrell-Bond, Elizabeth E. *Imposing Aid.* Oxford: Oxford University Press, 1986.

Henkel, Joachim. "The International Protection of Refugees and Displaced Persons: A Global Problem of Growing Complexity." Washington, D.C.: U.S. Committee for Refugees, 1985.

Hendricks, Glenn L., Bruce T. Downing, and Amos S. Deinard, eds. *The Hmong in Transition.* Center for Migration Studies of New York, and the Southeast Asian Refugee Studies of the University of Minnesota, 1986.

Herdt, Gilbert and Robert Stoller. *Intimate Communications: Erotics and the Study of Culture.* New York: Columbia University Press, 1990.

Holborn, Louise W. *Refugees: A Problem of Our Time.* The Work of the United Nations High Commissioner for Refugees, 1951–1972. Volumes 1 and 2. Metuchen, N.J.: Scarecrow Press, 1975.

Huffman, Franklin E. "The Ethnolinguistic Background of the Khmer." Paper presented at the Asia Society, Washington, D.C., November 20, 1980.

Hugo, Graeme. "Postwar Refugee Migration in Southeast Asia: Patterns, Problems, and Policies." In John R. Rogge, ed., *Refugees: A Third World Dilemma,* pp. 237–252. Totowa, N.J.: Rowman and Littlefield, 1987.

Hurlich, Marshall, Neal R. Holtan, and Ronald G. Munger. "Attitudes of Hmong Toward a Medical Research Project." In Glenn L. Hendricks, Bruce T. Downing, and Amos S. Deinhard, eds., *The Hmong In Transition,* pp. 427–446. Center for Migration Studies of New York and the Southeast Asian Refugee Studies of the University of Minnesota, 1986.

Kahnert, Marianne, David Pitt, and Ilkka Taipale. *Children and War.* Proceedings of Symposium at Siuntio Baths, Finland, 1983.

Kamm, Henry. "A Broken Country." *The New York Times Magazine.* September 20, 1987, p. 96ff.

Karnow, Stanley. *Vietnam, A History.* Middlesex, England: Penguin Books, 1984.

Keely, Charles. *Global Refugee Policy: The Case for a Development Oriented Strategy.* Public Issues Paper, The Population Council, New York, 1981.

Keller, Stephen L. *Uprooting and Social Change: The Role of Refugees in Development.* New Delhi: Manohar Book Service, 1975.

Kelly, Gail Paradise. *From Vietnam to America: A Chronicle of the Vietnamese Immigration to the United States.* Boulder, Colo.: Westview Press, 1977.

Keyes, Charles F. "Introduction." In Charles F. Keyes, ed., *Ethnic Adaptation and Identity: The Karen On The Thai Frontier With Burma,* pp. 1–23. Philadelphia: Institute for the Study of Human Issues, 1979.

Kitagawa, Joseph M. "Some Reflections on Immigration and Refugee Problems." In *American Refugee Policy: Ethical and Religious Reflections,* pp. 136–158. Minneapolis, Minn.: Presiding Bishops Fund for World Relief, The Episcopal Church in collaboration with Winston Press, 1984.

Krieger, Susan. "Fiction and Social Science." In *The Mirror Dance: Identity in a Women's Community,* pp. 173–199. Philadelphia: Temple University Press, 1983.

Kunstadter, Peter. "Health of Hmong in Thailand: Risk Factors, Morbidity and Mortality in Comparison with Other Ethnic Groups." *Culture, Medicine, and Psychiatry* (1985), 9:329–351.

Lake, Anthony. *After the Wars: Reconstruction in Afghanistan, Indochina, Central America, Southern Africa, and the Horn of Africa.* U.S.-Third World Policy Perspectives, No. 16. Overseas Development Council. New Brunswick, N.J.: Transaction Publishers, 1990.

Langness, L. L. and Gelya Frank. *Lives: An Anthropological Approach to Biography.* Novalo, Calif.: Chandler and Sharp, 1981.

Lanphier, Michael C. "Indochinese Resettlement: Cost and Adaptation in Canada, the United States, and France." In John R. Rogge, ed., *Refugees: A Third World Dilemma,* pp. 299–308. Totowa, N.J.: Rowman and Littlefield, 1987.

Lebar, Frank M., Gerald C. Hickey, and John K. Musgrave. *Ethnic Groups of Mainland Southeast Asia.* New Haven: Human Relations Area Files Press, 1964.

Lemoine, Jacques. "Shamanism in the Context of Hmong Resettlement." In Glenn L. Hendricks, Bruce T. Downing, and Amos S. Deinard, eds., *The Hmong in Transition,* pp. 337–348. Center for Migration Studies of New York and the Southeast Asian Refugee Studies of the University of Minnesota, 1986.

—— *L'initiation du mort chez les Hmong.* Bangkok: Pandora Press, 1983.

—— *Un village Hmong vert du Haut Laos.* Paris: Editions du Centre National de la Recherche Scientifique, 1972.

LeVine, Robert A. *Culture, Behavior, and Personality.* 2d ed. New York: Aldine, 1982.

Lévi-Strauss, Claude. "The Sorcerer and His Magic." In *Magic, Witchcraft, and Curing,* pp. 23–41. John Middleton, ed. Austin: University of Texas Press, 1967.

Levy, Barry S. and Daniel C. Susott. *Years of Horror, Days of Hope: Responding to the Cambodian Refugee Crisis.* New York: Associated Faculty Press, 1986.

Loescher, Gil and John A. Scanlan. *Calculated Kindness: Refugees and America's Half-Open Door, 1945 to the Present.* New York: Free Press, 1986.

Long, Lynellyn. "Literacy Acquisition of Hmong Refugees in Thailand." In Fraida Dubin and Natalie Kuhlman, eds., *Cross-Cultural Literacy: Global Perspectives on Reading,* 23–30. Englewood Cliffs, N.J.: Prentice-Hall, 1992.

—— "Language and Literacy Shifts in Refugee Populations." In *Language and Literacy Roundtable.* Background paper. World Conference on Education for All. Jomtien, Thailand, 1990.

—— *The Floating World: Laotian Refugee Camp Life in Thailand.* Ann Arbor, Mich.: University Microfilms, 1988.

Luche, Jenna E. *Socio-Economic Analysis of the Lao/89/550 Highland Integrated Rural Development Project.* Field report. United Nations Fund for Drug Abuse and Development, Laos, 1991.

Lutz, Catherine. "Depression and the Translation of Emotional Worlds." In Arthur Kleinman and Byron Good, eds., *Culture and Depression,* pp. 63–101. Berkeley: University of California Press, 1985.

Malkii, Liisa. "Context and Consciousness: Local Conditions for the Production of Historical and National Thought Among Hutu Refugees in Tanzania." In Richard G. Fox, ed., *Nationalist Ideologies and the Production of National Cultures,* pp. 32–62. Washington, D.C.: American Ethnological Society Monograph Series 2, 1990.

Marcus, George E. and Dick Cushman. "Ethnographies As Texts." *Annual Review of Anthropology* (1982), 11:25–69.

Marcus, George E. and Michael M. J. Fischer. *Anthropology as Cultural Critique: An Experimental Moment in the Human Sciences.* Chicago: University of Chicago Press, 1986.

Marshall, E. "Yellow Rain Evidence Slowly Whittled Away." *Science* (July 4, 1986), 233:18–19.

Marx, Karl. "Economic and Philosophic Manuscripts" In Loyd D. Easton and Kurt H. Guddat, eds. and trans, *Writings of the Young Marx on Philosophy and Society,* pp. 283–358. New York: Anchor Books, Doubleday, 1967.

Mason, Linda and Roger Brown. *Rice, Rivalry, and Politics: Managing Cambodian Relief.* Notre Dame, Ind.: University of Notre Dame Press, 1983.

McCallin, Margaret. Report of a Pilot Study to Assess Levels of Stress in a Sample of 90 Refugee Children in Central America. Geneva: International Catholic Child Bureau. n.d.

McCoy, Alfred W. With Cathleen B. Read and Leonard P. Adams II. *The Politics of Heroin in Southeast Asia.* Singapore: Harper & Row, 1972.

Melander, Goran and Peter Nobel. *African Refugees and the Law.* Uppsala: Scandinavian Institute of African Studies, 1978.

Miller, Tony. "Sample Survey of Refugee Needs and Problems." Report. Ban Vinai, Thailand: Catholic Organization for Emergency Relief and Refugees, 1984.

Montero, Daniel. *Vietnamese Americans: Patterns of Resettlement and Socioeconomic Adaptation in the United States.* Boulder, Colo.: Westview Press, 1979.

Mottin, Jean. *Allons faire le tour du ciel et de la terre: Le chamanisme des Hmongs vu dans les textes.* Bangkok: White Lotus, 1982.

—— "Le dragon prive de ses poissons (Suav Hwb Xeeb thiab Zaj Laug)." In *Contes et legendes Hmong blanc.* Bangkok: Don Bosco Press, n.d.

Nakavachara, Netnapis and John R. Rogge. "Thailand's Refugee Experience." In John R. Rogge, ed., *Refugees: A Third World Dilemma,* pp. 269–281. Totowa, N.J.: Rowman and Littlefield, 1987.

Nichols, J. Bruce. *The Uneasy Alliance: Religion, Refugee Work, and U.S. Foreign Policy.* New York: Oxford University Press, 1988.

Nietzsche. Friedrich Wilhelm. "Thus Spake Zarathustra." In *The Portable Nietzsche,* pp. 183–439. Selected and translated by Walter Kaufman. New York: Viking Press, 1968.

O'Brien, Jay. "Sowing the Seeds of Famine: The Political Economy of Food Deficits in Sudan." *Review of African Political Economy* (1985), 33:23–32.

Olney, Douglas. "Population Trends." In Glenn L. Hendricks, Bruce T. Downing, and Amos S. Deinard, eds., *The Hmong in Transition,* pp. 179–183. Center for Migration Studies of New York, and the Southeast Asian Refugee Studies of the University of Minnesota, 1986.

Outsama, Kao. "Laotian Themes." Paper disseminated by the MERIT Center, Temple University, Philadelphia, June, 1977.

Pear, Robert. "Some Doors Are Closing." *New York Times.* August 21, 1988, p. E3.

Pitterman, Shelly. "Determinants of International Refugee Policy: A Comparative Study of UNHCR Material Assistance to Refugees in Africa, 1963–1981." In John R. Rogge, ed., *Refugees: A Third World Dilemma,* pp. 13–36. Totowa, N.J.: Rowman and Littlefield, 1987.

Pluvier, Jan M. *A Handbook and Chart of South-East Asian History.* Kuala Lumpur: Oxford University Press, 1967.

Ranard, Donald. "Thailand: The Last Bus." *The Atlantic* (October 1987), 260:26–34.

Read, James M. *Magna Carta for Refugees and The Text of the Convention.* Preface by G. J. Van Heuven Goedhart. New York: United Nations Department of Public Information, 1951.

Ressler, Everett M., Neil Boothby, and Daniel J. Steinbock. *Unaccompanied Children: Care and Protection in Wars, Natural Disasters, and Refugee Movements.* New York: Oxford University Press, 1988.

RMC Research Corporation. *The Effects of Pre-Entry Training on the Resettlement of Indochinese Refugees.* Portsmouth, N.H.: RMC Research Corporation, 1984.

Roberts, T. D., Mary Elizabeth Carroll, Irving Kaplan, Jan M. Matthews, David S. McMorris, and Charles Townsend. *Area Handbook for Laos.* Washington, D.C.: GPO, 1967.

Robinson, Court. "Laotian Refugees in Thailand: The Thai and U.S. Response, 1975 to 1988." In Joseph J. Zasloff and Leonard J. Unger, eds., *Laos: Beyond the Revolution,* pp. 215–240. London: Macmillan, 1991.

Rosaldo, Michelle Zimbalist. "Women, Culture, and Society: A Theoretical Overview." In Michelle Zimbalist Rosaldo and Louisa Lamphere, eds., *Women, Culture, and Society,* pp. 17–42. Stanford, Calif.: Stanford University Press, 1974.

Rosaldo, Renato. "Ideology, Place, and People Without Culture." *Cultural Anthropology* (1988), 3(1):77–87.

—— "Ilongot Hunting as Story and Experience." In Victor W. Turner and Edward. Brunner, eds., *The Anthropology of Experience,* pp. 97–138. Urbana and Chicago: University of Illinois Press, 1986.

Rothkopf, Carol Z. *Jean Henri Dunant: Father of the Red Cross.* New York: Franklin Watts, 1969.

Rubin, Gary E. *Refugee Protection: An Analysis and Action Proposal.* Washington, D.C.: American Council for Nationalities Service, 1983.

Sapir, Edward. "Culture, Genuine and Spurious." In *Culture, Language, and Personality: Selected Essays,* pp. 78–110. David G. Mandelbaum, ed. Berkeley: University of California Press, 1970.

Sartre, Jean-Paul. *Being and Nothingness: A Phenomenological Essay on Ontology.* Translated with an introduction by Hazel E. Barnes. New York: Washington Square Press, 1956.

—— *La Nausee.* Paris: Editions Gallimard, 1938.

Schein, Louisa. "The Miao in Contemporary China: A Preliminary Overview." In Glenn L. Hendricks, Bruce T. Downing, and Amos S. Deinard, eds., *The Hmong in Transition,* pp. 73–86. Center for Migration Studies of New York, and the Southeast Asian Refugee Studies of the University of Minnesota, 1986.

Schoenmeier, Hermann W. "Refugee Policy: The Need to Include Psychological Aspects." In John R. Rogge, eds., *Refugees: A Third World Dilemma,* pp. 66–72. Totowa, N.J.: Rowman and Littlefield, 1987

Scott, George M. Jr. "The Hmong Refugee Community in San Diego: Theoretical and Practical Implications of Its Continuing Ethnic Solidarity." *Anthropological Quarterly* (1982), 55(3):146–160.

Sesser, Stan. "A Reporter At Large: Forgotten Country." *The New Yorker.* August 20, 1990, pp. 39–68.

Shawcross, William. *The Quality of Mercy: Cambodia, the Holocaust, and Modern Conscience.* New York: Simon and Schuster. 1984.

—— *Side Show: Kissinger, Nixon, and the Destruction of Cambodia.* New York: Simon and Schuster. 1979.

Shweder, Richard A. and Robert A. LeVine. *Culture Theory: Essays on Mind, Self, and Emotion.* Cambridge: Cambridge University Press, 1984.

Simmace, Alan J. F. "The Impact of Large-Scale Refugee Movements and the Role of UNHCR." In John R. Rogge, ed., *Refugees: A Third World Dilemma,* pp. 9–14. Totowa, N.J.: Rowman and Littlefield, 1987.

Simmonds, Stephanie, Patrick Vaughan, and S. William Gunn. *Refugee Community Health Care*. Oxford: Oxford University Press, 1983.

Smalley, William A., Chia Koua Vang, and Gnia Yee Yang. *Mother of Writing: The Origin and Development of a Hmong Messianic Script*. Chicago: University of Chicago Press, 1990.

Smyser, W. R. "Refugees: A Never Ending Story." *Foreign Affairs* (Fall 1985), 64:154–168. New York: Council of Foreign Relations.

Stuart-Fox, Martin. "Foreign Policy of the Lao People's Democratic Republic." In Joseph J. Zasloff and Leonard Unger, eds., *Laos: Beyond the Revolution*, pp. 187–208. London: Macmillan, 1991.

—— "National Defense and Internal Security in Laos." In Martin Stuart-Fox, ed., *Contemporary Laos: Studies in the Politics and Society of the Lao People's Democratic Republic*, pp. 220–244. St. Lucia: University of Queensland Press, 1982.

Tabori, Paul. *The Anatomy of Exile: A Semantic and Historical Study*. London: Harrap Press, 1972.

Thao, Xoua. "Hmong Perceptions of Illness and Traditional Ways of Healing." In Glenn L. Hendricks, Bruce T. Downing, and Amos S. Deinard, eds., *The Hmong in Transition*, pp. 365–378. Center for Migration Studies of New York, and the Southeast Asian Refugee Studies of the University of Minnesota, 1986.

Thayer, Carlyle A. "Laos and Vietnam: The Anatomy of a "Special Relationship." In Martin Stuart-Fox, ed., *Contemporary Laos: Studies in the Politics and Society of the Lao People's Democratic Republic*, pp. 245–273. St. Lucia: University of Queensland Press, 1982.

Tollefson, James W. *Alien Winds: The Reeducation of America's Indochinese Refugees*. New York: Praeger, 1989.

—— "Functional Competencies in the U.S. Refugee Program: Theoretical and Practical Problems." *TESOL Quarterly* (December 1986), 20:649–664.

—— "Research on Refugee Resettlement: Implications for Instructional Programs." *TESOL Quarterly* (December 1985), 19:753–764.

Tribal Research Institute. *The Hill Tribes of Thailand*. Bangkok: Technical Service Club, Tribal Research Institute. 1986.

Turner, Victor. *Dramas, Fields, and Metaphors*. Ithaca: Cornell University Press, 1974.

—— *The Forest of Symbols: Aspects of Ndembu Ritual*. Ithaca: Cornell University Press, 1967.

United Nations. *Demographic Yearbook: 1959*, pp. 138–141; *1968*, pp. 117–118; *1977*, pp. 160–161 and 170–174. New York: UN.

United Nations High Commissioner for Refugees. "Interview with Ken Kragen USA for Africa." *Refugees* (April 26, 1986), 28:40–41.

—— *Brief on Ban Vinai Refugee Camp*. Field Office in Ban Vinai, 1986.

—— *Handbook for Emergencies*. Part One: *Field Operations*. Geneva, 1982.

—— *Report on the Status of Refugees in Thailand*. Bangkok, December, 1981.

—— *Statute of the Office of the United Nations High Commissioner for Refugees*. Geneva:Palais des Nations, 1951.

United States Committee for Refugees. *World Refugee Survey, 1985: In Review*. Washington, D.C.: American Council for Nationalities Service, 1986.

—— *World Refugee Survey, 1986: In Review*. Washington, D.C.: American Council for Nationalities Service, 1987.

————— *World Refugee Survey, 1987: In Review.* Washington, D.C.: American Council for Nationalities Service, 1988.

————— *World Refugee Survey, 1989: In Review.* Washington, D.C.: American Council for Nationalities Service, 1990.

United States Congress. House of Representatives. *Reports on Refugee Aid, UN High Commissioner for Refugees, Refugees in Somalia, Refugees in Pakistan, Bataan Refugee Processing Center.* Reports of Staff Study Missions to the Committee on Foreign Affairs, U.S. House of Representatives, Washington, D.C., 1981.

United States Congress. Senate. *Midyear Consultation on U.S. Refugee Programs for Fiscal Year 1986.* Hearing before the Subcommittee on Immigration and Refugee Policy of the Committee on the Judiciary, United States Senate, Washington, D.C., 1986.

————— *U.S. Refugee Program in Southeast Asia: 1985.* Report prepared for the Subcommittee on Immigration and Refugee Policy, Committee on the Judiciary, U.S. Senate, Washington, D.C., 1985.

————— *Refugee Problems in Southeast Asia: 1981.* A Staff Report, Subcommittee on Immigration and Refugee Policy, Committee on the Judiciary, U.S. Senate, Washington, D.C., 1981.

United States Department of Health and Human Services. *Southeast Asian Mental Health: Treatment, Prevention, Services, Training, and Research.* Tom Choken Owan, Bruce Bliatout, Keh-Ming Lin, William Liu, Tuan D. Nguyen, and Herbert Z. Wong, eds. Washington, D.C.: Social Security Administration, Office of Refugee Resettlement, 1985.

————— *Refugee Resettlement Program.* Report to the Congress. January 31, 1983.

United States Department of State. *World Refugee Report.* Bureau for Refugee Programs, Washington, D.C., September 1992.

————— *Progress Report: Recommendations of the Indochinese Refugee Panel.* Washington, D.C., 1986.

Van Der Kroef, Justus M. "Refugees and Rebels: Dimensions of the Thai-Kampuchean Border Conflict." *Asian Affairs: An American Review* (Spring 1983), pp. 19–36.

Van-es-Beeck, Bernard J. "Refugees from Laos, 1975–1979." In Martin Stuart-Fox, ed., *Contemporary Laos: Studies in the Politics and Society of the Laos People's Democratic Republic,* pp. 324–334. St. Lucia: University of Queensland Press, 1982.

Vansina, Jan. *Oral Tradition As History.* Madison: University of Wisconsin Press, 1985.

Wekkin, Gary D. "The Rewards of Revolution: Pathet Lao Policy Towards the Hill Tribes Since 1975." In Martin Stuart-Fox, ed., *Contemporary Laos: Studies in the Politics and Society of the Laos People's Democratic Republic,* pp. 181–198. St. Lucia: University of Queensland Press, 1982.

Westermeyer, Joseph. "Mental Health of Southeast Asian Refugees: Observations Over Two Decades from Laos and the United States." In Tom Choken Owan, Bruce Bliatout, Keh-Ming Lin, William Liu, Tuan D. Nguyen, and Herbert Z. Wong, eds., *Southeast Asian Mental Health: Treatment, Prevention, Services, Training, and Research.* pp. 65–112. Washington, D,C.: U.S. Department of Health and Human Services, 1985.

————— *Poppies, Pipes, and People: Opium and Its Use in Laos.* Berkeley, Los Angeles, and London: University of California Press, 1982.

————— "Use of Alcohol and Opium by the Meo of Laos." *American Journal of Psychiatry* (1971), 127:59–63.

Williams, Carolyn L. and Joseph Westermeyer. "Psychiatric Problems Among Adolescent Southeast Asian Refugees: A Descriptive Study." *The Journal of Nervous and Mental Disease* (1983), 171:79–85.

Winter, Roger. *Testimony of Roger P. Winter,* Director, U.S. Committee for Refugees Before the House Judiciary Committee, Subcommittee on Immigration, Refugees, and International Law. Washington, D.C., 1989.

Women's Commission for Refugee Women and Children. *Repatriation and Reintegration: Can Hmong Refugees Begin To Look Homeward?* Report of the Women's Commission for Refugee Women and Children, International Rescue Committee. New York, 1991.

Zolberg, Aristide R. "The Formation of New States As a Refugee-Generating Process." In Elizabeth G. Ferris, ed., *Refugees and World Politics,* pp. 26–42. New York: Praeger, 1985.

—— "International Migration in Political Perspective." In M. M. Kritz, C. B. Keely, and S. M. Tomasi, eds., *Global Trends in Migration,* pp. 3–27. New York: Center for Migration Studies, 1981.

Zwingmann, Charles and Maria Pfister-Ammende. *Uprooting and After.* New York: Springer-Verlag, 1973.

Meetings and Interviews

Bateson, Wendy. May 1988. In Washington, D.C. Former American Friends Service Committee Representative in Laos (1980–85). United Nations Development Programme, Pakistan.

Bertrais, Yves. July and August 1986. In Chiang Khan, Thailand. Catholic priest, co-author of Hmong dictionary, and author of numerous articles on Hmong culture, history, and language.

Lim, Janet. July 1986. In Bangkok. Operations Officer, United Nations High Commissioner for Refugees, Bangkok.

Pitterman, Shelley. June 1989. In Geneva. Desk Officer, United Nations High Commissioner for Refugees, Geneva.

Robinson, Court. May 1988. In Washington, D.C. Policy Analyst, U.S. Committee for Refugees, Washington, D.C.

Yang, Long. June-August 1988. In Greenbelt, Md. Former officer and American liaison in Vang Pao's forces. Currently businessman.

Conferences

Annual Meeting of the Committee for Coordination of Services to Displaced Persons in Thailand, Bangkok, July 11, 1986.

Conference on Indochinese Relations, Foreign Service Institute, U.S. Department of State, Washington, D.C., March 10–11, 1987.

Conference on Current Developments in Laos, Foreign Service Institute, U.S. Department of State, Washington, D.C., May 4, 1988.

Index

(page numbers in *italics* indicate charts, tables, etc.)

229